Fight the Good Fight

To my mother and father, who fought the good fight in their own distinct ways; to Rosa, Sophia and David in the hope they may grow to fight worthy fights; and to Dawn, who has been my soul mate throughout this journey.

Fight the Good Fight

Voices of Faith from the
First World War

John Broom

Pen & Sword
MILITARY

First published in Great Britain in 2015 by
Pen & Sword Military
an imprint of
Pen & Sword Books Ltd
47 Church Street
Barnsley
South Yorkshire
S70 2AS

ISBN 978 1 47385 415 4

Typeset in Ehrhardt by
Mac Style Ltd, Bridlington, East Yorkshire
Printed and bound in the UK by CPI Group (UK) Ltd,
Croydon, CRO 4YY

Pen & Sword Books Ltd incorporates the imprints of Pen & Sword
Archaeology, Atlas, Aviation, Battleground, Discovery, Family
History, History, Maritime, Military, Naval, Politics, Railways, Select,
Transport, True Crime, and Fiction, Frontline Books, Leo Cooper,
Praetorian Press, Seaforth Publishing and Wharncliffe.

For a complete list of Pen & Sword titles please contact
PEN & SWORD BOOKS LIMITED
47 Church Street, Barnsley, South Yorkshire, S70 2AS, England
E-mail: enquiries@pen-and-sword.co.uk
Website: www.pen-and-sword.co.uk

Contents

Acknowledgements

The genesis of this book arose from some research undertaken for the Bible Society on the importance of the Bible in the First World War. Some of that research appeared on the World War One section of their website, www.biblesociety.org.uk. What appears here is further information gathered during that project. I acknowledge their patronage in providing support for expenses to unearth these stories.

In a work covering twenty-seven different individuals and families, the advice, understanding and encouragement I have received from relatives, copyright holders, historians interested in the subject and archivists has been huge.

I am grateful to the Estate of David Jones for permission for photographic reproduction rights and to quote from *In Parenthesis*; to Jurgen Imschoot for his translation of information about Father Dergent from Flemish into English; to the family of Joseph Garvey for permission to quote from his reminiscences, for use of the photograph and for further information on his post-war life; to Jonathan Greaves for permission to quote from the diary of Philip Bryant and photographic reproduction rights; to David Blake, Curator of the Royal Army Chaplaincy Museum at Amport for his helpful suggestions and support; to the staff at the Special Collections Department at the University of Leeds Library for their work in guiding me towards accessing permissions to quote from the wonderful Liddle Collection; to staff at the Imperial War Museum Department of Documents for clarifying the copyright of the Mrs Hayman collection; to Linne Matthews for her continuing advice and guidance through the writing and publishing process; to the staff at Pen and Sword Books for the smoothness in which my first foray into book writing has been handled; to Charles Beresford for leads provided on The Hon. Edith Gell; to the Cadbury Research Centre at the University of Birmingham and Dominic Cadbury for permission to quote from the papers of Laurence Cadbury; to Noelle Dowling at the Dublin Diocesan Archive for her assistance and advice regarding the papers of Francis Gleeson; to the family of Corder Catchpool for permission to quote from his published works and for access to recent source material; to Brian Gell for the photograph of Edith Gell; to Michael Snape for the benefit of his huge wisdom and experience in the art of writing history; to Dai Pike for his comprehensive Welsh Revival blog, which led me to further information about Lewis Valentine; to Arwel Vittle for insights into Valentine's life; to Norman Ching for permission to use the Sunday School exercise book of his uncle, Samuel Ching; to John Tucker of the Soldiers' and Airmen's Scripture Readers Association (SASRA) for permission to quote from the Rough Journal of Harry Wisbey.

In the cases where copyright has not been acknowledged, the author has made strenuous efforts to trace the holders, and would be pleased to correct any omissions in future publications of this work.

Belgian towns and cities typically have two place names; the French and the Flemish, e.g. Ypres / Ieper, Malines / Mechelen, Louvain / Leuven. In every case I have used the version that was known to or referred to by that individual. This is also the case for the names of towns that have reverted between German and Polish control in Eastern Europe.

Foreword

The First World War changed Britain forever. In many ways it marked the true beginning of the twentieth century, setting events in motion that would shape people's lives for generations to come. It was a conflict that touched every family, affected every community and fundamentally altered Britain's place in the world. It took the lives of 16 million soldiers and civilians across the globe, including 900,000 servicemen from Britain and the Commonwealth.

The centenary anniversaries that began last year provide us with an important opportunity to pay tribute to their service and sacrifice. There were 16,000 towns and villages across Britain in 1914, but only forty of them would reach 1918 without having lost someone in the conflict. So every community has its own story to tell.

In my constituency of Barnsley Central, men responded to Lord Kitchener's famous recruitment poster in 1914, and formed the 13th and 14th battalions of the York and Lancaster Regiment, the famous Barnsley Pals. They included miners, glassworkers, stonemasons and clerics – many of them friends and neighbours. They joined up together, trained together, went to war together, and ultimately many of them died together. I am pleased to see the story of one of their number, Philip Brocklesby, included in this book.

Last year I travelled to Serre in northern France, where the Barnsley Pals fought at the Battle of the Somme. I walked the ground over which the Pals had fought – open rolling fields that have changed little this past century. I tried to imagine what it must have been like, what must have been going through their minds.

Before departing for France, my 9-year-old daughter had lent me a replica 1916 trench whistle that she'd got from a school trip. I had it in my pocket and I thought that I might blow it from one of the trench positions that still scar the countryside. When I got there, I simply couldn't bring myself to blow that whistle. It wasn't that it seemed inappropriate, although maybe it would have been. Standing in front of their graves, in the pouring rain, thinking about the sound that signified the start of the attack, the sound that so many men must have dreaded, it was hard not to be overwhelmed by the emotion of it.

Later we visited the Memorial of the Missing at Thiepval. And it was there, as I read the names inscribed on the memorial, that I saw my own name staring back at me – D. Jarvis. Two things hit me at that moment. The first was the profound scale of the sacrifice. Our country's recent deployment in Afghanistan lasted over three times longer than the First World War; 453 servicemen died, and we've felt the pain of each one of them. So it's hard to imagine now what it must have been like to live through a conflict where about seven times that many soldiers would lose their lives each week, or to appreciate how much of a scar was left on the country by the first day of the Battle of the Somme – a beautiful summer's day on 1 July 1916 – when 20,000 men were cut down in a single day.

However, the commemoration of the First World War is about more than the remembrance of those who fought and died in the front line. It is also about those who worked so hard on the home front to keep the country going, those who cared for the wounded, those who strove to improve the political and social position of women in British society, and those whose sincere beliefs led them to oppose the war as conscientious objectors.

The moments when we all reflect on our history together are both precious, and few and far between. This centenary is an opportunity we will not have again as a country, so we must not fail to tell that wider story.

I am pleased to commend this book of case studies of Christians from all walks of life, of many different denominations and displaying a wide spectrum of political views. It includes accounts from the Western Front, the home front and from the prisons of Britain that held conscientious objectors and those on the Continent that held prisoners of war and spies. The religious faith of so many in Britain and other combatant nations is often overlooked when remembering the mentalities and world view of those who now stand a century apart from us. These stories help us to understand better an aspect of the rationale behind the response of so many to the challenge of global warfare, and further increase our admiration for the depth of belief and of personal character that so many were called upon to show.

As a nation, we can only own our futures if we stay connected with our history, and the publication of this book gives further strength to that connection.

Dan Jarvis OBE MP
Labour Spokesman of First World War Commemoration

Introduction

Why a book on Christians in the First World War? With the current centenary commemorations of a conflict that has now passed from living memory, it is evident that much of this retrospective has been through the lens of twenty-first-century values. Concepts of bravery and sacrifice are still seen as relevant today, whilst those of a sense of moral duty to abstract notions such as God, nation and empire are sometimes seen as a quaint aspect of a long gone past. One aspect of the commemorations that is always present, yet strangely frequently overlooked, is the huge importance that religion, more specifically the Christian faith, played in the lives not just of millions of individuals of all nations, but in the contemporary public discourse of the main protagonists.

Through simple observation of those permanent recollections of the sacrifices of 1914 to 1919, the public war memorials that grace the British landscape, it is clear that Christian faith played a central role in coming to terms with the scale of loss that the war brought. The phrase chosen by the Imperial (later Commonwealth) War Graves Commission to adorn their monuments was *Their Name Liveth for Evermore*, taken from the book of Ecclesiasticus in the Apocrypha of the Bible and suggested by Rudyard Kipling. Frequently, the memorials contain biblical quotes, such as John 15:13: *Greater Love Hath No Man Than This, That A Man Lay Down His Life For His Friends*. Often they are in the shape of crosses and sometimes contain a crucified Christ on that cross. They make reference to fighting for 'God, King and Country' and were usually unveiled as part of a Christian service. Often they are found within the consecrated ground of a parish church, with rolls of honour and memorial inscriptions almost always on display within the church. Therefore, for millions of people the war was fought and commemorated within a broadly Christian framework.

As the importance of Christianity in the collective public life of Britain has crumbled in recent decades, so has the appreciation of some of the values that spurred our great-grandparents to action. This book is not intended as a comprehensive overview, or even a representative sample of the ways in which Christianity was manifested in people's experience of war. It does not seek to judge the decisions people made or to apportion degrees of devotion. What I hope it does achieve is to keep alive the thoughts, feelings and beliefs of people a century on and to appreciate the moral and spiritual strength of a generation of people from all walks of life thrust into a world of new and frightening challenges. It is written for people of all faiths and none, and most of all it is written out of a profound respect for a generation that faced challenges that for the most part they were ill-prepared for, but who met those challenges head on with a sense of duty and purpose we can respect and admire.

Part I

Christian Britain in 1914

'Onward Christian Soldiers, Marching as to War'

'W ithout appreciating its religious and spiritual aspects, we cannot understand the First World War.'[1] So wrote Philip Jenkins, Professor of History at Baylor University, Texas. That war was of immense scale in the way it affected life in these islands. In Britain alone there were 705,000 fatal casualties, with a further 300,000 fatalities from men as far afield as India, New Zealand, Australia, Canada and South Africa fighting as Empire forces.[2] From 1914 to 1918, nearly 5 million British men volunteered or were conscripted to join the regular army of 800,000 – one in every five males in the country.[3] Of these, nearly 80 per cent were English, 9.6 per cent Irish, 8.6 per cent Scottish and 2.4 per cent Welsh.[4] Due to the relatively small size of the British Regular Army, Lord Kitchener created a 'New Army' of thirty divisions of volunteers in 1914–15. This new army had strong local connections, being identified with certain counties or cities, most notably in the 'Pals' battalions. After the introduction of conscription across Great Britain (but not Ireland) in 1916 and the need to fill the massive gaps in the regionally based battalions after the horrific losses during the Somme campaign of that year, that sense of local identity became diluted. Within this changing nature of the British Army, Christianity had a strong hold at all levels, from Sir Douglas Haig through to the modest private.

In pre-war England, as opposed to the whole of Britain, 60 per cent of the population was Anglican, 15 per cent Nonconformist and 5 per cent Catholic, with the other 20 per cent agnostics or belonging to other denominations.[5] However, for many this was a nominal adherence. Figures have been produced that show there were 5,682,000 official adherents of Protestant denominations across the whole of Britain, out of a total population of 42 million.[6]

The church had grown marginal in working-class areas, especially in the north of England and particularly amongst men. The Church of England in particular had many nominal adherents whose church attendance ranged from patchy to almost non-existent. To some extent, Nonconformism had filled the religious gap in urban areas and Wales. Due to the somewhat fundamentalist nature of Nonconformism, members tended towards a more active faith than many Anglicans.

In the early 1900s there was still institutional discrimination against Catholics in many sections of society. Despite the presence of a handful of large landowners in the House of Lords, there were relatively few members of the Catholic middle class. Where there were larger numbers of adherents of Catholicism was in the industrial cities of the north. Joseph Garvey, whom we shall meet in this section, is an example of this milieu. There was little reason to be a nominal Catholic or Nonconformist, so, whilst lacking the numbers that the Church of England could claim, there was perhaps a higher level of belief and devotion amongst their adherents. Catholics and Nonconformists were very different in their approach to ritual and symbolism but to be a member of either was to stand outside of the mainstream Church of England.

This advance of Nonconformism, the growth of Catholicism particularly as a result of Irish immigration, and the resultant increased efforts of the Church of England to maintain its supremacy as the national denomination had led to a situation in which 'the generations alive in 1914, particularly among the working classes, had been exposed to greater religious influence than at any previous time.'[7] However, this did not mean that Christianity was all-triumphant. Archaeological and scientific criticisms of the traditional interpretation of the Bible had challenged the infallibility of scriptural knowledge, whilst some objected that Christian evangelisation smacked too much of the middle classes preaching down to the working classes, and many in the Anglican church were wary of people being nominal, rather than active, Christians.

In general, British Christians gave full support to Britain's war effort. For Nonconformists, the 'rape of Belgium' could be equated with the Nonconformists' struggle against the dominance of the Church of England. Up until 1916, army recruitment followed the voluntary system, which appealed to their sense of free, individual moral choice. The Church of England had given official credence to the just war theory in its Articles of Religion of 1571, one of which stated, 'It is lawful for Christian men, at the commandment of the Magistrate, to wear weapons and serve in the wars.'[8] One of the obligations of being the established church of the state was allowing Christians to fight for that state. The Church of England also played an important role in wartime propaganda. It helped to transform a war begun for strategic political and economic interests into something approaching a holy war. Many clergy preached patriotic sermons and senior churchmen emphasised the moral and spiritual superiority of Britain's war aims. Arthur Winnington-Ingram, the Bishop of London, put this case in December 1915: 'No one believes more absolutely than I do in the righteousness of this present war; as I have said a thousand times, I look upon it as a war for purity, for freedom, for international honour, and for the principles of Christianity. I look on everyone who fights for this cause as a hero, and everyone who dies in it as a martyr.'[9]

The tradition of British Protestantism and the right of the individual to read and interpret the teachings of the Bible in a personal manner, stretching back to the time of the Reformation and beyond to John Wyclif, still held strong. Thus a huge spectrum of interpretations of its perspective on warfare led people to advocate the most ardent nationalism through to the most passionate pacifism. Some recalled that the most prominent influencer of the Reformation, Martin Luther, was himself German and therefore saw beyond national boundaries, whilst others saw Britain in the tradition of Cromwell, Wesley and Bunyan and accused Germany of being the source of a more liberal and critical attitude towards the Bible.

Lloyd George, the then Chancellor of the Exchequer of the Liberal government, addressed an audience of 3,000 Nonconformists at the City Temple on 10 November 1914, calling for them to show sympathy with the cause of justice and the small nationalities. The chair of the meeting declared, 'If we had not been Christians, we should not have been in this War. It is Christ ... who has taught us to care for small nations and to protect the rights of the weak ... The devil would have counselled neutrality, but Christ has put His sword into our hands.'[10] He compared Britain to the Good Samaritan coming to the aid of the stricken. The painting *The Great Sacrifice* by James

Clark, published in *The Graphic* magazine in 1914, counterposed Christ's crucifixion with that of a slain British soldier. Some saw the war as a chance for Britain to turn its back on materialism, social division and selfishness and embrace that idea of sacrifice leading to a state of grace.

In Ireland, 92,000 men had enlisted by 1916, about half of whom were Catholics.[11] John Redmond, the nationalist MP, calculated that a display of loyalty from Ireland would advance the cause of Home Rule. In a similar tone, the Irish Catholic *All Hallows Journal* argued that support for the war would advance Irish independence.

Historians have argued for the notion of a 'diffusive Christianity', or the underlying strain of popular religion that permeated much of British society – a cultural ideal of Christian behaviour that was widely shared.[12] This was a Christianity that went beyond mere church attendance; 'Even if Christian belief was declining, which is a proposition difficult to prove, and one which is more questionable than secularisation theorists suggest, this does not mean that the habits of thought and the unspoken assumption had disappeared.'[13] Regular church-going was common among the upper classes and therefore Christianity played a large role in the public life of the country.

In addition, Britain had a history of Sunday school education stretching back to the 1780s and by the mid-nineteenth century religious education, either in day or Sunday school, had extended to most rural and urban areas. In 1888 about three out of four children attended Sunday schools. In 1906, Wesleyan Sunday schools taught more than a million children.[14] The Primitive Methodist movement could point to 'a continued enlargement of Sunday school work', and significantly, 'the retention for a longer period than formerly of the Scholars in the Schools, the increasing number of select and Adult Bible Classes'.[15] However, for many, this was where their experience of religion ended, leading to a disconnection between the juvenile and adult male and the daily life of the churches.

As well as bringing forth the notion of a Christ-like sacrifice, it was also seen that the war provided a biblical backdrop to some of its events. Damascus had seen the empires of Babylon and Nineveh rise and fall, and was now witnessing the impact of 'the Kaiser's ill-starred and horrible war'.[16] *The Times* reported how British soldiers had 'camped near to the rivers where the exiles of Israel hanged their harps; they have pursued the fleeing enemy along the road which led from Egypt to Babylon; they have known the cities to which St Paul wrote.'[17] One soldier wrote to his parish magazine in Cheshire to say the war had taken him to Hebron and Bethlehem, and he had received a special commemorative card from his padre for receiving Easter communion in Jerusalem.[18] Three of the case studies in this book – Philip Bryant, Russell Barry and J.V. Salisbury – refer to their war in those biblical lands.

That people could relate their war to stories from the Bible shows its importance in the British culture. 'The English Bible is the first of treasures,' King George V had stated in 1911.[19] The War Office already had well-established protocols for handing out religious literature to regular soldiers, but the vast expansion of the British Armed Forces between 1914 and 1918 meant that Christian trusts and charities enhanced this provision. The Young Men's Christian Association (YMCA), the Society for Promoting Christian Knowledge (SPCK), the Religious Tract Society, the British and Foreign Bible Society, the Scripture Gift Mission (SGM), the Pocket Testament League and the Trinitarian Bible Society all endeavoured to provide whole Bibles, New Testaments, individual Gospels, Psalms and the Book of Proverbs, as well as prayer cards and hymn books. Whilst estimates are very difficult to come by, Alan Wilkinson suggested a number of 40 million pieces were distributed from 1914 to 1916.[20]

In the front of the SGM Bible was found a message from Lord Roberts, a hero of the Afghan and Boer Wars, to the troops, dated 25 August 1914:

I ask you to put your trust in God. He will watch over you and strengthen you. You will find in this little Book guidance when you are in health, comfort when you are in sickness, and strength when you are in adversity.

These particular Bibles contained a section at the back where the serviceman could sign a personal commitment to Christ. It is claimed that many grieving families were comforted by the sight of that page signed by their loved one when the deceased's possessions were returned. Richard Schweitzer has identified three main areas of the use of the Bible for the British serviceman in the First World War: drawing general strength and comfort from its possession; providing solace in wounding and death; and the importance of specific readings or quotations that were marked or commented on in letters or diaries. Schweitzer concluded that the Psalms were the most popular texts in the final context, followed by the Gospels of St John and St Matthew. In general, the Psalms excepted, the New Testament proved more popular than the old.[21]

However, in some ways the Bible had been at relatively low ebb by 1914. James Bryce, former ambassador to the United States, commented in early 1914 that, 'It is with great regret that one sees in these days that the knowledge of the Bible seems to be declining in all classes of the community.'[22] Just a year later, the mayor of Bath was able to comment that one of many results of the war was a rediscovery of the Bible, and it was 'being read in England more readily that it had been for many a long day.'[23]

A *Times* article on 19 August 1916 considered the changed importance of the Bible in wartime.[24] The anonymous correspondent claimed that the words of the Bible had shown a personal understanding of the situation of British people in wartime in a number of ways. As the war demanded new standards of service and sacrifice, the correspondent thought that the Holy Scriptures had presupposed this demand, and that a link had been created between the prophets and apostles on the one hand, and the members of the modern British nation on the other. There was a 'feeling of intimacy with something living and personal in the words of the Bible'. The article identified four separate parts of the Bible as being of particular significance during the war. Firstly, the Psalms had developed a particular resonance. After a period of relative neglect, 'they needed the leaping up of the fires through the crust of life to make them clear.' The Psalms had given the nation a prayer for the Belgian refugees, 'When the Lord turned again to the captivity of Zion' (Psalm 126:1). The Book of Revelation had echoes of the 'death struggle ... the Church and the Beast' and gave credence to the idea that issues are decided in conflict. The Bible also gave examples of 'deliverance through the shedding of blood', and the examples of Job and Jeremiah were cited as men who faced extreme challenges in life. The Gospels offered comfort to those in distress and overall the Bible gave a 'smile of recognition by singers and thinkers and prophets'. Finally, the Bible offered the reassurance that eventually the clash of armies will be replaced by the 'nobler enterprises of the commonwealth of nations'.

In a similar vein, the *Derby Daily Telegraph* reported on an address to the local auxiliary of the British and Foreign Bible Society by the Reverend Dr Jones.[25] His contention was that the war had ended the period when the Bible had become seen as a book just like any other, to be analysed and criticised:

> In the cloistered seclusion of their studies critics had in the past written nice little essays to prove that the Bible was just like any other book, and they had tried to deny its inspiration, but the tragic events of today were blowing their pretty little theories sky high and bringing them to utter scorn. They might say that it was nothing but an ordinary, fallible human book, but the men facing death in the trenches and the people sitting in show homes knew different; they knew that it was the word of God.

This sentiment was echoed by C.T. Studd, the famous missionary who had also played Test cricket for England in his youth. The war had not been caused by the nation, but by the lack of faith in the Bible as God's truth. 'Look at the way we picked the Bible to pieces, like the Germans picked the Belgian Treaty to pieces. If we had held to the Bible the nation would have been in a different state today.'[26] *The Times* agreed that 'it has not retained the place it held in the lives of our predecessors even fifty years ago.'[27] Biblical criticism had altered people's conception, and had to some degree relegated the Bible to the level of myth and folklore.

However, this increased profile for the Bible does not seem to have translated into a general religious revival. In 1916 the Church of England saw fit to begin a National Mission led by the archbishops to remove misconceptions about the Gospel, to call people to nationwide and personal repentance and to claim that the only hope for the nation lay in the Living Christ. Its message began with a passage from Deuteronomy 30:15-19: 'See, I have set before thee this day life and good, and death and evil ... therefore choose life.' This mission failed to have the desired impact and in 1919, the Reports of the Archbishops' Committees of Inquiry described the Church's failures to evangelise, encourage worship, provide efficient administration and a relevant message for the nation's problems. One of the suggested solutions was to teach less of the Old Testament and more of the New to children: 'The first eleven chapters of Genesis are not fitted for them. Nor are the plagues, though the deliverance from Egypt is.'[28] A further report identified a decline in the habits of prayer, worship and Sunday observance. It had been hoped by churchmen that the war would stem the tide of secularism and revive religion by bringing the reality of death into focus.

Thus it would appear that whilst the First World War had marked a decline in the traditional markers of Christian faith, it provided an opportunity for those who had embraced its fundamentals while young to have those beliefs reinforced and strengthened.

The six individuals examined here display the complexities of that faith. John Reith's Scottish Presbyterianism led him to broadcast his message of faith as he was later to broadcast to the world through the BBC. David Jones entered the war with some degree of Anglican faith, but found for himself the true nature of Christianity while witnessing a simple mass held in a barn on the Western Front, lighting the way for a future conversion to Catholicism. J.V. Salisbury saw God's metaphorical and literal protection through the Bible he had purchased before heading off to war, whilst Joseph Garvey maintained a solid Catholic faith through a long captivity as a prisoner of war. Lewis Valentine found he was able to maintain his Baptist beliefs through service in the Royal Army Medical Corps (RAMC), that service fuelling his emerging senses of both pacifism and Welsh nationalism. Philip Bryant drew on his sincere Nonconformist beliefs to give him strength in times of adversity.

It is my hope that in their stories, the reader may find connections with the truth, humanity and sincerity displayed in these men's war experiences, and respect in the ways in which they conducted their lives during those difficult four years through the prism of their Christian beliefs.

Chapter 1

John Reith

'There remaineth, therefore, a Sabbath rest to the people of God'

John Reith was the founder of the BBC and one of the titanic figures of British public life in the twentieth century. To this day, the term 'Reithian' refers to a set of values that permeate public service broadcasting. These were set out by John Reith in 1922 as being 'to educate, inform and entertain'. Had a sniper's bullet seven years previously been half and inch higher, then John would not have been alive in 1922, and the shape of public service broadcasting in the United Kingdom and beyond may have taken a different path in the proceeding five decades.

John Charles Walsham Reith was born on 20 July 1889 at Stonehaven, Kincardineshire. His father, George, a graduate of the University of Aberdeen and New College, Edinburgh, was the minister at the Presbyterian College Church in the West End of Glasgow. He also served as the first chaplain for the Boys' Brigade, founded in the same city. John's mother, Adah, had been raised an Anglican. There were six older children in the family, with John being the youngest by ten years. He recalled his mother teaching him hymns and psalms and stories from the Bible.[1]

John attended Sunday school from an early age, and at the age of six was enrolled into the Band of Hope, promising to abstain from all 'intoxicating liquors and beverages'.[2] He was enrolled at Glasgow Academy, but did not enjoy his education there. Despite the constant encouragement of his father he coasted through his studies and developed poor relationships with many of the staff and students. When he was fifteen, his father was advised to transfer him elsewhere, so John was sent away to Gresham's School in Norfolk. In his second term there he ran away from school, but was leniently dealt with. However, he refused to attend Sunday evening concerts as they offended his faith, which would not condone such frivolity on the Sabbath.

On leaving school he reluctantly undertook a career in engineering, something he felt to be an 'affront to one's intelligence and intellect'.[3] He enrolled at the Glasgow Technical College (now the University of Strathclyde) in 1908 and worked long hours. On some evenings, he paraded with the Glasgow University company of the 1st Lanarkshire Rifle Volunteers. He was soon promoted to sergeant and claimed to have 'war in my bones'.[4] Membership of the Territorial Army seemed to have given John the sense of purpose, status and satisfaction that his career had not, despite the awarding of some first class certificates. He was commissioned into the 5th Scottish Rifles in 1911 but found the formality of mess life trying. He was 'not a good mixer, nor had I entered into the spirit of the thing; intolerant, reserved and aloof.'[5]

During this time John began a diary – which he would keep for the next sixty years – with the florid inscription: 'My Diary – being a Chronicle more or less Faithful of the Doings both in Public and Private of J.C.W. Reith, Likewise a Survey of his Thoughts Expressed or Otherwise, and a Record of his Transactions with Others.'[6]

From 1912 John developed an intense, affectionate but seemingly platonic relationship with a boy named Charlie Bowser, seven years his junior. His biographer claimed that, 'For the best part of ten years ... Reith's friendship with Charlie was the most important thing in his life.'[7] Charlie's family had moved to London in 1913, prompting John to take a position with Pearson & Son, a large civil engineering contractor based in the capital. John impressed his new employer with the intensity of his work. John and Charlie took a holiday together, during which they would spend many hours reading the Bible. When on the Western Front, John carried two photographs with him constantly; one of his father and one of Charlie. Throughout the war, Charlie wore a ring that John had bought for him.

John joined the London Scottish Rugby Club and had ambitions to make the First XV and then the Scotland team, but the onset of war in July of 1914 excited him more. In August he returned to Glasgow to rejoin his territorial regiment and was presented with his dog tag, inscribed 'Lieut. J.C.W. Reith Pres 5th SR' – 'Pres' being short for Presbyterian. After four weeks he was made transport officer, a move very pleasing to John as it meant that he was excused routine parades and orderly duties, and was to a large extent his own boss. As he put it, he was 'a somebody; an object of mystification, envy and even respect among [my] brother officers'.[8] It also meant he could wear spurs on his riding boots, something of which he was inordinately proud and which provided the title for his wartime autobiography five decades later. He found himself in charge of fifty men and commanded them to up their game, including attending church parades with the rest of the battalion. At the end of October the 5th Scottish Rifles was transferred to France. John continued to try to observe the Sabbath as best as he could, and thought badly of his commanding officer when no such observance took place. However, on one occasion when the battalion had joined the 19th Brigade, there was a Presbyterian service, which made John yearn his father's College Church.[9]

By mid-December 1914, John's transport section was stationed in Armentières, which received heavy shelling. The section remained unscathed and John recalled the words of Psalm 91 of God being a refuge and a fortress, and made a note of those from Hebrews 4:9: 'There remaineth, therefore, a Sabbath rest to the people of God'.[10] He also recited Psalm 23 to himself while having a bath, in order to console his mind after a sharp disagreement with his adjutant. John was starting to consider himself responsible not only for the physical well-being of the men under him, but also their spiritual well-being. When he discovered that his batman, Tudhope, did not know the words of this psalm, he was sent off to learn it and recite it the next day.

During Easter 1915, John urged his non-commissioned officers to read their Bibles, and noted that they added this to their list of routine duties. Of the fifty-five men under his command, only nine were church members. On Good Friday his persuasive powers meant that twenty-two of them were admitted into the Presbyterian Church by the army chaplain. John felt compelled to record their names and to list them in his account of the Great War written five decades later: Whitelaw, Anderson, MacLelland, Tudhope, W.D. Wallace, Webb, Henderson, Mackie, Munro, T. Reid, H. Reid, Bulloch, Brown, Massey, Edmiston, Dick, Paton, Paul, Harker, Ferguson, Strang, Christie.[11] In May he received a parcel from his mother containing twenty-two Bibles, one for each of those men. John inscribed each one with their names and the words 'Easter Sunday 1915 JCWR'.

John read his Bible every day and also referred to a small book of devotional readings called *Daily Light*. On two occasions, his dedication to the teetotal pledge he had made at the age of six caused him some illness as the water available was not always clean, whereas the beer in the mess was safe to drink.

John felt that after the war he would like to achieve more academically and wrote to his father asking if he could be supported to go to Oxford University as, 'I believe God has given me intellect, which is an exceedingly rare and precious gift.'[12] He then wanted to follow a career in politics. His father contested these wishes, advising him to stay at Pearson's and, citing Carlyle, that the best university was a good library. He was reminded of the advice from Proverbs that 'before honour is humility'. John wanted to study the works of great philiosophers, historians and economists, and complained that he was forced to work with 'ill-educated rude mechanics who aruge about the size of a screw – the pettiness of the whole thing is not only distasetful but utterly revolting to anyone constituted as I am …'[13]

He did not find his relationships with his superiors easy, and frequently fell out with his adjutant and commanding officer, and actively considered a transfer to the Royal Engineers. He admitted finding it hard to find Christian forgiveness within himself. Having completed an interview for the transfer, he had to wait two months for it to be confirmed, and after much prayer it eventually came through in August 1915. He approved of a new fellow officer – a teetotal, non-smoking Wesleyan – but took a dislike to the Roman Catholic padre whom he had seen downing whiskies.

John was active on the front line of the trenches, rigging telephone connections. He showed little regard for his personal safety. During the preparations for the Battle of Loos in the autumn of 1915 he stood with his head above the parapet surveying the scene through his field glasses. On the morning of 7 October, John decided that the route along the communication trench to the front line was too congested so he climbed up onto the open ground, then jumped down again. However, the defences had been disturbed by German shelling and suddenly John felt a smack against his left cheek. He had been hit by a bullet and blood poured out onto his tunic. As a sergeant attempted to dress the wound John asked for some paper and wrote his mother's name and 'I'm all right', later claiming this was meant to be interpreted that he was ready to meet his death. He also wrote a note to Charlie, exhorting him to 'cheer up'.

John was moved to a general hospital, where he read a prayer book through his one good eye. He acknowledged some disappointment at being taken out of the action but also saw that he had had a narrow escape from death. He was invalided back to London and then heard news that Pearson's had been awarded a contract to organise munitions supplies from the United States to British forces. After a short time with the company in a position at Gretna Green, in February 1916 he sailed for New York, having first bought expensive presents for his parents and Charlie and also having prayed and joined in family worship with them. Psalm 91 was read, which nearly reduced John to tears.

John was to spend the next eighteen months in America. He made contact with the 2nd Presbyterian Church in Philadelphia and had a part to play in an improvement in quality and number of weapons being supplied to Britain. He was based in Swarthmore – home to a large Quaker community as well as a high number of Presbyterians – and took some pleasure in upsetting the pacifist sensibilities of the Quakers with his tales of action on the Western Front. Due to his imposing stature and war wound on his face he became a recognisable celebrity and was invited to speak at dinners. He spoke passionately about Scotland and the British war effort, and against the attempts of some Americans to accept German peace proposals to prevent America entering the war. He cited the oppression of Belgium, the massacre of Armenians, the destruction of Serbia and Poland and the starvation of Jews in the Holy Land, as well as the more domestically striking theme of the sinking of the *Lusitania*.

In one speech, delivered to the Presbyterian Social Union in January 1917, he quoted from the Book of Judges: 'Curse ye Meroz, said the angel of the Lord, curse ye bitterly the inhabitants thereof; because they came not to the help of the Lord, to the help of the Lord against the mighty.'[14] Thus he equated the British war aims in biblical terms, setting up his nation and undertaking the Lord's will on earth. In another address, this time to the Pennsylvania Scotch-Irish Society, he accused the Americans of making excuses not to take up arms and profiting from the war financially whilst their cousins in Britain were losing sons.

John built such a reputation that he was awarded an honorary Master of Science degree by Lafayette University. He left America in August 1917, having succeeded not only in improving the supply of munitions to the British Army, but having won many hearts and minds to the Allied cause. He had, in effect, talked himself out of a role, as American armaments manufacturers were now supplying their own army, which had entered the war in April 1917.

John Reith spent the rest of the war in England, being promoted to major and overseeing various engineering projects with the Royal Marine Engineers. After the war he set up an engineering company in Glasgow, with Charlie Bowser as his assistant, then in 1922 became the first general manager of the newly formed British Broadcasting Company. He came into conflict with Winston Churchill over the coverage of the 1926 General Strike, with Reith attempting an impartial reporting and anaysis of events. Under his directorship, there was no Sunday broadcasting before 12.30 pm so that people could observe the Sabbath. He served as Minister of Information in Chamberlain's wartime government and then in the Ministry of Transport under Churchill, being created Baron Reith. He became Rector of Glasgow University in 1965 and Lord High Commissioner of the General Assembly of the Church of Scotland in 1967, having previously turned down this highly coveted position in the 1940s as he could not bring himself to accept the offer from Churchill, whom he had detested since 1926.

John Reith showed a detemination not just to display personal courage, but to follow in his father's footsteps in the propogation of Presbyterian Christianity and an understanding of the Bible amongst his men. His, at times, awkward and forthright character produced both many enemies and admirers. This intensity drove him on to achieve great things in public life and, like many other characters in this book, he certainly fought his fight with all his might.

Chapter 2

David Jones

'I felt immediately the oneness between the Offerant and those toughs that clustered around him in a dim-lit byre'

David Jones is responsible for some of the most stunning poetry written about the First World War. His 1937 epic, *In Parenthesis*, is an outstanding work covering themes of classical and British history, culture and the relationship between the Celts and the English. W.H. Auden considered it 'the greatest book about the First World War'.[1] However, it has not gained a similar level of recognition to the work of other war poets such as Rupert Brooke, Wilfred Owen and Siegfried Sassoon. Unlike these three, David spent his whole war as a private, despite his lower middle-class upbringing and undoubted artistic skills, and so his work documents life from the point of view of the ordinary solider. (See plate 4.)

Born in Brockley, Kent, on 1 November 1895, David was the son of James Jones, a native of Flintshire who worked as a printer overseer for the Christian Herald Company and served as a lay preacher. His mother, Alice Bradshaw, a Londoner, was a former governess and Sunday school teacher. The family attended the local Anglican church. Although christened 'Walter David Michael Jones', by the age of eight he had persuaded his friends and family to call him David due to an emerging affinity with his father's Welsh roots. This was despite James himself having been discouraged from speaking Welsh in the home by his own father from the fear that it would restrict his opportunities in life. By the age of ten David was producing paintings and drawings of animals and entering them into national children's exhibitions.

He was educated at Brockley Road School, and then from 1909 to 1915 at Camberwell School of Arts and Crafts. His tutor, A.S. Hartrick, had worked with Van Gogh and Gaugin. On the outbreak of war the 19-year-old Jones tried to enlist in the Artists' Rifles, but was rejected on account of his chest measurement being too small. By January 1915, the physical entry requirements for the army were relaxed and after his father had written to Lloyd George, David enlisted as a private in the Royal Welsh Fusiliers, a rank at which he remained for the duration of the war. He also took the opportunity to see the Chancellor and future Prime Minister speak at the Queen's Hall in September 1914, comparing the nation of Wales to Britain's plucky allies of Belgium and Serbia, and referring to the Welsh spearmen who had helped the English win the Battle of Crecy in 1346.

After initial training in Llandudno and Winchester, he was sent to France in December 1915, and undertook sentry duty on the Richebourg Sector, undertaking fatigues such as repairing barbed wire and deepening trenches. On Christmas Day 1915, David, in a rest area behind the front line, heard news of an unofficial Christmas truce. Although nowhere near as extensive as the 1914 truce in which John Esslemont Adams took part (see Chapter 8), it began with British and German troops trying to out-sing each other. This news moved him and he wished he had been able to take part in it, the incident ending up as a reference in his later poem, *The Anathemata*.

In the summer of 1916 David's battalion was transferred to the Somme and, with the 38th (Welsh) Division on 10 July, after a few abortive moves up to the front line and back again, was ordered to attack Mametz Wood. The Welsh battalions went into battle, having beforehand sung *Jesu, Lover of my Soul*. As they began the attack, David's platoon officer, Lieutenant Rees, was shot in front of him. This incident was later recalled in *In Parenthesis*:

> *He sinks on one knee*
> *and now on the other,*
> *his upper body tilts in rigid inclination*
> *this way and back;*
> *weighted lanyard runs out to full tether,*
> > *swings like a pendulum*
> > *and the clock run down.*
> *Lurched over, jerked iron saucer over tilted brow,*
> *clampt unkindly over lip and chin*
> *nor no ventaille to this darkening*
> > *and masked face lifts to grope the air*

and so disconsolate;
enfeebled fingering at a paltry-strap –
buckle holds,
holds him blind against the morning.[2]

David walked on for 500 yards through a turmoil of bullets and shrapnel, the walk taking four minutes. He and the other survivors reached the first German trench, tripping and falling into it. It was full of corpses. They pushed on further, and were then ordered to dig in at night-time to hold their gains. After midnight, as David had been sent into the wood to clear a path for the morning, he felt a sharp pain in his left calf. Realising from the blood that he had been shot, he discarded his pack and crawled back towards the British trench. He was soon forced to abandon his rifle as it was impeding his progress. As he had spent each day of the previous seven months cleaning and oiling the weapon, he felt 'a sense of shame and … real affection … the feeling of leaving a mate … or as when a child has to leave a toy it has had affection for'.[3] David was found by a corporal from his battalion and carried some of the way back before the latter was ordered to 'drop the bugger here' by a Major Edwards as manpower was needed to fight the enemy. David crawled some more until he was found by stretcher bearers. In Part 7 of *In Parenthesis*, David relived the moment he received the injury and his subsequent mental struggle on having to leave behind his rifle in order to crawl to safety, leaving it perhaps for a future battlefield tourist to claim as a souvenir:

And to Private Ball it came as if a rigid beam of great weight
flailed about his calves, caught from behind by ballista-baulk
let fly or aft-beam slewed to clout gunnel-walker
below below below.
When golden vanities make about,
you've got no legs to stand on.
He thought it disproportionate in its violence considering
the fragility of us.
The warm fluid percolates between his toes and his left boot
fills, as when you tread in a puddle – he crawled away in the
opposite direction.

It's difficult with the weight of the rifle.
Leave it — under the oak.
Leave it for a salvage-bloke
let it lie bruised for a monument
dispense the authenticated fragments to the faithful.
It's the thunder-besom for us
it's the bright bough borne
it's the tensioned yew for a Genoese jammed arbalest and a
scarlet square for a mounted mareschal, it's that county-mob
back to back. Majuba mountain and Mons Cherubim and
spreaded mats for Sydney Street East, and come to Bisley
for a Silver Dish. It's RSM O'Grady says, it's the soldier's
best friend if you care for the working parts and let us be 'av-
ing those springs released smartly in Company billets on wet
forenoons and clickerty-click and one up the spout and you
men must really cultivate the habit of treating this weapon with
the very greatest care and there should be a healthy rivalry
among you — it should be a matter of very proper pride and
Marry it man! Marry it!
Cherish her, she's your very own.
Coax it man coax it — it's delicately and ingeniously made
— it's an instrument of precision — it costs us tax-payers,
money — I want you men to remember that.
Fondle it like a granny — talk to it — consider it as you would
a friend and when you ground these arms she's not a rooky's
gas-pipe for greenhorns to tarnish.
You've known her hot and cold.
You would choose her from among many.
You know her by her bias, and by her exact error at 300, and
by the deep scar at the small, by the fair flaw in the grain,
above the lower sling-swivel —
but leave it under the oak.

Slung so, it swings its full weight, With you going blindly on
all paws, it slews its whole length, to hang at your bowed neck

like the Mariner's white oblation.
You drag past the four bright stones at the turn of Wood Support.
It is not to be broken on the brown stone under the gracious tree.
It is not to be hidden under your failing body.
Slung so, it troubles your painful crawling like a fugitive's irons.

* * *

At the gate of the wood you try a last adjustment, but slung
so, it's an impediment, it's of detriment to your hopes, you
had best be rid of it – the sagging webbing and all and what's
left of your two fifty – but it were wise to hold on to your mask.
You're clumsy in your feebleness, you implicate your tin-hat
rim with the slack sling of it.
Let it lie for the dews to rust it, or ought you to decently
cover the working parts.
Its dark barrel, where you leave it under the oak, reflects
the solemn star that rises urgently from Cliff Trench.
It's a beautiful doll for us
it's the Last Reputable Arm.
But leave it – under the oak.
Leave it for a Cook's tourist to the Devastated Areas and crawl
as far as you can and wait for the bearers.[4]

David was then carried to a forward dressing station to have the bullet removed. A medical orderly described his wound as a 'beautiful Blighty', the term used to describe a wound serious enough to mean a period of convalescence in Britain but not serious enough to cause significant permanent damage. An ambulance took him away from the fighting sector to a casualty clearing station, where he fell asleep. He was woken by the sound of a female nurse's voice, 'the nicest thing in the world', bringing back thoughts of a 'civilised world' that he had 'almost forgotten existed'.[5] David would remember the events of the Somme every July until his death. By the end of the encounter, more than 4,000 men of the 38th Welsh Division were killed, wounded or missing in battle.

David returned to England on the hospital ship *St David* for some initial recuperation in Birmingham before being transferred to the Cotswold village of Shipston-on-Stour. Here he formed a romantic attachment with an unregistered Voluntary Aid Detachment (VAD) nurse, Elsie Hancock. By visiting her house for tea, he broke the hospital rules and was discharged by the manager, a Dr McTaggart, who quoted the Ten Commandments to him in the context of obeying principles and regulations. He spent two weeks' convalescent leave at home, being taken aback by the ignorance of civilians of the real situation in the trenches and their concern with domestic matters. However, there was some amusement for him in a visit to a great-aunt who spoke to him about fighting the Prussians, who, she thought, had been right in 'the other war', referring back to the Franco-Prussian War of 1870–71.

It was October 1916 before David returned to the front, initially to reinforce trench defences for another big push the following summer, but then working from battalion headquarters drawing maps and sketches of enemy positions. From here he was transferred to the 2nd Field Survey Company of the Royal Engineers to make observations and sketches from positions on the Ypres Salient. Despite his artistic talent he found it challenging to focus on and record the rapid bullet traces and was subsequently returned to his battalion.

At this time David was still nominally an Anglican, and wrote a letter to his local vicar, the Reverend Edwin Davies of St James's, Hatcham. An edited version of it appeared in the *Christian Herald* in May 1917 in which David, despite the war dragging on, optimistically pointed out that whenever it would end, they were now nearer to peace. He recounted being keen to find out the truth behind alleged German atrocities to Belgian and French civilians during the opening months of the war in 1914 (see Chapter 17), and had found a French woman who recounted ten days of 'bare-faced cruelty and unheard-of arrogance', which David was inclined to believe.[6]

After his leg injury in 1916, David experienced another brush with death in 1917 when a mine exploded near him and a large piece of metal struck his helmet, leaving a pattern inside it and him unconscious. Again, a friend carried him to safety. However, it was early in 1917 that two events occurred that would see the young Anglican begin his journey to conversion to Catholicism.

One Sunday David was out searching for firewood to keep warm in the trenches when he came across a byre. He peered through a crack in the wall to see an altar made out of ammunition boxes surmounted by two candles. Half a dozen infantrymen were kneeling on the floor as a robed priest conducted Holy Mass. Two aspects greatly impressed him; the unity of spirit he sensed from the service and the fact that it was taking place so close to the front line. He noticed a large Irishman and a naturalised English–Italian, both of whom he knew. The former's devotion particularly impressed him: 'I felt immediately the oneness between the Offerant and those toughs that clustered around him in a dim-lit byre – a thing I had never felt remotely as a Protestant at the Office of Holy Communion.' He later described it as a 'great marvel'.[7]

In the spring of 1917 he became friendly with a Jesuit Catholic chaplain, Father Daniel Hughes. Hughes had won the Military Cross for administering the sacraments to the dying in no-man's-land and lent Jones a classic Catholic text, St Francis de Sales' *The Introduction to the Devout Life*. David was increasingly being drawn to the idea that the virtues of heroism, love between soldiers and sacrifice he had witnessed over the past two years were spiritual ones, and the book echoed this view of the spiritual virtues found in ordinary people. For David, Anglicanism had become a matter of routine, a sentiment echoed by Russell Barry (see Chapter 9). Whilst some nominal Anglicans became sceptics or agnostics, he was drawn to what he saw as a deeper, richer faith with a tradition stretching further back than the Church of England. He later claimed that from this point he was 'inside, a Catholic'.[8] However, he did not formally convert until after the war – partly because he wanted to give more thought to such a huge decision and partly so that he could explain any conversion in depth to his staunchly Anglican parents.

In February 1918 David contracted trench fever and returned to England, where he spent some months recuperating before being posted to Limerick. He remained in Ireland until being demobilised in the middle of January 1919. Although he was anxious to join the British forces in Russia, his father persuaded him not to go. He returned to his studies, this time at the Westminster School of Art from 1919 to 1922.

On 7 September 1921, David formally converted to Catholicism, choosing 'Michael' as his confirmation name, and he joined a small community of Catholic artists, the Guild of St Joseph and St Dominic, headed by craftsman Eric Gill. He continued to combine his art and his faith, including producing wood engravings for a Welsh translation of the Book of Ecclesiastes.

David Jones branched out from engraving and painting to publish his epic poem about the war, *In Parenthesis*, in 1937. It had taken him nearly ten years to write and had been stimulated by his response to reading Erich Maria Remarque's *All Quiet on the Western Front*: 'Bugger it; I can do better than that. I'm going to write a book.'[9] It had been a painful experience, reliving scenes of horror, and had led to a severe nervous breakdown in 1932.

The poem won him the admiration of W.B. Yeats and T.S. Eliot, the latter being 'deeply moved … I still regard it as a work of genius … A work of literary art which uses the language in a new way.'[10] In the poem, David takes on the character of an English private, John Ball, serving in a combined English and Welsh regiment. The work covers the period of seven months from embarkation from Southampton to the assault on Mametz Wood, which had left an enduring impression on David. A mixture of verse and prose, the poem makes frequent allusions to Irish and Welsh mythology, as well as references to Mallory and Shakespeare. David also turned to the Bible, with references to 'seventy times seven times' of (Matthew 18:21-3) and the 'Helmets of Salvation' (Ephesians 6:14). Halfway through the poem, David introduces the character of Dai (David) Greatcoat, a typical soldier who has fought in wars of legend, the Bible and history and who re-emerges in the twentieth century proving the maxim that 'Old Soldiers never die, they just fade away'.

David's second epic poem, *The Anathemata* (1952), demonstrated his belief that all art should be a form of worship, and that all worship to God should be a form of art. For David it was the act of the Mass that encapsulated this artistic form. The scene he had witnessed back in 1917 in the byre near the front line had stayed with him and become the centrepiece of his understanding of man's relationship with God.

David Jones continued to write and paint until his death in 1974. His war experience had been a near continuous grind from the winter of 1915–16 through to his demobilisation in 1919. He saw action at the Somme and Passchendaele, being wounded twice. The fight led to a transformed and deeper faith, one that his talent allowed to be expressed through art and literature, including the remarkable *In Parenthesis*, essential reading for anyone seeking to understand the interplay between the First World War and the development of poetic forms.

Chapter 3

J.V. Salisbury

'I got a piece of shell half through the Bible in my Pocket. Which was much better than tearing through my guts at such short range'

Of the many millions of Bibles handed out by groups such as the British and Foreign Bible Society and the Scripture Gift Mission, few can have been as valuable as that purchased by a young Lancastrian, John Salisbury, from the Manchester outlet of the Bible Society shortly before he departed for war.

John Victor Salisbury was born in industrial Lancashire on 17 May 1887. By his early twenties he was a grocer's assistant near Preston. Like many of his generation, he volunteered for active service, and enlisted into the Royal Marines Medical Unit of the Royal Naval Division on 28 June 1915. He was described as being 5 feet 6¾ inches in height and of a fresh complexion.

Following some basic medical training, on 21 August that same year, his unit left Blandford Camp in Dorset to travel to Southampton to embark on their voyage to the Dardanelles. The Dardanelles, or Gallipoli, campaign had seen British and Empire forces suffer a humiliating series of reversals at the hands of Turkish forces since the initial landings at Sulva Bay in April 1915, and Salisbury was being sent out to back up the August offensive in what was to prove one final but futile attempt to establish a firm footing in the enemy Ottoman Empire.

Sailing on the hospital ship *Oxfordshire*, bound for Malta, Salisbury's faith was frequently in evidence. On 23 August a service was held on board ship during which gospel hymns were sung by moonlight. When the ship docked at Valetta on 23 August he attended the garrison church and heard a sermon on Naaman, the leper from the Book of Kings, with the message 'Wash and be clean'. While there he also took the opportunity to visit the medieval cave dwellings where sacrificial human bones were displayed, a potent reminder of the modern-day sacrifice to be exacted from Salisbury's generation.

He then embarked on a 'dirty cattle boat', sleeping uncomfortably on deck en route to Alexandria. On 4 September a submarine was spotted, and a French cruiser had to follow Salisbury's vessel into the harbour for protection. On leaving the boat, the men marched through the ancient city to camp, witnessing 'Priests, Rabbis, Camels, perfectly groomed Donkeys with what looked like desert chiefs astride them', and spread their blankets out on the desert sand to rest.[1]

While exploring the city of Alexandria, John was able to appreciate the faith of the Islamic religion. He paused at an entrance to a mosque and saw 'a completely engrossed Mahomedan at Prayer'.[2] On 9 September the party left Alexandria on the *Ionian* to endure a rough passage to Crete. Many men were seasick, including Salisbury – 'my turn came at about 9 o'clock' – as his attempt to sleep on deck was foiled by the choppy sea wetting his blanket, and, going down below, 'deposited my tea on the floor.' He was criticised by a colleague for not leaving it on the deck. 'The thought that I had specially brought my Vomit below for him made me laugh between gulps.'[3] Salisbury spent the next day on a fast!

On 11 September he had his first sight of Crete and this was followed by passing the Greek islands. Finally, on 14 September the unit arrived at Cape Helles, at the foot of the Gallipoli Peninsula. Salisbury could see and hear the flashing and roar of the guns. The next day he marched to the ambulance dressing station and the reality of the danger of war was brought even closer as a shell dropped 60 feet from him. This continued as intermittent fire from a Turkish gun, christened 'Asiatic Annie' by Australian troops, kept the men on full alert.

Salisbury's job on the peninsula was explained, to assist the doctors of the different naval battalions treating the sick and wounded. He was assigned to the Hawke Battalion, which was due to move up to the forward trenches within seven days. In the meantime he tended to the sick and wounded in the battalion sick bay and enlarged a dugout for extra shelter. Remarkably, one of the men Salisbury treated showed him his New Testament, which had a bullet embedded in it, the Bible having saved him from more serious injury or death. As the man admitted to having strayed away from the prayerful habits taught by his mother, Salisbury advised him to get back to them.

On 22 September John went up to the trenches, just 200 yards behind the firing line, and quickly 'learnt to keep cover from Bullets cracking and whizzing around.' This new duty involved attending to men wounded when scanning through the periscope. He was kept busy as 'Johnny Turk was good at sniping.' However, he did note a 'lovely sunset, and looked over the Plain of Troy, the scene of ancient battles.'[4]

The sick bay received a visit from Sir Ian Hamilton, commander of the whole Dardanelles campaign on 10 October, just six days before he was recalled to London, the campaign having failed to meet its objectives. Salisbury noted 'his neat uniform and snow white collar – a marked contrast to our muddy and unclean condition.'[5] Another incident involved the commanding officer of the Hawke Battalion, Colonel Leslie Wilson MP and future Governor of Queensland. He had been admitted to the sick bay suffering from dysentery, and one orderly, in the absence of the bay's dispenser of drugs, accidently gave him an overdose of opium, which nearly killed him!

By 9 November an outbreak of jaundice, combined with increasing flooding and cold, had brought about 'a Peninsula of sick and discouraged men'.[6] The cold soon turned to snow but this did not dampen Salisbury's faith and his desire to share worship with fellow Christians. On Sunday, 29 November there was a mouth organ sing-song, with everyone joining in singing old hymns.

In early December, after ten days in the trenches, the incident occurred in which the Bible purchased months previously in Manchester literally saved the life of John Victor Salisbury. (See plate 2.)

Sick Bay duties. Sick Bay and enlarged Portion of Trench covered with Tarpaulin, Turkish shell dropped in Sick Bay. Doc attending to some sick had his Stethoscope cut in two, all in Bay wounded. I was bandaging a chap with wounded wrist. The shell exploded beside us. We were blown down, faces blackened with the explosion. I had just turned the chap to get a better light on his wrist; this proved the Salvation for us both. He was slightly wounded. I got a piece of shell half through the Bible in my Pocket. Which was much better than tearing through my guts at such short range.

I found the best antidote to shock was to carry on with my job & finally we got the Doc & other chaps off to Hospital. I was ordered to rest awhile. Next day, on having a sponge down, I fisked from my legs with a Penknife a few tiny shell splinters, not worth reporting.[7]

He later reflected on the incident:

Why a Bible in one's Pocket. Well, along with other Christian chaps, we got a group of chaps together for Bible reading, Prayers & Hymn singing. I was C of E. Some of the others were Methodist or other Christian denominations. When opportunity offered we had H.C. [Holy Communion] with Padres of our respective churches. But often we were closer to the man. Padres were expected to be good – a Christian in the Ranks was in very close and critical observation, especially when under fire. Was he a coward? Did he grab the best in food, or most comfortable billet? Did he swear? Did he booze? His behaviour was watched at every turn.[8]

In late December orders came that the Gallipoli Peninsula was to be evacuated. Although the Turkish forces made a determined attack to try and cut off the beach to the retreating British and French forces, Salisbury and his comrades managed to transfer to Imbros, a Mediterranean island. Here the Hawke and its sister battalion, the Drake, installed a sick house which 'was, to us, the Lap of Luxury,' staying there until May 1916 before being transferred to France.[9] The evacuation, although not on the scale of that achieved at Dunkirk nearly twenty-five years later, was still regarded at the time as an excellent piece of strategic withdrawal.

Salisbury reflected that Gallipoli had been 'a romantic but dangerous experience'. As well as the Bible having saved his life, the episode had also given him wider appreciation of the Bible as he had had the opportunity to see the lands in which many of the stories had taken place. 'The Greek Isles, with the association of St John, Paul. Samothracia, Salonica, Patmos all mentioned in the N. Test: were interesting to a Bible student.'[10] But this romantic backdrop was contrasted with the reality of war: 'The stink of Death, the corpses rotting away, unburied from previous battles or the skulls peeping, half buried in the trenches we occupied were not romantic at all.'[11]

John put these conflicting thoughts into verse form while on the island of Imbros in January 1916:

> *Thy clay is soaked with British blood;*
> *'Twas freely given, that crimson flood,*
> *For freedom's cause and brotherhood*
> > *Gallipoli*
>
> *Thy deep ravines the graves enfold*
> *Of them who would the right uphold;*
> *Their valiant fight shall e'er be told:*
> > *Gallipoli*
>
> *They stormed thy cliffs and ventured far*
> *From Anzac cove and Sedd-el-Bahr,*
> *By sea and land on thee made war:*
> > *Gallipoli*
>
> *Shall we forget their noble deeds,*
> *These sons for whom the Empire bleeds?*
> *Thy corpse strewn shore their memory reads:*
> > *Gallipoli*
>
> *They bravely strove and suffered loss,*
> *Their deeds apparent failure gloss –*
> *Thine is the Crescent, theirs the Cross:*
> > *Gallipoli*
>
> *Nor have they suffered this in Vain,*
> *Tho' Victory's prize they did not gain:*
> *Their great example shall remain*
> > *Gallipoli*

J.V. Salisbury
RND[12]

In later life John emigrated to New Zealand, where he died in October 1980 at the grand age of ninety-four, having donated the Bible that had saved his life to the Liddle Archive at the University of Leeds.

J.V. Salisbury experienced warfare in biblical lands, being fascinated with seeing the places he knew of so well from his Bible studies. He worked under dangerous conditions to tend to wounded men in what was retrospectively seen as a poorly planned campaign. However, it was his copy of the book in which those stories were written that saved him in 1915 and allowed a subsequent long life.

Chapter 4

Joseph Garvey

'My formula was the simple one of never failing to say my prayers once in the morning and again at night each day'

Joseph Garvey was of working-class Irish ancestry. His physical, psychological and spiritual strength enabled him to endure nearly four years in captivity as a prisoner of war (see plate 3). He emerged with his faith intact and his moral fibre strengthened. His recollections were recorded in the 1950s and shine a fresh light on those forgotten souls who spent their war working at the behest of the Germans hundreds of miles from their comrades and their homes.

Joseph was the youngest of seven sons born to Thomas and Mary Ann Garvey (née Baines), being born on 16 September 1888 in Halifax, in the West Riding of Yorkshire. His father was a 'delver's bearer' at a quarry and the family was poor but strong. All the boys slept together in the bedroom whilst the parents had a pull-up bed in the living room. When Joe was a young boy, his father was killed in a quarrying accident, and his mother died a few years afterwards from the strain of holding together a large family by herself. All six of the brothers who survived childhood served in the army during the first two decades of the twentieth century. Joseph was a keen sportsman as a young man, having had the talent to have played football or rugby league professionally, had he taken the opportunities offered to him in these fields.

His Catholic faith was a hugely significant influence on him as a young man. Being from a family with Irish Catholic roots, Joe felt a loyalty to his religion, and carried on going to Mass throughout his teens. This was particularly challenging to a young, active sportsman as it meant refraining from food and drink from midnight until the act of Communion. Unlike many at this time, Joe did not attend Mass due to family ritual but as an orphan who had made an active decision to stay true to his faith. He attended St Bernard's Church in Halifax, which had been built by the voluntary labour of Irish immigrants. Joe later expressed his appreciation of the work of those who had preceded him:

> The least one could do was to remain loyal and when the time came to do what I could to support those who had gone before me in upholding my beliefs in a practical way and being faithful in all things attending to religious duties, giving a portion of my earnings towards the upkeep of the pastors, above all staying inside the church and working for its continuation and where possible its extension.[1]

Joe's early working life was spent in factories in Halifax and Manchester, but despite rising success in his work life, he decided that the only way he was going to see the world was by joining the army, so in 1907 he volunteered for the Scots Guards. He soon found himself able to adapt to the iron discipline of the sixteen-week training course. Due to hours previously spent at the Albion Street Gymnasium in Halifax, Joe was the best in his group and promoted to 'No. 1', meaning he undertook each gym exercise first after the instructor had demonstrated.

While stationed in Aldershot with the Scots Guards, Joe continued with his spiritual life, attending the garrison church for church parades, which were at that time compulsory for all in the army. He then spent a year based at Wellington Barracks, near Buckingham Palace, and would frequently undertake guard duty for the royal family, as well as sometimes guarding the nation's wealth at the Bank of England in Threadneedle Street. Joe kept his faith strong during this year by regularly attending Mass at a small church behind the barracks and also, occasionally, in the newly built Westminster Cathedral, the mother church for the Catholic faith in England and Wales.

A further year was spent at Windsor, including being on duty during the funeral of Edward VII in 1910. On the day after the funeral he was on sentry duty outside Windsor Castle when a uniformed figure approached and said, 'Good morning, sentry', in good English. Joe sloped arms and presented as he recognised the figure as Kaiser Wilhelm II of Germany. Little was he to know that he would see the Kaiser again just over four years later in very different circumstances.

In 1910 Joe left the army and worked as a canteen waiter at an army camp and then as a postman under a scheme whereby a certain number of jobs in the General Post Office had to be kept open for ex-servicemen. He continued with his sporting and academic interests, as well as becoming active as a trade unionist, 'to get the bottom dog a fair deal.'[2] During this time he also met Louise Beaumont, who became his fiancée. She was a Protestant at that time but became increasingly interested in the Catholic faith and was eventually received into the Catholic Church in early 1915.

As Joe was still on the army reserve list, he was immediately recalled on the outbreak of war. On 5 August 1914 he left Halifax for London, and after meeting up with former comrades went to the Tower of London for a medical examination. He was classed as A1 and therefore fit for immediate front-line service. He transferred to Aldershot for a week's training before leaving England on 13 August bound for Le Havre. By 22 August he was near Mons, the scene of the first major engagement between British and German forces in the First World War.

Joe's first experience of warfare came the following day, when a German cavalry group about fifty strong was spotted and his platoon was sent up as part of an ambush party and they opened fire on them from above a main road. Most of the Uhlans were killed. Joe recalled:

> I had taken a human life for the first time. I was only concerned at that stage in obeying orders from my superiors and doing the work I was sent out to do with zeal and efficiency.[3]

However, instead of advancing after this success, the Retreat from Mons was ordered and Joe marched 177 miles in fourteen days until he was south of Paris. This march was carried out in scorching conditions while carrying a 105lb pack and a rifle. He then took part in the Battle of the Marne, the engagement that saved Paris from falling to the Germans, and then spent thirty-four days at the Aisne, frequently patrolling no-man's-land. He felt a 'Guardian Angel' working very hard on his behalf: 'From the beginning to the end of the war my formula was the simple one of never failing to say my prayers once in the morning and again at night each day.'[4] He then entrained for Belgium to see more action in the crucial first few battles of the war.

On 19 October the battalion marched to Poperinghe and engaged in the First Battle of Ypres. Ten days later, Joe lost a man named Stringer, someone he had grown to love dearly: 'He died in my arms with the loveliest smile on his face that I have ever seen.'[5] On the same day, 29 October 1914, after relentless attacks on their line, Joe and a man named Roff made for cover in a farmhouse 30 yards back. But the building was swarming with Germans and they were made to surrender at gunpoint. They joined a handful of others who had also been taken prisoner, and then were marched towards Menin to form a larger party of prisoners. During this march the party was ordered to halt as a very important person was in a field by the side of the road. It was Kaiser Wilhelm II, in close proximity to Joe for the second time in four years. Joe reflected that for all his confidence at seeing so many 'Old Contemptibles' captured, the Germans had made few gains despite overwhelming superiority in numbers.

About 240 prisoners were taken to Schneidemühl, in modern-day Poland. This was one of what eventually amounted to nearly 300 prisoner-of-war camps under German authority. They travelled in cattle trucks, packed forty to each one with limited opportunities for exercise, eating and toileting. This journey lasted more than a hundred hours and the train covered over 500 miles.

Two miles outside of the town there was a large camp that already housed 150,000 Russian prisoners of war. It was soon clear that prisoners were being captured by the Germans faster than they were able to accommodate them. Many of the Russians had no shelter and were expected to spend the harsh winter in holes dug into a hillside, with straw, blankets and sleeping close together the only means of keeping from freezing at night. The problem of accommodation was not unique to the German authorities as all nations struggled to meet the terms of the Hague Convention of 1907 to provide adequate shelter and nourishment for prisoners.

The Russians were suffering from malnourishment and in these conditions typhus fever flourished. The situation improved slightly by mid-January as the British prisoners were given new barracks, which at least meant some shelter and warmth, and the ability to cook food from the regular supply of parcels that were now coming through. However, about 10 per cent of British prisoners at this time died from typhus fever and the Russians had an even higher death toll as they were not accorded many of the privileges granted to the British.

Joe himself became seriously ill with typhus fever in February 1915; he was in such a bad condition that his personal effects were sent home to his fiancée. He was treated by being starved of food so the typhus germs had nothing to feed on, and then was nursed back to strength on goat's milk and seed cake. Conditions began to improve as 1915 progressed, with the typhus death toll decreasing and a new camp commandant, Bond, being appointed. Joe found him a kindly man, willing to improve the welfare of the prisoners.

Joe mixed and made friends with men of many nationalities, including Russians, French, Belgians, Serbs and a range of British Army troops – black and white – from all around the globe. Parcels were of particular importance, with about 9 million food parcels and 800,000 clothing parcels being received by British prisoners abroad (see also Chapter 11).

As well as the parcels containing foodstuffs, Joe was particularly delighted to receive, from his future father-in-law, a parcel containing a full football kit, including his old football boots. Some of the football matches that took place within the camp attracted crowds of up to 5,000 people. Games took place daily but on Sundays there were special exhibition matches featuring the best players in the camp. Joe often featured in these matches as centre half or full back.

As many as 750,000 British prisoners of war were employed in agriculture and about 300,000 in industry. Joe's first experience of what were called working commandos was in October 1915, when he was sent to work on a farm near Bromberg. The farmer was a severe taskmaster and Joe soon found a way to be removed from that job, aided by the local policeman. Many of the prisoners found good commandos in farms or factories and worked right up until the end of the war.

Joe's next job was also on a farm, where he was given his own room, good food and there was central heating in the farmhouse. He would drive the family trap into town, but declined the invitation from the lady of the household to attend the local Evangelical church, insisting on going to the Catholic church on the same street. This caused some surprise as she had assumed that all British soldiers were Protestants (in fact between 10 and 15 per cent were Catholics). This often meant missing the end of Mass, as the lady's stipulation was that he could attend the Catholic service as long as he was ready to pick her up at the end of the Protestant one.

This job lasted little over a month, as once again Joe refused to undertake excessively heavy and unpleasant work on the farm, so he was sent back to the prison camp. He found himself favoured by one of the sergeant majors, a man named Kunze, for whom Joe had previously acted as an interpreter, and was given the option of staying in camp or only being sent out on a job that would prove relatively pleasant.

At Joe's request, he was sent on another farm commando with three other British prisoners to join four French prisoners who had been captured at Verdun. The main task on this one was hoeing potatoes, and once again food proved plentiful and nutritious. However, Joe's command of languages soon became apparent to the landowner, Herr Jochami, and he was asked to give lessons in English to Jochami's son, with his wife also taking part.

On his return to camp following this commando, Joe found some serious matters of national pride to attend to. The influx of French prisoners had meant that their football team had drawn 2–2 with the British one and there was a danger that in the next fixture there would be a French victory. Joe was invited to join the selection committee for the next match and was eventually given the job of selecting the team by himself. He dropped four of the most prominent players, a decision he later likened to dropping the legendary Billy Wright from the England team. Fortunately for Joe's reputation the game ended in a 3–0 victory for the English.

The prospect of regular football matches was just one of the reasons why Joe appears to have preferred being inside the prison camp rather than on a work commando. He would take part in the French soldiers' debating society, the discussion on one occasion being 'Confessions in the Catholic Church'. Joe put forward his belief that confessing one's sins kept one humble, avoiding the sin of pride that had led countries to wage war, and was well received by most in the debate. In general, Joe loved to discuss language and culture with men of all nationalities.

Although the Hague Convention allowed for the freedom of religious observation in prisoner of war camps, it was not always possible to provide chaplains of every faith. However, after the influx of French prisoners in

1916, a centre for observing Mass was established, with a French priest who had also been captured sharing the centre along with a Lithuanian Roman Catholic priest who ministered to the Russian-speaking soldiers. Joe would attend these Masses, which were conducted in French. Overall he considered Schneidemühl quite a good camp, with its sport, religion, theatre, educational and exercise facilities, and thought that quite a lot of the time he spent in captivity was enjoyable and beneficial. He even had the luxury of spending evenings with his French friends, sipping wine.

By 1917, German war losses meant that manpower was in short supply, so some of the fitter prisoners were detailed to work in the strategically important coalmines of Westphalia. Joe, being one of the strongest and fittest men in the camp, felt he was almost certain to be one of those chosen. But a clever manoeuvre that saw him dodge the medical inspection by entering then exiting a building almost immediately meant that he escaped this draft. At his own request, Joe was put in charge of a party of twenty prisoners sent to work at a local gravel pit, and found the opportunity once again to keep his faith strong through attendance at the Catholic church in Czarnikou. However, the fact that two of the party were habitual thieves threatened trouble for Joe, as the prisoner in charge of the group, so he escaped and was caught, being sent back to Schneidemühl with no more than ten days' solitary confinement as punishment.

After nearly four years as a prisoner, most of which seem to have been spent in relative safety and comfort, a dramatic turn of events in the spring of 1918 nearly meant that Joe did not survive the war. He had been sent as an interpreter with another work party, this time at a starch factory in Schneidemühl. Initially things went well but then more and more of the men started reporting sick in order to avoid work. It was Joe's job to liaise with the sentry in charge, and he accused Joe of allowing the men to malinger. He began to hit Joe with the butt of his rifle and ended up receiving a thrashing from Joe for his action. The incident then escalated as the sentry rushed to collect his Mauser pistol, pressed it against Joe's body and pulled the trigger.

Despite being a non-smoker, Joe had a cigarette case in his pocket containing pictures of his family and newspaper clippings. The bullet flattened the case and he fell to the floor in a faint. The sentry believed he had killed him and arrangements were made to take Joe to the mortuary. He quickly came round and was taken to the guardroom, where he was ordered to strip before being whipped and lashed by a group of six German soldiers. He fought back bravely using his boxing skills but was eventually knocked unconscious. When he awoke he was in a cell, awaiting a German court martial for 'disarming and assaulting a German soldier'. One might have expected the severest penalty for such a charge, but the combination of Joe's good character and the disdain in which the sentry was held – even by his own men – meant that Joe was sentenced to three months' detention in the camp prison, a sentence he served in relative comfort with access to food parcels and a kitchen.

On release Joe was transferred to a new camp for the last few months of the war, on Dänholm Island, near Straslund. His new job was to act as an interpreter in camp for British officers. Once again, Joe found Catholic fellowship in the shape of a major from the Royal Engineers and an Irish priest. He helped to establish a new Mass centre, which was well attended each Sunday, and made friends with a German corporal called Steyn. Steyn had four children who were in various stages of malnourishment due to the severe food shortages in Germany. Joe would scrounge food parcels for him to help the situation. During the final few weeks of the war, Joe was witness to acts of mutiny by German soldiers in the revolutionary atmosphere sweeping parts of the country.

Joe was eventually freed and he sailed to Denmark for a fortnight's decontamination procedure. In mid-December he sailed from Aarhus to Leith, where his party was given a civic welcome and breakfast. From there he entrained to Clipstone Camp in Derbyshire, and finally to the Wellington Barracks in London to rejoin the Scots Guards. Joe was expected to resume normal solider duties, undertaking guard duty at Buckingham Palace once again. At the end of one stint, when he had just presented arms to Queen Alexandra and Queen Mary, he was demobilised and put on a train to Bradford that very night, arriving in Halifax the next morning 'to commence my struggle as a civilian, at thirty years of age, from scratch.'[6]

Joe Garvey was a man who experienced the extremes of war, from the early war on the Western Front and then four long years as a prisoner of war. His faith mirrored his character; one of unyielding strength and certainty of moral purpose. It enabled him not only to survive the First World War, but to provide inspiration and leadership to others. Although a soldier of a private's rank, he was a Christian and character of the top rank.

Chapter 5

Lewis Valentine

'Tomorrow I go into the lines again … If it is thy will protect me from all harm for the sake of aching hearts at home. Amen'

Lewis Valentine was a Welshman whose Christianity was combined with a passionate national identity and abhorrence of the idea of war. However, in 1916 he took the decision to be conscripted into the British Army rather than object to military service, and shared the horrors and hardships of his generation in a non-combatant role in the Royal Army Medical Corps. His faith and his political beliefs were shaped in the furnace of that war and he became one of the leading figures of Welsh nationalism in the twentieth century.

Lewis Valentine was born in Llanddulas, near Colwyn Bay, North Wales, on 1 June 1893. His father, Samuel, was a checkweighman at a local quarry and deacon of the Bethesda Baptist Chapel, also serving as a lay preacher. His mother, Mary, was the daughter of Robert Roberts, who was minister of the local Salem Wesleyan Chapel. Nonconformist faith and lifestyle exerted a strong hold on the area, with there being no public house in the vicinity.

Lewis was the fourth of seven children. He received firebrand preaching in the chapel and a solid grounding in the Bible at Sunday school. He was just eleven years old when the great Welsh Revival of 1904–05 took place, with meetings taking place late into the night, but it was a couple of years later that Lewis was converted due to the examples of Christian living set by others at the chapel. He started work as a pupil-teacher at Llanddulas School and began preaching in 1912. In 1913 he went up to Bangor University to study Welsh and Semitic languages in order to prepare himself for Baptist ministry.

On the outbreak of war, Lewis inclined towards pacifism, but upon the introduction of conscription in 1916, he was one of approximately 240 men to enlist in the Welsh Students Company of the Royal Army Medical Corps at Rhyl Town Hall on 28 January. The company earned the nickname 'God's Own' due to the high proportion of Nonconformist ministers and theological students in its ranks. It had been especially created 'to enable men with conscientious objections to serving in combat units to serve their country without violating those objections'.[1] Pressure for its formation had been brought to bear on the War Office by Brigadier General Owen Thomas.

During their initial training at Llandrindod Wells it was reported that the men had enjoyed the snow, with tobogganing being popular, and that one Sunday evening the service had been held at the Baptist Tabernacle with three addresses being given by serving privates, including Lewis.[2] He also spoke at their last parade at the Congregational church in the town before the unit was transferred to Hillsborough Barracks, Sheffield.

Lewis was sent to the Western Front in October 1916 and over the next two years he kept a diary, firstly in English then latterly in Welsh, which was eventually published in the Baptist denominational quarterly magazine *Seren Gomer* from 1969 to 1972 in an untranslated version. According to his biographer, Arwel Vittle, Lewis had developed a dislike of the English officer class and the change from Welsh to English was an act both of resistance to English domination and of love for his native tongue. An early entry described the action at La Boisselle, where he was acting as a stretcher bearer. On 21 October, having witnessed the desolation of dead German lads and officers, a prayer meeting took place, with 'divine presence illuminating the place.'[3] The next day he spent bringing the wounded back from no-man's-land, something he found exhausting and dangerous, being struck on the boot by a bullet.

During a brief respite from the action in late October, Lewis saw Albert Cathedral, heavily damaged by the bombardment of that town (see plate 5). It used to have a statue of a mother presenting her child to heaven. To Lewis it now appeared as if she was dashing the child to the ground. Lewis considered the Christian Church in Britain to be in peril, to the extent that its future needed safeguarding. He expressed the Calvinist view of God being the Rock and Refuge, and being content to place the future in His hands. Like many who had been forced by circumstances to take part in warfare, he reflected on the worth of his life, resolving to give his life more fully to God's service. He felt a longing for God, home and Wales.

On 14 November, Lewis wrote a poignant soldier's prayer: 'Tomorrow I go into the lines again ... If it is thy will protect me from all harm for the sake of aching hearts at home. Amen.'[4] He again took a typically Welsh Calvinist view of his fate, having faith in God's protection and rejecting the thought of accidents or fatalism in God's design.

During this period, Lewis became close friends with Frank Carless, an Englishman and schoolteacher from Oswestry. Frank taught Lewis to speak German, while he in turn learned Welsh. One day they went for a long walk behind the lines, stopping eventually to rest in a haystack. Both men fell asleep. When they awoke, Frank informed Lewis that he had had a dream that he himself would soon die, but that Lewis would return safely home.

By early 1917 Lewis was back in the lines on the Ancre, based in Regina Trench, a scene of bitter fighting by the Canadians during the Battle of the Somme of the previous year. Lewis saw this landscape, and the destruction of human life, in biblical terms:

There was one continual stream of wounded all the day. The Royal Fusiliers are badly mutilated and the Northants lose heavily in prisoners. At dusk we move further up the ravine a veritable 'Valley of the Shadow of Death'. It was indeed 'ghoulish'. The march of the years can never dispel its weirdness from my mind. Its two sides were buried with dead, and this added to the weirdness of the place.[5]

By 1917, the strain of stretcher-bearing and medical work in conditions of danger was beginning to tell on Lewis. He wrote of veering between extreme jubilance and madness and of the desire to behave recklessly, running over shell-riddled ground in the danger zone. Lewis was attached to the 56th Field Ambulance, and on the front at Arras, serving in a casualty clearing station, where the work was often grim. He saw the intense sufferings of the wounded brought in from the battlefield and dozens of amputations, many of them unsuccessful.

In July 1917, having experienced the Somme, Ancre and Arras, Lewis's unit moved further north to Poperinghe to prepare for the big push of 1917, the Third Battle of Ypres, also known as Passchendaele. Now serving in the 54th Brigade, he described his 'helpless despair' at the sacrifice of young men, 'before the nations' senseless lust for blood is satiated.'[6] On the eve of the push on 30 July his thoughts turned to hearts of the womenfolk at home about to be broken. He wrote in prayer:

> Give the courage born of faith in thee to all who are left desolate by this war. Especially do we pray for the mothers of Europe. They have loved much. Help us to destroy this order of things which makes this great suffering possible. Forgive us our sins against humanity and against thee. Amen.[7]

One of those killed in the push was Lewis's closest friend, 25-year-old Frank Carless. He recorded, 'He was a great scholar. He learned Welsh, lived his religion and the Bible not only at the tips of his fingers but also deep in his heart.'[8]

Many years later, Lewis was invited to preach at Penuel Baptist Chapel in Oswestry. He felt as if someone was whispering the name 'Carless' in his ear. When he had finished preaching, he asked the deacons if they knew the Carless family. He was introduced to a man who had been at school with Frank, and then Frank's father, Frederick, who had tried unsuccessfully several times to find out more about the circumstances of his son's death from the War Office. Lewis was able to share with him everything he knew about Frank.

Lewis's bitterness against the fruits of war intensified. In August, while the battle continued to rage he wrote, 'Hell! Hell! Hell! O merciful God, what is man?' and 'Woe – blood – madness! ... Torn flesh, shattered bones. Halt, O God this mad fever ...'[9]

Lewis felt an increasing sense of isolation, feeling that many of the army chaplains lacked sympathy for the men: 'It appears to me that many of them think more of their status than of the kingdom of God.'[10] He was horrified on hearing one of the chaplains preaching to the men in a way that sought crudely to justify the war: 'The service was so cold, the message so poor, the words so anti-Christian ... He attempted to justify war. We listened not to a servant of Christ expressing the convictions that burned in his heart but a military officer addressing soldiers according to the convention.'[11]

Iorweth Davies, a comrade of Lewis's going right back to the initial training period at Llandrindod Wells, wrote of how seriously the latter thought of the role of Christianity on the battlefield and the events of 25 October 1917:

> He went through something I can tell you. He went over the top as a stretcher-bearer when he was in France with his group. I think there were 200 in units, and I think it was fifty-seven that came back, and the chaplain was killed and a couple of the Officers were killed. And Valentine survived and came back.
>
> And the officer, Colonel of this little group asked him: 'Mr Valentine, I want to ask you a favour. The Chaplain's been killed, as you know, and this little lot that are left are going over the top again tonight. I've sent down to the base to get another to fill up, to make 200 to go over the top again tonight. And several men have asked me; they'd like to get Communion before they go. And the Chaplain's equipment is here.'
>
> Well Valentine said, 'I'm not an ordained man,' he said, 'but I'm going in for the church I admit.'
>
> 'Well that's quite all right,' he said, 'you do it.'
>
> So he gave Communion to them, and went over with them as a stretcher bearer that evening. And indeed, after he went into the No Man's Land and so on, a shell came over and buried Valentine, and he insisted on staying with these chaps because he'd given Communion to them the night before and he couldn't leave them. And he was deaf, dumb and blind for three months after that.[12]

Lewis Valentine had so nearly paid the ultimate sacrifice. He was invalided back to Britain and spent three months in a military hospital at Walton-on-the-Naze, Essex. He was then transferred to Ireland, which was then in a state of political turmoil following the reprisals enacted as a result the Easter Rising of 1916 and growing calls for independence from the United Kingdom. Lewis met members of Sinn Fein and was impressed with their approach to national self-determination:

> Went to a village not far from our camp where there were a large number of Sinn Fein. They were very noble people, and among them many Scots and Englishmen who had fled the British Army because

they were sympathetic to the Irish cause. I went with a friend who is an Englishman … SF is taken very seriously and people join here. We would have been welcomed and sheltered by them.[13]

Lewis had been conscripted to fight in a war ostensibly fought to ensure the rights of self-determination of small nations such as Belgium and Serbia. However, it was becoming increasingly clear that those rights only applied to certain nationalities, not including the Irish and Welsh. This provided a further grounding for the Welsh nationalist agenda that he would pursue for the rest of his life.

In 1919 Lewis was demobilised and returned home to Llanddulas, and thence back to his studies in Bangor, where he remained for a further two years. He then became minister at the Welsh-speaking Tabernacle Baptist Chapel in Llandudno, the largest in North Wales. He grew to equate the propagation of the Gospel with that of the Welsh language. Neither could survive and grow without the other. In 1929 he became the first person to stand for Parliament on a Welsh nationalist platform and became a founding member of Plaid Cymru.

In 1936 Lewis was imprisoned for setting fire to an RAF base at Penyberth that had been created by destroying an ancient Welsh manor house. For Lewis and others this demolition was an act of English vandalism against Welsh culture, as well as being emblematic of the arms race leading inexorably to another world war, possibly worse than the one he had experienced two decades previously. He linked what he saw as his act of patriotism and pacifism to his duty as a Christian, an act for which he served a nine-month sentence in Wormwood Scrubs. For the next four decades he continued to preach and write, becoming increasingly disillusioned with the secularisation of Welsh society. He wrote the Welsh spiritual anthem *Dros Gymry'n Gwlad* (*For Wales Our Land*), and his war diary, *Dyddiadur Milwr* (*A Soldier's Diary*), was collated and published posthumously in edited format in 1988. Lewis Valentine died in 1986 aged ninety-two.

Lewis fought on three fronts during his life: firstly, to spread the word of the Gospel; secondly to preserve the Welsh language and culture; and thirdly, to promote the cause of pacifism. His First World War experiences had strengthened his belief in all three causes, and imbued him with an extra sense of urgency and purpose to make a stand for his beliefs. Like many others in this book, he did not see his Christian faith as being isolated from the world, but the central feature of his engagement with the great issues of war and nationhood in his time. He is considered one of the great Christians and great Welshmen of the twentieth century.

Chapter 6

Philip Bryant

'Rarely in ordinary life have I enjoyed such an overwhelming sense of
the Master's nearness'

Philip Bryant's experience of the First World War lay untold for nearly
a century as his diary remained in private family hands. However,
the decision of his grandson, Jonathan Greaves, not only to publish
the diary in its raw format, but also to undertake meticulous research into
Philip's pre-war life and service, has left us with a remarkable insight into
the mind of a devout and evangelical Christian who saw active service both
before and during the First World War. (See plate 1.)

Philip, a native of Kilburn, London, was born on 5 December 1881. His
first job was as a blacksmith's assistant. At the age of nineteen Philip travelled
to Gloucester to volunteer for the Royal Garrison Artillery, becoming a
gunner with the 31st Company of the Western Division. He spent three
years training in the use of heavy artillery in Devenport at the new garrison
training school in Plymouth, before sailing from Sheerness to arrive in
Madras, India, on 4 February 1904. Here British interests were defended by
the garrison at Fort St George before this was closed, and Philip transferred
to Rangoon in 1906.

He was assigned to the Public Works Department, which oversaw the
development of the infrastructure in the area. In March 1909 he returned to
Madras and was placed on the army reserve, Section B. This meant a return
to civilian life, with the requirement to spend twelve days per year on military
training and to be available for mobilisation if required. Philip remained in
India for a year before returning to England in April 1910 and received his
full decommission from the army having finished his army reserve time in
January 1913. This extra year in India meant a lower grade of army reserve
pay, as he was not considered available for immediate mobilisation in the

United Kingdom. Some of this time was spent assisting at the American Baptist Mission Training School in Bapatla in southern India. This work included helping with general education at the school and leading Sunday school lessons described as 'interesting, full of faith and devotion'.[1]

This time in India saw the most significant and formative episode in Philip's life. His army record indicates that he became a committed Christian and, furthermore, explored the possibility of missionary work. The American Baptists were active in Rangoon during Philip's time there and an entry on his military enrolment record was changed on 1 September 1904 from the nominal Church of England that would be attested by 70 per cent of soldiers in 1914 to Baptist, meaning an active choice of a specific denomination. It is probable that he would have been physically baptised at a local church mission, along with thirty others recorded in the American Baptist Missionary Union report.

However, for Philip, who later worshipped in Methodist churches in England, the denominational label was of less importance than the fact that he now had a personal evangelical faith. This meant a belief that he was in the tradition of the New Testament followers of Jesus, unencumbered by the centuries of religious dogma and practice that had grown in the established churches during that time. A belief in the Bible as God's revelation to mankind and as a means of conducting one's own life was an important part of this faith, along with the belief that God became human through Jesus Christ. The importance of the cross as the place where man's broken relationship with God was healed was central, as well as the need for a personal conversion to follow Christ. Another key part of Philip's faith required the Christian to make a practical difference, both by evangelising, or sharing the good news of Christ, and seeking to improve the social conditions people live in.

As part of this evangelicalism, Philip preached his first sermon on 26 August 1906 on the subject of 'Walking with God'. He chose readings from Leviticus 26:3-13 and 2 Corinthians 6&7 and in his sermon notes are the words:

Most of us are more or less conversant with the thought of God dwelling in us. God reveals Himself and His goings in each individual saint. When God walks in me, I am walking in some measure worthily of God. It is not my simply making a desperate effort. Whatever God is, is to come out in my life. Oh what a humbling theme we have.[2]

On his return to England in 1910, Philip undertook work as a representative for correspondence schools, acting as a salesman to enrol people onto courses, and visiting and encouraging those students who had already subscribed. He lodged in Hull, Yorkshire, and then in Seaton Sluice, Northumbria, where he met an active Wesleyan Methodist, Millie Smith, from York. Following his army decommission in 1913, Philip moved to York to be near to Millie and took a post as a commercial clerk. Here he became involved with the Grove Wesleyan Methodist Church, where he and Millie were married on 6 September 1915. They lived in Haxby, a village 4 miles from the centre of York, and were active in the life of both Grove and Haxby chapels. On his conscription into the army in August 1916, Philip gave his religion as Wesleyan, making no reference to his former Baptist ties.

Due to his previous military experience, Philip was assigned to the East Riding Royal Garrison Artillery based in Ripon, and then to Winchester as an assistant instructor in gunnery in June 1917. In August he set sail with the Egypt Expeditionary Force (EEF) bound for the Middle East. Philip's service there covered the biblical lands of Northern Egypt, Beersheba, Gaza and Jerusalem. This was a great relief to Philip, who had complained of 'thin blood', meaning that he found cold environments difficult to cope with. The warmth of the Middle East contrasted favourably to the potentially bitter winters experienced by soldiers in France and Belgium. It also meant less prolonged exposure to the constant artillery noise that had caused him nervous problems while in India.

Following a journey by boat from Southampton to France and then a long train journey through France and Italy, Philip finally arrived in Egypt on 21 October 1917 and was posted to the 181st Heavy Battery Royal Garrison Artillery. In late October, Philip's detachment successfully took Beersheba from Turkish control. Gaza was then seized and Philip remained there in a defensive position while other parts of the EEF pressed on to capture Jaffa and Jerusalem. Suffering from lumbago, Philip was assigned to animal duties during what turned out to be a cold, wet winter.

Throughout this period Philip kept a diary, the reasons for which were stated in an early entry: firstly, as an expression of gratitude to those who were praying for his safety; secondly, for his wife, 'whose unfailing courage, cheerfulness, and unceasing prayerfulness has been under God the chief factor in keeping me cheerful'; thirdly, for those friends and family in York who had supported him and Millie; and fourthly and most importantly, 'to the glory of God Whose loving care, gracious providence, and tender long sufferance with my very many failings has made such a record as the following possible.'[3]

That set the tone for the diary entries, laced with biblical allusions and quotes from Christian hymns. It displayed Philip's close personal relationship with God. For Philip this was not in the form of a miraculous deliverance, or direct divine intervention in a particular episode. It was more that God was a constant presence by his side rather than someone to be called on in moments of crisis. God also transcended denominational labels. Philip was originally a nominal Anglican, converted into the Baptist Church and then later became active in Methodist circles. When he came across Methodists, or a 'fine evangelical preaching' of an Anglican padre, or a Salvationist in the army, he felt a sense of fellowship with them.

His relationship with the physical manifestations of Catholicism proved more complex. As a Nonconformist he had a wariness of excessive ritual or iconography. However, while travelling across France he saw a number of roadside shrines similar to the one in front of which Father Gleeson delivered the Last Absolution (see Chapter 7). He wrote:

The religious character of the people was very evident in the fairly numerous shrines and images seen from the train. As a rule, the images, if apart from the shrines, stood on prominences, and one huge image of Christ stood on an isolated high rock facing the valley sloping downwards. However one may condemn and deplore the system and belief represented by these shrines and villages, there was something beautiful and spiritual about these marks of devotion, for the images at least, if not the shrines were probably placed in these positions out of love to God and of a desire for service toward the fellow countrymen of the donors. I felt too something of the irresistible appeal it must make to the devout Catholics, the sight of this magnificent image of the Lord with arms outstretched in eternity to a world of suffering, sinful humanity.[4]

On entraining through the Alps, he saw a similar sight in Italy with a similar mix of misgiving and wonder:

> High up on a huge solitary rock, reaching heavenwards was a huge crucifix. Ah yes, the emphasis of direction, even of the Cross is upward to God. This crucifix suggested the supremacy of the Cross, standing as it did so high and commanding. Really, I am after all something of a ritualist, for I felt profoundly impressed by this sight. Much as I object to any 'aid' which tends to obscure the real Object of all true 'worship', or which befogs the simple path of approach to God, I feel bound to recognise the value of such tangibilities to those whose minds and temperaments are such as to be humanly incapable of sensing God without such assistance, or who find in them the means of grace that I feel grateful I can do without. I remember too, that these things must have meant much indeed to Brother Lawrence, Bernard of Clairvaux, Thomas à Kempis, and other saints of God through whom He has enriched the Christian world. Let me pray 'Lord make me very tolerant, very charitable'.[5]

In this piece, Philip showed not only an appreciation of how others may be drawn to God, but a range of knowledge of classic Christian theologians and writers through the ages. Thomas à Kempis's work, *The Imitation of Christ*, was the same text from which Edith Cavell drew comfort on her final night (see Chapter 14). But this broadening appreciation did not divert him away from the ways he felt close to God – through nature and man's interaction with it and in a more planned devotional manner through prayer, hymn-singing and reading his Bible.

Philip's love of nature was in that he saw God's handiwork in it. He wrote:

> These high flung peaks remind me of their Creator Who is my God and Father. To me, they represented in some measure the strength of

Him Whose eye turneth to and fro throughout the whole earth, to show Himself strong on my behalf. The hand that shaped the Alps, guards me and mine.[6]

A series of dwellings nestling in a rock reminded him of the song *Rock of Ages* and he found time every day to be close to God in what he called his 'Bethels', which in wartime would be any place he could meet with God. On arrival at camp in Cimino in Italy, Philip found:

At first there were no facilities for religious services, but owing to the untiring efforts and steady persistence of a Wesleyan padre ... a reading marquee was eventually erected, and a concert platform built nearby, so that we enjoyed some really fine services ... But personally, I best enjoyed those quiet times I had 'on my own' behind timber stacks, under trees, by the sea, or beside a bush. Oh how sweet those times were. Every spot a Beracah [blessing], every place a Bethel. Only those who have had to seek for such blessings can realise what I felt, only those who have ever been denied the usual means of grace, the quiet room, the hushed stillness, the help of books, etc. can sympathise with my difficulties. And yet, rarely in ordinary life have I enjoyed such and overwhelming sense of the Master's nearness. He revealed Himself so fully, that I got into the habit of conversational talks with Him.[7]

Philip's prayerfulness was not just a solitary practice, or even one taken in fellowship with others in his battalion. It took his mind and spirit to those at home whom he knew would be praying at the same time in the Methodist congregations he had left behind. However, he was able to find new congregations with whom to pray and worship God, although due to the demands of war, this was not always possible on a Sunday. His prayers were not given to seek God's protection, but for the strength to act as a good Christian and to seek God's closeness.

For Philip the Bible was of supreme importance. He saw it as his lifeline to God and turned to it during times of joy and times of difficulty. On 27 October 1917, Philip reached the front line near Abu Shawish at 2.00 am and dug in to the sand. He recalled the words of Psalm 121 and this brought reassurance to his mind and allowed his tired body to sleep. The ability to memorise portions of the Bible would have been ingrained in many soldiers through attendance at Sunday schools and Bible classes, as well as continued reading into adulthood for those of a more active faith.

> *I will lift up mine eyes unto the hills, from whence cometh my help.*
> *My help cometh from the Lord, which made heaven and earth.*
> *He will not suffer thy foot to be moved: he that keepeth thee will not slumber.*
> *Behold, he that keepeth Israel shall neither slumber nor sleep.*
> *The Lord is thy keeper: the Lord is thy shade upon thy right hand.*
> *The sun shall not smite thee by day, nor the moon by night.*
> *The Lord shall preserve thee from all evil: he shall preserve thy soul.*
> *The Lord shall preserve thy going out and thy coming in from this time forth, and even for evermore.*

(Psalm 121)

This closeness to the Bible was enhanced by the fact that Philip's war action took place in biblical lands. He could see a landscape and relate it to events that had taken place there many millennia ago. 'One and one only well worn track could be distinguished, and that was the oldest highway in the world along which the travellers long before the time of Abraham and Abraham himself passed.'[8]

In addition to having biblical passages on which to draw, Philip also drew on the great Methodist tradition of hymnody. He would sing them to himself as part of his devotional time and on one occasion even found an Arab taxi driver joining in with the singing, albeit making up his own words! Three hymns he mentioned in particular were *And Can It Be?*, *Who Fathoms the Eternal Thought?* and *No Not One.*

This combination of prayer, belief in the Bible and constant Christian fellowship provided the strength to see Philip through his war. He saw sights that moved him greatly, and formed the opinion that whilst the war was necessary, those who gloried in its necessity should be made to 'taste its horrors, share its privations, feel its hell'.[9] In August 1918 he was granted extra proficiency pay before the final surrender of Turkish forces in October 1918. After a frustrating period of waiting, Philip finally returned to England on 4 March 1919. He was said to have shed a tear at seeing the greenness of the British countryside following the long period in a dry landscape.

After the war Philip and Millie settled back in Haxby, where they purchased the village grocery shop and post office and Philip served on a variety of Methodist committees. He served as a lay preacher, with his daughter Barbara playing the organ. In 1949 Philip and Millie moved to Devon to care for their son John, who suffered from respiratory problems. Here they also ran the local shop and post office as well as being active in the life of Zion Chapel, Beaford. Philip was described as formal and outwardly austere in his later years, befitting a man of military and Nonconformist background.[10] He died on 30 May 1963, his final words being 'Lord, I come'.

Philip Bryant took with him to war a firm and active Nonconformist and evangelical faith, albeit one that broadened to appreciate elements of Anglicanism and Catholicism through his wartime experiences. This faith meant that despite periods of anxiety and danger he never felt alone, as God was constantly by his side. It was a faith built on the firm rocks of the Bible, a belief in Jesus as his personal saviour. It was the defining characteristic of his life before, during and after the war. He was not a natural soldier, but saw himself as a 'camouflaged civilian'.[11] However, Philip, like hundreds of thousands of other Christians, did what he saw as his duty to God and his country with courage and integrity throughout.

Part II

Three Chaplains and an Army Scripture Reader

'Ambassadors of Christ you go, Up to the very gates of hell'

The Army Chaplains Department (AChD) had been established by Royal Warrant in 1796. Initially, army appointments were open only to Anglican chaplains but from 1827 Presbyterian chaplains were permitted too. In 1836 Catholic emancipation extended to there being allowed chaplains of that faith, and Wesleyan chaplains were first appointed in 1881. The first Jewish chaplain was appointed in 1892. Legally, all chaplains had to be non-combatants although, in exceptional circumstances, as we shall see in the case of Father Francis Gleeson, they could serve in combat too.

During the early months of the First World War, as huge numbers of men volunteered to join the army, many of them from Nonconformist religious backgrounds, spiritual provision had to be made for them when on service. The Wesleyan Methodists assigned fourteen acting chaplains to be recognised by the War Office to serve in England, Malta and Cairo. However, a decision soon had to be made whether the Methodist movement was comfortable with its chaplains being embedded in battalions and receiving commissions from the War Office in the same way that Anglican and Catholic chaplains were. This decision was a positive one, and for the first time Methodists became commissioned members of the Army Chaplains' Department.

In 1915, after representations from the Free Church Council and support from David Lloyd George, a United Board was created with supplied chaplains from the Baptist, Congregationalist, Primitive Methodist and United Methodist denominations. The regular role of chaplains included the conducting of church parades, providing pastoral care for their men, writing condolence letters home and, as the war wore on, ministering to the wounded and dying and conducting huge numbers of burial services (see plate 6).

During the First World War some 4,400 army chaplains were recruited and 179 lost their lives on active service. Three chaplains – Theodore Bayley Hardy, Noel Mellish and William Addison – received the Victoria Cross. Another 250 received the Military Cross. In addition it should not be overlooked that many hundreds of civilian chaplains decided to enlist in the armed forces as regular soldiers. Many were awarded gallantry medals. Among their number were Bernard William Vann, who was awarded a Victoria Cross in combat, and the Reverend George De Ville Smith, a curate at St Thomas Church in Worsbrough, Barnsley. Smith had joined the autumn 1914 rush to enlist in the 13th York and Lancaster Regiment, the 'Barnsley Pals', and was made a captain. He died alongside so many of them at the Somme on 1 July 1916.

By November 1918 there were 3,475 serving army chaplains, broken down into the following denominations: 1,985 Anglican, 649 Roman Catholic, 302 Presbyterian, 256 Wesleyan, and 251 United Board.[1] Fortunately, recent historiography has challenged the myths of brave working-class Catholic chaplains outperforming their more middle-class and reserved Anglican counterparts. A study of accounts written by men who experienced the war first-hand would challenge the impression given in the musical, and then the film, *Oh! What a Lovely War* of Anglican chaplains merely aping the nationalistic outpourings of the British propaganda machine.

In this section we meet three army chaplains: one Anglican, one Roman Catholic and one from the United Free Church of Scotland. For the author, they represent the best of human and Christian spirit. They sought to serve their men in the finest manner possible despite their civilian backgrounds. In Russell Barry's case, the 'prevailing wisdom … that [Anglican chaplains] were peripheral and ineffectual figures who were either sanctimonious misfits or worldly malingerers' is given lie to.[2] John Esslemont Adams was involved in the iconic Christmas Truce of 1914, conducting a moving burial service before going on to gain the respect of men of all denominations for his work in the war. Francis Gleeson, an Irish Catholic priest, was a man of deep humanity and compassion. Consideration of his life brings a realisation of the true meaning of Christian love and charity.

In addition to army chaplains, 2,000 men, all ex-soldiers, served as army scripture readers.[3] Their work was mostly in home camps where Bible classes and devotional meetings were organised as the readers sought to convert men to Christianity. Nineteen of their number went to the Western Front, and one of them, Harry Wisbey, left a remarkable account of his time with the Suffolk Regiment during the retreat of August 1914 through Belgium. Here we learn of the momentous events he witnessed while seeking to bring men to Christ.

Men whose job it was to provide a Christian framework for men in the army endured hardship and privations whilst striving to provide moral and spiritual leadership. Their good fight was on both the physical and temporal plane, and their stories continue to inspire after a century has passed.

Chapter 7

Father Francis Gleeson

'Spent all night trying to console, aid, and remove the wounded. It was ghastly to see them lying there in the cold, cheerless outhouses, on bare stretchers with no blankets to cover their freezing limbs'

Francis Gleeson's general absolution of the Munsters before the Battle of Aubers Ridge in 1915 became the subject of an iconic painting widely reproduced in the war (see plate 7). Behind the image of piety and devotion lay a great man, one who dedicated his life to the service of his flock, be it with the visually impaired of Dublin, the men for whom he served as chaplain, or the forces of the Irish Free State after the war. Despite living through some of the most contentious and divisive times in the history of his troubled country, he emerged with a sense of dignity and compassion that serves as an inspiration to the true meaning of Christianity to this day.

Francis Gleeson was one of thirteen children and was born on 28 May 1884, in Eastwood, Farrenderry, just outside Templemore, County Tipperary. Having decided to become a priest, he was educated at the Holy Cross College in Dublin and St Patrick's College in Maynooth. He was ordained as a priest in 1910 and went to live in Glasnevin, Dublin, before becoming chaplain at St Mary's Home for the Blind in March 1912.

On the outbreak of war he volunteered for service and was commissioned into the Army Chaplains' Department and attached to the 2nd Battalion, Royal Munster Fusiliers. But despite his swiftness in volunteering he soon became less than enthusiastic about what the war meant.

If … advocates of war were made to be soaked and caked and crusted with cold, wet trench mud, like these poor soldiers, and to wear those mud-weighted coats, they would not be so glib with their treatises on the art of war. These militants should be made to undergo a few nights in cheerless billets [and] mud-river trenches to teach them a lesson. What is it all for at all?[1]

Francis served with the Munsters at the First Battle of Ypres in November 1914. It was during this battle that he is said to have taken command of the battalion after all the officers were incapacitated by the enemy. Having removed his chaplain's insignia that indicated his non-combatant status, he took command of the unit and held it until relieved. This action earned a mention in Robert Graves's autobiography *Goodbye to All That*, in which Francis became 'Jovial Father Gleeson of the Munsters'.[2]

Francis was highly regarded by his men for tending to the wounded under fire, visiting the front-line trenches and bringing gifts. On Christmas Day 1914, the Munsters were in part of the front line unaffected by the Christmas Truce and Francis chose to conduct a Mass in one of the front-line trenches that was frequently under fire. Francis was an advisor to men of all faiths in the regiment and kept careful records of their names and addresses so that he could write to the families of those that died. He ended each letter with the words 'They paid a great sacrifice'. Francis made frequent visits to the front lines and often conducted burial services there using wooden grave marker crosses that he made himself. His men said that they were always sure of a cup of tea from him when he visited the trenches late at night and he was certain to check that they were not short of ammunition. Francis sent requests to Ireland for hymn books for the men in the field and also bought mouth organs for their entertainment.

On 8 May 1915, on the eve of the Battle of Aubers Ridge, Lieutenant Colonel Victor Rickard ordered the battalion to halt at a roadside shrine in Rue du Bois, near Fleurbaix. Francis gave the general absolution, the subject of a painting by Fortunino Matania that was made at the request of Mrs Victor Rickard, the widow of the battalion's commanding officer.

The painting was initially reproduced in *The Sphere* magazine. It depicts Francis mounted on horseback in front of one of the many roadside shrines found in France as the men stand in front of him and their fellow officers with their heads bowed. A contemporary report in *The Tablet* recounts how the men then strung out along the road, with Francis moving between them, offering words of comfort.[3] The account given in *The Sphere* claims the

Te Deum was sung, whilst *The Tablet* refers to the popular Catholic hymn *Hail Queen of Heaven*. In Francis's own diary, he recorded the hymn as *Hail Great St Patrick*. The battalion suffered heavily in the battle.

Francis noted the event in his diary:

> We march out from Tombe Willot (Locon) about 900 strong, our Commanding Officer being Major Rickard and the Adjutant, Captain Filgate – two of the kindliest men I have come across. We leave about 7.00 pm. The scenes of enthusiasm are outstanding. I ride my horse. Give Absolution to Batt. during rest on road. Opposite La Couture Church between the shrine of 'N.D. de la Bonne Mort' and another shrine we have another rest. The men all sing hymns *Hail Great St. Patrick*. I go further up – near the trenches and bid good bye to all. So Sad!![4]

Sergeant Louis Moore of the 2nd Royal Munster Fusiliers wrote a letter describing the episode:

> On his way up to our position on that Saturday evening, and just before reaching our trenches, we passed one of those little shrines. The Major halted his Regiment, and the Father, still mounted, gave the whole Regiment a general absolution. After that they sang the *Te Deum*. I know you can see the whole picture. The semi-light, the Major on his horse in front, and the whole Regiment uncovered. It was a sight never to be forgotten.[5]

'What a day for all the Munsters,' Francis wrote in his diary on 9 May.

> We lose at least 350 men, between killed and wounded and missing. Spent all night trying to console, aid, and remove the wounded. It was ghastly to see them lying there in the cold, cheerless outhouses, on bare stretchers with no blankets to cover their freezing limbs ... Hundreds lying out in cold air all night at Windy Corner. No ambulances coming. They came at last – at daylight.[6]

Out of twenty-two officers and 520 men who made the assault, only three officers and 200 men returned. One of Francis's duties as chaplain was to write to the families of those who had been killed. An example of one of these letters, showing a depth of humanity beyond the sometime curt letters received from other officers, was published in the *Cork Examiner* on 9 June 1915:

HEROIC CORK BOY – PRIVATE CHRISTY BARRY'S DEATH – LETTER FROM FR. GLEESON – TOUCHING TRIBUTE TO BRAVE DEED

Rev. Father Francis A. Gleeson, chaplain to the Munsters at the front, writes as follows to Mrs Barry, 89 Douglas Street, Cork, mother of Private Christy Barry, 2nd Battalion, Royal Munster Fusiliers, who was killed in action on May 9th

2nd June, 1915 – Dear Mrs Barry – By this time you will have heard of the death of your heroic boy in the attack of Sunday, 9th May, 1915. The greatest consolation I can offer you is to tell you that your son was well prepared for death, as the battalion received Holy Communion the Sunday before the battle and were given absolution a few hours before the terrible ordeal. You need have no worry regarding your son's soul, for he was careful and zealous about it, and was one of the best boys in the battalion. I knew him quite well, and to know him was to love him, for he was one of the most cheerful and good-natured young fellows I have met. I buried his body in a little cemetery beside the trenches, and several comrades lie beside him. A little cross marks his grave. He has made an immortal name for the gallantry and unselfishness with which he rescued the body of Captain Hawkes. He had not the faintest idea of what fear was. There could not be greater heroism displayed than that shown by your son.

   You may well feel proud of being the mother of such a son. He has, by his thrilling acts of bravery, imprinted his name on all our hearts, and no honour, no matter how high, could be at all adequate to mark the greatness of his action. Out of a battalion of cheerful and daring heroes, Barry stands out supreme and admired of all, and his glorious death has inspired it. He was shot three times during his rescue of Captain Hawkes – still, in spite of loss of blood and a tornado of bullets and shells, he held on to his task till he got the captain in safety over the parapets. Having done this, he fell down exhausted and mortally wounded, into the British lines, where he died a saintly and easy death a few hours afterwards.

You will not grudge the good God such a good boy, and will be compensated for his death by the greatness and glory which marked it. On his pure and saintly soul may Jesus have mercy.

Yours sincerely, Francis A. Gleeson, Chaplain, Munsters [7]

The emotional toll of receiving letters from distressed relatives, and writing such heartfelt letters as the one above was exacting on Francis. In June 1915 he recorded:

I got 12 letters today; just after reading them. What answering they will take tomorrow. I like to give these poor people all the solace I can, anyhow, but still there's no limit to the sorrowing inquiries. The tragedy of these letters ... One letter was from a broken-hearted girl ... Then, the mothers! Oh![8]

Francis held frequent Masses for his men, recording one:

I said Mass in the distillery yesterday and preached very strongly on St Paul in the Corinthians. ('He who striveth for the mastery refraineth himself from all things. They indeed that they may gain a corruptible crown, but we are incorruptible.') I preached on these words both in Cuinchy battered distillery & at 11 oc AM in Beuvry to C. Company (Captain Hawkes).[9]

He also organised a preaching mission in July 1915 and issued a certificate to all who attended. It was beautifully designed and was surrounded the names of the major battles fought by the Royal Munsters up to that point (Mons, Ypres, Festubert and Rue du Bois), the flags of the Allied nations and representations of Irish culture including a Celtic cross and a harp. In the middle were the exhortations 'To live a temperate life, To shun all occasions of sin' and 'To make frequent use of prayer and the Sacraments'. Jesus was depicted hanging on the cross, perhaps a reference to the huge sacrifices already made by the Munsters, with the words from Matthew 16:24, 'Go, take up thy cross and follow Jesus'.

At the end of his year's service as a chaplain, exhausted by the physical and spiritual exertion of his work and further shaken by the losses of the Munsters at the Second Battle of Loos, Francis returned to Dublin in late 1915 and became a curate in the newly opened Church of Our Lady of Lourdes, Gloucester Street, Dublin. He stated that 'I am sorry to be leaving the dear old Munster lads, but I really can't stand it any longer. I do not like the life, though I love the poor men ever so much.'[10]

Following his ministry at the Church of Our Lady of Lourdes, he volunteered to return to army service. He was recommissioned as a Chaplain 4th Class (equivalent to a captain) on 15 May 1917 and served another two years until his discharge in 1919. After the war Francis returned once more to Ireland, encountering some hostility with Irish republicans during this violent and divisive period after the war due to his association with the British Army. It is said that the Bishop of Cork deliberately chose challenging parishes for Francis to serve in.

He returned to Dublin, serving for a year in Gloucester Street before being appointed as a Curate in St Michael's Parish, Dun Laoghaire, on 13 July 1920. On 4 June 1922, he attended the dedication of Étreux British Cemetery, Aisne, which holds the remains of 110 men of the Royal Munster Fusiliers who were killed in the defence of Étreux against superior German forces while acting as a rearguard for the Great Retreat of August 1914.

On account of his previous experience in the First World War, Francis was appointed as a Command Chaplain with the Dublin Army Command of the National Army of the Irish Free State on 12 February 1923. He was appointed as a curate in Bray Parish on 18 May 1924, and then Parish Priest of Aughrim Parish on 20 January 1941. Finally, he was appointed Parish Priest of St Catherine's, Meath Street, Dublin, on 30 August 1944 and was elected Canon of the Metropolitan Chapter of the Archdiocese of Dublin in 1956. He died on 26 June 1959.

Francis was buried at the Glasnevin Cemetery in Dublin, the resting place of many prominent figures in Irish history including Daniel O'Connell, Charles Stewart Parnell, James Larkin and Éamon de Valera. A stone tablet at the Island of Ireland Peace Park near Ypres, Belgium, is inscribed with a quote from Francis describing his efforts to comfort the wounded:

SPENT ALL NIGHT TRYING TO CONSOLE AID AND MOVE THE WOUNDED

IT WAS GHASTLY TO SEE THEM LYING THERE IN THE COLD CHEERLESS OUTHOUSES ON BARE STRETCHERS WITH NO BLANKETS TO COVER THEIR FREEZING LIMBS

The opening of the park marked a step along the road to the Irish Republic becoming reconciled with the role of the Irish soldiers who fought in the British Army during the Great War, with President Mary McAleese standing alongside the Queen of England at the ceremony on 11 November 1998.

Francis Gleeson gave comfort and strength to others under the most trying of circumstances. As a Catholic Chaplain from a city where many of the inhabitants were openly hostile to the British state, his humanity and compassion superseded ideological considerations. He provided moral and practical leadership during times of danger and felt the full weight of the emotional burden of twentieth-century warfare. His faith and his example provided comfort for the wounded and the bereaved and his works touched the lives of thousands of people.

Chapter 8

John Esslemont Adams

'Most chaplains hope sooner or later to be posted to duty at the front. There, in the rattle of rifle fire and the roar of artillery, they feel the thrill of battle and taste the stern reality of war'

On Christmas Day 1914, a series of informal truces occurred along the Western Front. As thousands of British, French, Belgian and German troops voluntarily and spontaneously laid down their arms for a brief respite from the fighting, cards, cigarettes and personal items were exchanged. Rumours circulated of football matches involving some troops. However, one episode we can be sure occurred is the joint burial of British and German dead near Fleurbaix, Northern France. At the centre of the burial service was the Reverend John Esslemont Adams, Chaplain to the Gordon Highlanders (see plate 8).

Son of a schoolmaster from Gilbertfield, Hamilton, John Esslemont Adams was born in Lanarkshire, on 25 May 1865. Esslemont (as he was known) matriculated in Latin and Greek from the University of Glasgow at the young age of fourteen. He also studied Mathematics, English and Natural Philosophy.

He was very successful in his studies and won a Coulter Prize, of £2 10*s*., for the best Latin essay on *The Cases Which Led to the Decline of Sparta in the Fourth Century BC*. He then graduated in 1892 with a BD (Bachelor of Divinity) having studied at the Free Church Training College. His first charge was as Minister for Dreghorn and Perceton in Ayrshire. On 13 August 1902 he married 28-year-old Marion Gallacher from Dreghorn. Their marriage took place in the United Free Church in Newhaven, Edinburgh.

By the time the First World War broke out Esslemont was Minister of the West United Free Church in Aberdeen, and he volunteered to serve with the Army Chaplains Department immediately. He was called up just a month after Britain had entered the war, on 4 September 1914. He was now a relatively mature forty-nine years old and was attached to his local Scottish Regiment, the Gordon Highlanders.

Esslemont's philosophy was that it was a chaplain's duty to serve as close to where the men needed him as possible. He wrote:

> Most chaplains hope sooner or later to be posted to duty at the front. There, in the rattle of rifle fire and the roar of artillery, they feel the thrill of battle and taste the stern reality of war.[1]

While at the front in December 1914, he took the time to remember the members of the Aberdeen Boys' Brigade, writing to their president to say, '"Sure and Steadfast" has given me the theme for more than one message to our men on parade before going into the trenches.'[2] However, it was an event later that month that ensured that Esslemont Adams's name would forever be associated with the iconic truce of 1914.

A field south-west of Fleurbaix, in northern France, had been the scene of an attack by the Scots Guards and Border Regiments on 18 and 19 December. The attack had been unsuccessful and six days later, many Scottish bodies still lay in no-man's-land. Esslemont was carrying out the burial of one of his own Gordon Highlanders who had been killed on 24 December. He then accompanied his commanding officer, Colonel McLean, on a tour of inspection. They saw some of their own men climbing out of the trenches to talk with the enemy. McLean initially ordered them to come back into the trenches, but they responded by saying that other British troops were visible out of the trenches further along the line, and German soldiers had come out of theirs too.

Esslemont then took control of the situation, telling McLean that this would be an ideal opportunity to bury the men who had lain dead for nearly a week, and strode out into no-man's-land. When he reached a ditch in the middle, he held up his hands and said to the Germans, 'I want to speak to your commanding officer. Does anyone speak English?' He was asked to step forward, saluted the senior German officer present, Baron von Blomberg, and put his suggestion of a joint burial service. This idea was agreed to, as well as that Adams should lead the service, and that prayers be said and Psalm 23 read out in both languages.

Both sides then proceeded to collect their dead. The British were allowed to bring their bodies beyond their side of no-man's-land, but the Germans would not allow them to retrieve the rifles.

Captain Giles Loder had led the Scots Guards' attack on 18 and 19 December and had survived. From further down the front line he could witness the unfolding events. He walked across the open farmland and discovered that there were twenty-nine dead Scots Guards. He was allowed to go through their uniforms to collect personal effects in order to send them home to relatives. 'It was heartrending to see some of the chaps one knew so well, and who had started out in such good spirits on December 18th, lying there dead, some with horrible wounds due to the explosive action of the high-velocity bullet at short range,' he wrote.[3]

A German major, Thomas, had been the one to negotiate with Loder for the return of the soldiers' personal effects. They agreed that it was a question of burying the dead of both sides who were lying between the trenches, and therefore a local armistice lasting until 1.00 pm was established to allow for this.

Altogether about 100 British and German bodies were gathered for burial and Esslemont conducted a service following the collection. This was described by Second Lieutenant Arthur Pelham-Burn of the 6th Gordon Highlanders in a letter to a school friend:

We then had a most wonderful joint burial service. Our Padre ... arranged the prayers and psalm etc., and an interpreter wrote them out in German. They were read first in English by our Padre and then in German by a boy who was studying for the ministry. It was an extraordinary and wonderful sight. The Germans formed up on one side, the English on the other, the officers standing in front, every head bared. Yes, I think it was a sight one will never see again.[4]

Esslemont read the 23rd Psalm, followed by the young German student:

The Lord is my shepherd: I shall not want
He maketh me to lie down in green pastures:
He leadeth me beside the still waters ...

Der Herr is mein Hirt: mir wird nihts mangeln.
Er weidet mich auf einer grunen Aue:
Und fuhrt mich zum frischen Wasser ...

The chaplain then stepped forward to salute the German commander. At the end of the service Esslemont saluted the German commander. They exchanged gifts, Esslemont receiving a cigar and the German a small card with a 'Soldier's Prayer' written on it, which he had retrieved from his cap. They shook hands and bade farewell. Even though Esslemont was a non-smoker, he graciously said he would keep the cigar as a souvenir, and subsequently showed it on a number of occasions during talks he gave on the war back in Scotland.

The Soldier's Prayer read:

Almighty and most Merciful Father,
Forgive me my sins:
Grant me Thy peace:
Give me Thy power:
Bless me in life and death,
        for Jesus Christ's sake.
                Amen

The Regimental Diary of the Gordon Highlanders recorded: 'It was an impressive sight, officers and men, bitter enemies as they were, uncovered, reverent, and for the moment united in offering for their dead the last offices of homage and honour.' Loder wrote in his diary: 'Both sides have played the game and I know this (German) Regiment anyhow has learnt to trust an Englishman's word.'

Following his Christmas action Esslemont took a brief holiday in his native Aberdeen, speaking to his congregation about the enormous losses the Gordon Highlanders had incurred, and the outstanding leadership they had received from Colonel McLean of Aberdeenshire.

In 1915 Esslemont wrote a book, *The Chaplain and the War*, in which he articulated his approach to his calling. A mixture of pastoral work, Christian ministry and communal singing was used to keep up morale:

Shoulder to shoulder with the men in their everyday life, securing their confidence, taking charge of their treasures, arranging their games and concerts with or for them, he paves the way for getting at their hearts and speaking with effect about the things of God. Every sing-song by a little manoeuvring may be made to end with worship. The men are glad that it should be so. A few verses are read, then comes a prayer, then in silence each man says his own prayers, and then the benediction is pronounced. Last of all comes *God Save the King*. The sing-song is over and the audience quickly scatters to the company billets.[5]

He went on:

It still remains strictly true that multitudes have had their faith deepened and multitudes have learned as never before the need and the value of faith in God. The book read most of all is the New Testament. A quartermaster tells how he found grooms reading it together in the battalion stable; a machine-gun officer writes to say that he never read much of it at home, but that it is the only book he can settle to read as he sits through the long nights in the trenches beside his gun; a platoon of Guards in the Ypres section in the early days of the war was grateful that although there was not a Testament among them, one man who was a Roman Catholic possessed a Douai Bible. Bibles are valued, and the National Bible Society of Scotland, with splendid appreciation of the situation, has promptly sent gifts of Scriptures to chaplains asking supplies for soldiers overseas.[6]

Reading of the Bible was not just of value while awaiting battle, but in the midst of the conflict itself:

They stand on the edge of the battlefield with bowed uncovered head whilst the chaplain prays, and go into battle with Psalms like the 23rd, 93rd, 103rd and 121st thrilling them. Their fortitude is fed on the faith they have in God the Father, Jesus Christ the Saviour, the Spirit of Christ in self-sacrifice and the assurance of life everlasting ...[7]

The importance of the words of the Bible in maintaining a familial link between those in service and those at home was shown in a heart-rending account Esslemont recorded:

> A widow in the North country, who with heroic industry has brought up her three children, sent forth in August last her only boy, aged nineteen, because his King and his country needed him. When he went away she took down the Family Bible, cut out the 23rd Psalm, and gave the page as a parting gift to her son. He put it in his pay-book, and many a time has told his mother in his letters that he was prouder of that gift than if he had received a Bank of England note, and that he 'Always takes out the torn page and reads the Psalm before he goes into the trenches'. When his effects come home the thing his mother says she will look for first and keep always as her comfort is the torn page she gave her darling who now sleeps his crimson sleep on the green fields of Flanders.[8]

Esslemont was promoted to become Assistant Principal Chaplain to the Forces. In 1916 he was working at a base hospital in Boulogne, ministering to men who had been badly wounded at the Battle of the Somme. He wrote to his congregation on 29 July 1916 of processions of motor ambulances bringing them into the hospital:

> Our own Congregation has not escaped. The names of its sons appear on the lists of wounded or killed ... Lieutenant Frederic Conner, Seaforth Highlanders, was born and brought up in and a worthy member of the Congregation. To me personally his death is heartbreaking. Dear, gallant 'Freddie' – one of the brightest, purest, most chivalrous boys in my friendship! And now he is 'alive for evermore'. ... He was indeed a good soldier of Jesus Christ – only twenty-one and yet a great example to all of us.[9]

Despite his action on Christmas Day 1914 displaying a common bond of Christian fellowship between the British and German sides, in 1917 Esslemont translated a book about German atrocities towards French and Belgian civilians. Titled *Their Crimes*, the chapter headings included 'Robbing', 'Incendiarism', 'Murder', 'Outrages on Women and Children', 'Killing the Wounded' and 'German Excuses: Lies and Calumny'. In doing so he echoed the martyrdom of Pastor Dergent and the impression formed by David Jones from speaking with French citizens.

Esslemont became hugely respected by men and chaplains of all denominations. When he left the Fifth Army Base in France in May 1918, having served there for two years, he had managed to unite the work of the chaplains that had previously been done independently by each denomination. A letter signed by chaplain representatives of the Roman Catholic Church, United Board (which covered Baptists, Methodists and Congregationalists), United Free Church of Scotland, Wesleyan, Presbyterian Church of Australia, Church of Scotland, a Jewish Rabbi and a Canadian Methodist Chaplain expressed 'our deep sense of gratitude ... the unfailing fairness of your administration, the kindness of your counsel, the soundness of your judgement, and especially the inspiration of your friendship.'[10]

Esslemont was a man of strong views and strong spirit. He mixed a passionate belief in the power of his Christian faith to embolden and comfort the men in his charge, with a personal courage and willingness to see the war in nationalist terms. He was awarded the Military Cross and the Distinguished Service Order and was twice mentioned in dispatches for gallantry in his duties.

After the war he returned to Aberdeen and became Doctor of Divinity at Aberdeen University. He also broadcast on the new medium of the radio, including an address from Aberdeen on Armistice Day, 1926. He died on 22 April 1935. Fittingly, at his funeral service, Psalm 23 was sung, twenty years after it had resonated across no-man's-land, at Adams's instigation, in two warring languages.

Esslemont strove to bring a spiritual dimension to the grim work of war. He was willing to show respect to his own men, and to those of the enemy when he considered it had been earned. However, he was also quick to condemn actions he saw as outside the pale of Christian spirit. He inspired the work of other chaplains and therefore his good fight had a much wider effect beyond those with whom he came into immediate contact.

Chapter 9

Russell Barry

'No man who was involved in that experience came out the same man that he went into it. And it was, as, I think, happened to many others, in war service that I was to find myself'

Russell Barry spent his whole life in the Church of England. From a young ordinand before the First World War, he rose to become Bishop of Southwell, and one of the most eminent theological thinkers of his generation. However, he could never forget the thousands of that same generation who sacrificed their chance to achieve eminence in the name of duty. This led him to a passionate belief that the message of the Anglican Church must be made relevant to all the citizens of England, and to question many of the orthodoxies with which he had been brought up.

Frank Russell Barry was born on 28 January 1890, into a world he later considered of 'unquestioning conformity'.[1] He was the eldest of six children of George Barry, a curate at St Peter's, Rochester, and Edith Reid. The family moved to Surbiton when he was three and lived in relative poverty, dressing in the cast-off clothes of wealthier parishioners. In fact, when his father lost a gold sovereign – a 'domestic tragedy' in those straitened times – a group of rich men in the congregation collected a total of five new sovereigns for him, causing Russell to be forever fond of the Parable of the Lost Coin from Luke's gospel. His father supplemented the family income by becoming an inspector of Church of England schools in the South London area.

A more permanent tragedy struck the family in 1898 when Russell's mother died in childbirth. With one child having already died in infancy, Russell's father was left desolate, with five young children to feed and feeling that 'the spring had gone out of his year'.[2] Russell himself became introverted and found it difficult to relate to other children. Two further sisters died young, leaving only three out of six siblings surviving into adulthood. George remarried in 1904 to Fanny Ekin, a former parishioner, and this union brought Russell two half-brothers.

Russell's initial education was provided at a dame school, learning reading, writing and arithmetic as well as the dates of the kings and queens of England. Aged seven he went to preparatory school, learning the classics, and from there in 1903 he won a scholarship to Bradfield College in Berkshire. He recalled the 'unthinking jingoism [and] imperial arrogance and optimism' of English society at the turn of the century.[3] Russell also had the opportunity to watch Queen Victoria's funeral in 1901, seeing King Edward VII and Kaiser Wilhelm II of Germany riding side by side.

The family moved to rural Norfolk for George to take up the country parish of Long Stratton, sacrificing any hope of intellectual and career advancement in the Church of England for stability and security for his family. However, for Russell it was a chance to learn about nature and he much preferred Norfolk to the suburbs of London. This did not blind him to the reality of the rural poverty of many of his father's parishioners, with those who spent all week producing food being on the verge of starvation themselves. They lived in cottages tied to the land and received no pensions, the only options being parish relief or the workhouse. He saw many men join the army or navy merely to gain sufficient food to eat. This was the beginning of Russell's development of the idea of a 'social gospel', that Christianity was of little use if divorced from the everyday lives of those to whom the message was being preached.

While at Bradfield College Russell received a religious education, but it was one that he saw as the 'sacralising of public school ethics'.[4] It left him dissatisfied, as he gained a lot of knowledge but little understanding of faith as questioning was discouraged. But he did gain a love of English literature and the classics, studying hard for a scholarship to avoid the necessity of causing further hardship for his father to fund a place at university. He was successful and in 1907 won an open scholarship to Oriel College, Oxford. He started there in the Michaelmas term, 1908, and although a decade after Maude Royden (see Chapter 12) had attended Oxford, women were still not yet allowed to take degrees, living in segregated colleges, and were not allowed to visit a man's room in college unless they were a sister or cousin. Russell wryly observed that some men seemed to acquire a remarkable number of cousins! The female students were chaperoned to and from lectures, creating for Russell an almost exclusively male social milieu.

Despite these restrictions, Russell found his mind began to blossom, attending lectures by men of great learning. He did note that he was from a privileged section of society, supporting a motion in the Oxford Union that the working classes should be admitted to the university and joining the Christian Social Union. However, there was a general acknowledgement that this privilege implied a debt to be repaid to society, with much good social work being done in the missions in the East End of London, including by those of quite a different political outlook to Russell such as Edith Gell (see Chapter 13).

The ultimate repaying of this debt was to come in the First World War, as 'that generation almost to a man flocked in its thousands to the recruiting offices, not grudgingly or of necessity, and supplied the leadership of the new armies ... They were conscious of a debt and, God knows, they paid it.'[5]

Like Maude Royden, Russell briefly flirted with ideas of Catholicism while at Oxford but on graduation in 1912 applied for an extension to his scholarship so he could read Theology as a prelude to ordination in the Church of England. The following year he was elected to a fellowship at Oriel to serve as a chaplain and tutor in Theology. Russell was now working in an environment in which textual criticism of the Bible was emerging, and debates within the church about traditional literal interpretations of Christ's life and ministry were causing divisions. For Russell, doubts and questions were positive forces but many older bishops and clerics felt threatened by the new debates.

Through 1913 and 1914 Russell spent considerable periods of time in Germany, studying with German theologians and in June 1914 was ordained as a deacon in Cuddesdon parish church, Oxfordshire.

Nearly all that gifted generation had been slaughtered before a year had passed ... The bitter arrow spares not the noblest. A voluntary system seems to entail that the finest spirits are the first victims ... From that holocaust of a whole generation, the potential leaders in Church and State, England has never yet recovered.[6]

At first Russell thought it his duty to try to maintain the life of his college, but as the casualty lists grew, he worked at a YMCA base during Easter 1915 and then was granted leave of absence by the college to accept a commission as an army chaplain. His first posting was to Egypt. As he had received no briefing or training on the work he was expected to do, he thought it best to take some formal services on board ship and to try to get to know the officers and men. This was successful and he became accepted by the territorial unit to which he had been attached. He then found himself in Ismailia as part of the Suez Defence Force, defending the canal against a possible Turkish attack. Russell, like J.V. Salisbury (see Chapter 3) saw himself as serving in biblical territory and used a commentary on Exodus to point out to his men places mentioned in the Bible, including Mount Sinai.

But as Russell realised, 'they needed more than knowing the route of the Exodus.'[7] He saw the men were fed up and had little to occupy their spare time. He had no other padre to work alongside in the unit but received advice from Alfred Jarvis, the Principal Chaplain in the Middle East, to use his own initiative. Russell obtained some funds from HQ and had a large tent erected, acquired some furniture and asked for volunteers to run a canteen. He spent the evenings there and the men warmed to him further, finding a social focus in the camp. This was also important in the development of Russell's self-confidence. For the first time in his life he was mixing with those outside the worlds of public school, the Church of England and academia. He admitted to having been 'scared stiff' at the thought of coming up against 'human life in the raw', but found himself not only accepted, but very popular in the camp.[8]

Before being reposted to France in 1916, Russell took the opportunity to ride into the desert, finding there a haunting sense of the presence of God in the lands of the Old Testament, and visited the Pyramids and the Sphinx near Cairo. By 1916, initial reservations from senior officers about chaplains being anywhere near the front line had been overcome and they had been given a greater freedom of movement. They would give Holy Communion in the dugouts, minister to the wounded and dying on the battlefield and try to share the privations of the troops. For Russell, the one thing he was glad that he did not share with his men was the 'worst thing of all … to kill other human beings'.[9]

On arrival in France he was sent straight up the line to the Somme and witnessed almost half his brigade being wiped out at the Battle of Mouquet Farm in late summer. This was Russell's first experience of seeing people die but he stayed ministering to his men in the heat of battle. For this act of bravery he was awarded the Distinguished Service Order (DSO), although he modestly played this down in his autobiography:

They thought I was brave, but in fact I was too innocent fully to appreciate the dangers! The real test of courage comes later, when a man's nerves are beginning to wear down. What needs courage and resolution then is not walking about in no-man's land but managing to hold on at all.[10]

Following this episode, Russell was transferred to the 20th Division and made senior chaplain, being with them during the horrors of the battle of Passchendaele in 1917 and at Cambrai in 1918 when tanks were used in battle for the first time. At the latter he found himself isolated from his men and accidentally walking down a German-controlled road until he came to the wrong side of a British barbed wire entanglement. He was wearing a German coat, which he had picked up from the field, and had to explain his predicament to some of the Indian cavalry who found him!

In 1918 he was promoted again, this time to Deputy Assistant Chaplain General with the 13th Corps, and was wounded at HQ when a German shell burst through a window. He then suffered from a severe bout of the Spanish influenza that killed nearly 5 per cent of the world's population from 1918 to 1920. This was effectively the end of his war.

Russell Barry had been brought up in the Anglican faith, but this did not mean that his faith was straightforward and unquestioning. 'No man who was involved in that experience came out the same man that he went into it. And it was, as, I think, happened to many others, in war service that I was to find myself.'[11]

Russell considered that the social and religious revolution began on the Somme and on the Salient. He, like thousands of other new army chaplains, had gone to war with minimal experience of life outside of 'academic or churchy circles' but were now ministering to men under the utmost moral and physical strain. It struck Russell that the Industrial Revolution had driven a wedge between the church and the workers, with religion meaning very little to the average soldier. He contrasted their bravery in battle with their lack of knowledge of the gospels, and concluded that there may have been something lacking in the way religion had been put across to people. He even accepted that it was possible to question the existence of God amongst all the suffering. Therefore:

> We had to re-examine our fundamentals and to hammer out a working theology which could stand the test of battle-conditions and give men a faith that could overcome the world ... We may not have said anything very startling ... But the chaplains were to have a decisive influence on the thinking and the practice of the post-war Church.[12]

In essence, that thinking, both after the First and Second world wars, involved relating Church of England theology and practice to the problems of the rest of the world, rather than existing within its own sphere. The gospel had to lead to more than an 'other-worldly salvation'. It had to challenge a world of 'glaring inequalities of wealth, education and opportunity ... Had the gospel nothing to say about ... labour conditions, housing, education, about the enhancement of human rights and dignity?'[13]

Part of this work for Russell meant taking on the role of principal of a new Army Divinity College at Knutsford in Cheshire, a centre for ex-servicemen who had felt called towards Christian ministry during the war. His later career led him to fulfil roles in Egypt, London, Oxford and Liverpool. During the early part of the Second World War he was Canon of Westminster, and as firebombs rained down on the ancient abbey, Russell saw the seriousness of the situation. He made a personal telephone call to Winston Churchill to urge the sending of a fire engine to the abbey, which the Prime Minister authorized. *The Times* reported in 1976 that 'The survival of Westminster Abbey during the "blitz" may be attributed to Barry's courage and vigilance.'[14] From 1941 to 1963, Russell served as Bishop of Southwell in Nottinghamshire, and became identified with the liberal wing of the Church of England. On his retirement he wrote prolifically, including his autobiography *Period of My Life*, published in 1970.

Despite his traditional Anglican upbringing, Russell Barry's experience of the First World War led him to a lifetime of questioning and challenging the accepted norms of the Church of England. He realised that belief and practice had to be made relevant to the challenges of the twentieth century. His career displayed both a physical and moral courage as he strove to make Christianity a true faith for all, not merely for those from privileged backgrounds.

Chapter 10

Harry Wisbey

'I just preached Christ to them. How they did listen!'

Harry Wisbey's war was one of trying to win souls to Christ while operating near the front line. As an Army Scripture Reader, he was not part of the regular army and had to rely on the goodwill of senior officers to permit his presence there, and of the ordinary ranks to provide him with food and shelter.

Following his birth in Nayland, Suffolk, on 12 July 1876, Harry had already served in the 1st York and Lancashire Regiment in the Boer War, being present at the relief of Ladysmith. He had been in the army for nearly five years before he was accepted to serve as an army scripture reader, joining the society on 18 July 1900. His service record held at the SASRA (Soldiers' and Airmen's Scripture Readers Association) headquarters in Aldershot states that he was an Anglican, a total abstainer and willing to serve at home or abroad.[1] He had served at York from 1900 to 1904, residing at 4 Sycamore Terrace at the time of his marriage to Florence Vellum in 1901. He had then briefly been with the Suffolk Regiment on the Isle of Wight and at Aldershot, and had been stationed at the Curragh, County Kildare, since 1904. By the time of the 1911 Irish Census he was thirty-four years of age and had been married to Florence for ten years. They had five children aged between eight and one.

Harry had already done significant work with the Suffolks, instituting an Old Comrades League 'to discourage gambling, drunkenness, and prevent bad language and disrespect to women.'[2] There were also between seventy and eighty members of the Pocket Testament League, and good daily attendance in the prayer room. Harry wrote, 'If ever a Regiment was prepared to meet their God it was the Second Suffolk Regiment.'[3] In 1914, when offered the chance by Lieutenant Colonel Brett, Harry took the decision to travel with the Suffolk Regiment as part of the British Expeditionary Force to France and Belgium.

He kept a record, or *Rough Journal,* of his experiences, which has been held at the SASRA headquarters for many decades and was recently published to mark the centenary of Harry's work as an army scripture reader in the First World War. It shows a man of Christian faith engaging in an active way in the early phases of the war, and is of great interest to those interested in Christianity, the First World War and social history alike.

Harry had been attached to the Suffolk Regiment as their reader for some years and was asked by Lieutenant Colonel Brett to accompany them to war. Harry made the decision to accede to this request on 12 August. He was soon kitted out with a soldier's uniform and equipment and busied himself with domestic preparations.

He left his house on 13 August having had a cup of tea; 'It may be the last my Wife will ever make for me.' He knew that he was going to face real suffering, having been in the Boer War. He conducted family prayers and found, 'To commend your dear ones into God's keeping for one knows not how long, it is very hard indeed.'[4]

Florence told him, 'You will come back. I am sure of that; I have already claimed that from God by faith, – and "Whatsoever ye shall as in prayer, believing, ye shall receive".'[5] Having entrained to Dublin, Harry was then smuggled onto the boat as he was not officially meant to be in the war zone. On his second day on board, he went actively seeking out other Christians. An evening prayer meeting was held in a cabin, and Harry heard two further men in the cabin 'avow … themselves to the Lord's side there and then.'[6]

Despite this Christian fellowship, separation was difficult for Harry. 'How I do miss my wife and little ones, and how I should just love to see them once more, and how nice a cup of tea would be.' He carried on his evangelical work, 'just going amongst the men and speaking about Christ from morning till night; there was no chance of a meeting, but I would go amongst them and talk to them in groups.'[7]

The Suffolks arrived in Le Havre and had to sleep in soaking conditions. It still proved impossible for Harry to organise a group service or prayer meeting and he was warned against talking with local civilians as there was the possibility that some may be German spies.

Harry was not deterred from his evangelical mission. 'I go round from tent to tent talking to the men about Christ during the afternoon, and speaking to and cheering the Christians. To my mind this is better than a Parade Service, and I think it does more good ... If my mission is to be successful, God must be in it throughout, for "Except the Lord build the house, they labour in vain that build it".'[8]

Harry described the commanding officer, Lieutenant Colonel Brett, as 'a godly man indeed, but says little about it; he lives it. He is not too keen to fight, but more than willing to do his duty.'[9] As Harry was not entitled to official army rations, he relied on the generosity of the men with whom he was serving to get enough to eat, and on the understanding of the officers to find him billets in which to sleep. He reflected in biblical terms that 'Foxes have holes, and the birds of the air have nests, but the Son of Man hath nowhere to lay His head.'[10]

Although attached to one particular company, Harry found himself free to go around different companies talking to men about Jesus and holding small prayer meetings. He was allowed to go to a farmhouse, where, as well as getting a tub of water in which to bathe, he was given a feast of plums and pears, and he talked to the old couple there about Jesus. He 'found them to be very religious, but of course, Roman Catholics.'[11] Each day of Harry's diary ended with a biblical quote and on this day he chose 'My God shall supply all your need according to his riches in glory in Christ Jesus'.

On 20 August, Harry took the opportunity to speak to about forty men after breakfast, urging them to 'decide for Christ'. He felt that they were too ashamed to cry and admit to being moved by his message, and that all he could do was to leave God to work through the results of his work.

Harry was under orders that, if captured, all he could say was that he was a scripture reader, something he thought might lead to him being shot for refusing to give information, but he was willing to agree to this. He reckoned there were about twenty-seven Christians in the regiment, presumably meaning active Christians rather than nominal ones. But he noted that a steady trickle of men were announcing to him that they had been converted since arriving in France.

On 21 August, Harry marched 16 miles to Valenciennes and was billeted in a hay loft. '[I] thought of my dear ones at home and the good bed I had left behind, but never mind, – to be with my dear comrades, and to win them for Jesus is more than worth it; so here goes to sleep thank God. Good night!'[12]

One man whom Harry did manage to convince to turn to Christ was a Private Cocle, who 'tells me that he is alright now with God, and if it pleases God to spare him he will again take his old Sunday School Class. I have been trying to win this lad for a long time; thanks be to God!' Some German prisoners had been taken by some of the Suffolk men, and Harry wrote, 'I am very sorry for these poor fellows, many of them love God, and have to fight whether they like it or not.'[13]

By this stage the Suffolks were very close to the front line, something that spurred on Harry in his efforts at conversion:

Now I have just appealed to some more of our men to give themselves to God, for things are looking very serious. Many of our men were fired at last night – 20 yards from where I was sleeping myself. Our master cook had a narrow escape. Terrible artillery fire going on now on our right; it is awful to hear it. We are now at a place called Hainin. Now the hills are on fire; now the guns roar again, and our men laugh, and say 'Let them have it, boys!' We are of course nearer the enemy than we expected we were; we cannot be but about 3 miles from the artillery fire, they could easily reach us. Two companies are now going out to help the East Surreys. 'Goodbye, lads – God bless you and preserve your lives,' said I.[14]

Harry also attempted to spread his message among the Belgian population:

The people here are very frightened; I tell them in the best way I can to look to God; they seem to understand. I place my hands together and I look up, and they know I mean prayer, and then they chat to each other, although I do not understand what they mean.[15]

The same day, 23 August, Harry reached Mons and stayed in the street opposite the railway station. On 24 August, as Harry's company moved down to the town and took up defensive positions, with Harry standing by the side of the road begging the men to lift their hearts to God and trust

Him. He did the same as the Duke of Cornwall's Light Infantry passed, and then other companies. He went back to wash, read his Bible and then returned to the firing line. However, as he was not allowed to talk to men in battle, he retired as this was an unnecessary risk. He advised the sergeant major to move the ammunition wagons further away from the firing line – advice that was taken. Further withdrawals took place as the British Army began the retreat from Mons.

Harry also witnessed the Belgian civilians fleeing from their homes, 'Poor old people, some cripples, little children trying to keep up with them; some of them carrying cradles on their head with babies in; some carrying food, some chairs, some tables. What a sad sight!'[16] As he wore a red cross on his arm to denote he was a non-combatant, he was asked to help wounded soldiers but sadly did not have the knowledge to do so. As German cavalry closed in on Harry's company, he believed he was close to death. The order was given for men to throw away everything except rifles and ammunition and do their best 'My word, the lads look quite white now, and I just say goodbye to my Wife and little ones myself, believing that the end has come.'[17]

However, the British ammunition was too much for the Germans and they were forced to retire. Harry noted that many men had promised to turn to God if he would spare them. The retreat was slow due to the sheer numbers of British troops using the road, and there were many close shaves with the advancing Germans. Harry's company reached Le Cateau, having marched 25 miles in the day. There they were forced to rest take up positions the next day to try to stem the German advance.

As wounded men were brought back from the front line, Harry recognised them as 'men whom I have many times urged to decision for Christ. I speak to them and try to cheer them on "It's a hell, sir, up there," says a man, "we shall be cut up." "Then lift your heart to God, lad, and ask Him to bring you through."'[18]

Harry heard that the colonel had been shot through the head. He escorted another wounded man down to the field hospital, talking to him about Jesus. The most dramatic part of Harry's account was about to occur. German cavalry broke through British lines. Harry jumped onto an ambulance with men from the Royal Army Medical Corps and the Red Cross, as well as some wounded men, then rode off at full gallop. Harry described the

British Army in full retreat as they discarded rifles but attempted to save as much ammunition as possible. Harry tended a sergeant who had had his jaw broken then, after 6 miles, heard that a Captain Blackwell had ordered the formation of a line to defend the ammunition trucks. Harry carried on with his wounded comrade, managing to board a train and reach a hospital in a French town, probably St Quentin. He then prayed. The expected German advance did not reach the hospital, even though they were in the town, saving him from capture. He reflected, 'Surely goodness and mercy shall follow me all the days of my life.'[19] The next day he got on a train to Amiens, thence to Rouen. Harry was advised to get on a hospital ship at Le Havre with the wounded, but refused as he wanted to meet up with the regiment from which he been separated.

By this time, 'I look very dirty, – long beard, hair straight up, teeth dirty; have lost everything except what I stand up in. My sole possessions are – Water bottle, small brown bag, some cash, loaf of bread and a tin of marmalade.'[20]

Another of Harry's possessions was his Bible, so at a rest camp:

I just preached Christ to them. How they did listen! Up came a lad and said 'I was once a lost sinner, but I put my trust in Jesus Christ, and He has saved me' – 'Blessed testimony, brother,' said I, 'thanks for it'; his name was Private Wallace King's Own. He supported me then for some time. The crowd was so great round me, I had to move on, but they followed me, and I took my stand again and preached Christ to them. I pleaded with them to surrender all to Jesus Christ; some of them must have made a decision, I am sure, there and then; one can tell by the look on their faces.[21]

Harry's situation was helped by the Reverend Patterson Talbot, a Presbyterian chaplain he had known at the Curragh Camp. Talbot arranged for Harry to be attached to a general hospital, and be given a coat and blanket. Harry was further encouraged to return to England but reflected that, 'My Society went to great expense to send me out here, and my mission is not ended yet.'[22]

There were further opportunities for Christian fellowship:

a Scotch lad came up to me just now, and said 'It did me good to see you kneeling down this morning; we were all looking at you. I am a Christian myself, and shall be all the better for meeting you.' We kept together fairly well all day after this. He left his name and address: Pte R. Cooper 'Black Watch'.[23]

Harry moved to Le Mans and there he found twelve men from his regiment. 'Christian brother Rifleman Tibbett, had a nice talk with him, and we cheered each other in the Lord. He too, had made his escape. Pte F. Rackham too, not a Christian, but a nice lad, willing to talk about Christ, gave me his address.'[24] At the barracks at Le Mans Harry was refused permission to organise an open-air service but was invited to join a different regiment as their scripture reader. However, as he had been away from his regiment for so long he was now seen by many as something of an anomaly in the war zone:

I fight hard against my feelings, but it is almost too much to bear – I am properly stranded, no one in authority cares for me, no one particularly needs me, but God is for me, Jesus loves me and I love Him – then Lord, what wilt Thou have me do?[25]

By 4 September Harry had been told that he had no right to be in a military barracks, but the military did not have the resources to send him anywhere else! His barracks was then evacuated due to an outbreak of fever and Harry took this as a sign that it was time for him to return home, spending a night with no bed and no shelter, sleeping in the rain. He attended a Roman Catholic church service on the morning of 6 September as there was no English one available, and finally his passage home was arranged by an army chaplain. He was evacuated out via St Nazaire in Brittany. Having been refused passage on a ship by an officer who said he had no business being there, Harry put his trust in God and within ten minutes a telegram arrived ordering that he was to travel home by the first boat available. After his tough time in the war zone, Harry experienced a rough journey back, having to sleep among German prisoners of war. He exchanged a watch with one of them.

As Harry saw troop ships passing in the other direction, he reflected:

I have been 80 hours in trains, I have slept in first and third class railway carriages, and in a Guard's Van, and Bullock Trucks, in streets, roads, cow-sheds, hay-lofts, fields, Barrack Square, tents, in the grounds of a Bishop's Palace, in a state-room on board ship; I have dined on a meal that would cost 3/6d. and I have dined on one that would cost ¾d.; either of them were sweet, God in either case being the giver.[26]

Harry was landed at Cowes, and then transferred to Southampton, then London, before returning to Ireland:

So ends the mission, it has been one of much anxiety, accompanied by great sacrifice and suffering, but it was a very blessed and successful one, but to my mind, the secret of success in this Regiment is due to the fact that the Regiment had its Reader with it for so long.[27]

Harry Wisbey continued to serve as an army scripture reader until the age of 75 in 1951. His part in the war came without position, status, or, following separation from his men at Le Cateau, much sympathy among the men he was with. He endured cold, hunger and deprivation to do what he saw as his duty in spreading the word of God in the army. His journal stands as a remarkable eyewitness account of the first weeks of the war from someone fully involved in the thick of the action.

Part III

Women in War

'The errand of angels is given to women; And this is a gift that, as sisters, we claim.'

For most working-class women living in Britain in 1914, the reality of life was hard work in factories, domestic trades such as dressmaking or millinery, or long hours spent in domestic service. This work also paid very badly, with an average weekly wage of 11s. 7d. For middle- and upper-class families, status was most usually achieved by ensuring that both mother and daughters did as little arduous and useful work as possible. If the daughters were to be educated, it was to make them decorative foils for their future husbands.

Some charity and voluntary work was undertaken by women to fill their leisure hours. Often this involved the development of considerable organisational skills. For a handful of women of this generation, educational opportunities were opening up. They could take degrees at the Scottish and English provincial universities, and female non-degree courses at some Oxford and Cambridge University colleges.

By 1914, the suffragette movement led by Emmeline and Christabel Pankhurst had reached the stage of civil disobedience and disruption in an increasingly frenetic attempt to make the Liberal government accede to their demands for the right for women to vote in public elections. However, this movement, in general, threw itself enthusiastically behind the war effort. Maude Royden stood out against this tide as an example of a former suffragist turned female pacifist.

One of the significant ways in which women of all classes and political persuasions could materially contribute was to encourage their menfolk to join up. The famous 'Women of Britain say- Go!' poster was symbolic of this. Recruiting meetings were addressed by society ladies such as Edith

Gell, as well as famous actresses and professional beauties. These meetings would include the singing of recruiting songs. Other women received some fame or notoriety depending on one's perspective for handing out of white feathers in the street for men in non-military uniform.

The Queen Alexandra's Imperial Military Nursing Service (QAIMNS) increased in membership from 463 in August 1914 to more than 13,000 by November 1918. Similarly, the Territorial Force Nursing Services (TFNS) increased from nearly 3,000 to about 10,500. In August 1918 there were more than 7,000 women employed in France working under the direction of the Royal Army Medical Corps. (See plate 9.) Over 1,094 were in the British Red Cross, with a similar number working for Christian organisations including the YMCA, Church Army, Soldiers' Christian Association and the Salvation Army.[1] These services had been augmented by the establishment of non-professional Voluntary Aid Detachments (VADs) in 1910, in which many girls enrolled as nurses. One British lady who had been a pioneer in the developing of nursing on the European continent was Edith Cavell, who has become an iconic figure of devotion to duty and faith in the hundred years since her execution in October 1915. This work considers her exceptionally moving story in the light of her intense faith as expressed during her intensely lived final hours.

The Women's Army Auxiliary Corps (WAAC) was created, with 40,000 women joining by November 1918.[2] They performed a number of jobs that did not involve fighting but were being carried out by men who could have been in battle. These included work in offices, canteens, transport, stores and army bases. This organisation later became known as the Queen Mary's Army Auxiliary Corps.

On the home front, many women sought to alleviate the day-to-day sufferings of their menfolk by the knitting of 'soldiers' comforts' such as socks, waistcoats, helmets, scarves, mitts and body belts. Other women, such as the formidable Lilian Hayman, whom we meet in this section, were active in Sunday school and Bible class work.

There were many books devoted to providing guidance for, and lessons to be delivered by, Bible class teachers. Elinor Lewis pitched her book for young women's Bible classes to 'arouse in the scholars an earnest thirsting after holiness, and a complete self-dedication to the service of God'.[3] The gendered nature of such holiness and dedication included exhortations in the lesson devoted to 'Taking Up the Cross Daily' to 'do a bit of extra work to save your mother', and in that devoted to 'Complete Self-Surrender' to say to Jesus, 'Lord, what wilt Thou have me to do?' before accepting an 'unsteady lover'.[4] In practice, Bible classes for girls and young women formed an extended social network to reinforce the values of the specific Bible teaching. For example, the Aberdeen Girls' class had an evening party with a church tea followed by songs, recitations and dancing to mark the moving on of the teacher, a Miss Lyon.[5] In Derby, a class had an annual tea followed by a 'Round the world with the Mothers' Union Lecture', followed by a lecture on Joan of Arc.[6] In Montrose the girls were given a lecture by a Dr Grant on the subject of 'Minor ailments – coughs colds headaches, rheumatism'. This was considered 'most helpful and admirably suited to the requirements of the pupils'.[7] On the coming of war, Bible classes identified themselves with the war effort and the relief of suffering. In 1916, the Holburn Girls' Bible Class, in Northumberland, collected ten shillings towards a New Testament Fund for soldiers.[8] Thanks to existence of both a remarkable collection of letters sent to one Bible class teacher, Mrs Lilian Hayman of Bournemouth, and an exercise book completed by one of her students, we can see the ways in which her teaching of the Bible had fed into the war experiences of her ex-students, and how the experience of war fed back into her teaching from 1915 to 1917.

In this section we meet four very strong-minded women who would probably have clashed violently on many political issues, but whose genuine concern for humanity and the advancement of womanhood reflected through a Christian perspective cannot be in doubt. In a society where their potential roles were limited by lack of opportunity, they seized what opportunities their relatively comfortable backgrounds gave them and fought very vigorous good fights.

Chapter 11

Lilian Hayman

'I will always bless you for the way you have helped me to keep on the very Narrow Path we have to tread'

Throughout the first four decades of the twentieth century, surgeon's wife Lilian Hayman, who had been born in Bristol in 1865, ran a boys' Bible class, firstly in Brighton, and then from about 1912 onwards from her large villa in Bournemouth. (See plate 10.) Both classes were part of Anglican communities – St Matthew's parish in Brighton and St Mary the Virgin parish in Bournemouth. Due to the existence of two unusual sources – a collection of more than a hundred letters written to her by ex-pupils serving in the war and an exercise book still in the possession of a pupil's family – it is possible to get an idea of the sort of Christianity that Mrs Hayman, as she was known to her 'boys', espoused during the war, and the effect it had on many young men.

Samuel Ching attended Mrs Hayman's class in Bournemouth from 1915 to 1917 and his neat, thirty-page Marks and Spencer's exercise book is still in his family today. One of the first lessons he had with Mrs Hayman took place on 28 February 1915. The subject was the betrayal of Jesus by Judas Iscariot. Mrs Hayman used the biblical story to draw parallels with the martyrdom of Father Joseph Dergent (see Chapter 17), whose betrayal was likened to that of Christ.

On 15 August 1915, work on Jonah shows him to be a 'missionary in a foreign land', whilst his experience with the storm and the whale is a 'time of terrible trouble and deliverance', with the message of the story being 'to stand by our religion at all times'. A strong connection between the journeys of St Paul in the New Testament and the journeys made by British forces in the war was emphasised. In a lesson entitled 'The Missionaries', Samuel learned that in Acts 16, Paul, Silas and Timothy answered the call to travel to Europe to 'Come over and help me'. The clear implication was that the British soldiers and sailors were answering a similar call from the Belgian and French nations, and thus they were fulfilling the will of God, positioning Britain's war aims on the same plane as that of the earliest biblical missionary journeys.

Another lesson examined the fate of the Jewish nation, drawing parallels between its dispersal due to a turning away from God and the perils that Britain faced in the war. Mrs Hayman had her boys consider the question posed in *Foxe's Book of Martyrs*, 'Who are following now – a noble army, men and boys, matron and maid?' The fate of Britain was in the hands of the modern-day noble army, willing to risk martyrdom for the Christian war. On a similar theme, a lesson on Joan of Arc posed the question, 'Was it cruel of God to let Joan of Arc fail?' The emphatic answer was, 'No, because it let Joan of Arc be a saint and sets an example to the French and English.'

A particularly apt lesson was delivered on 26 June 1916, a week before the commencement of the Battle of the Somme. Entitled, 'Sowing and Reaping', the lines written by Samuel were as follows:

1. They that sow in tears shall reap in joy. Ps. 126:6
2. Sowing in tears means doing something hard now, in order to reap a harvest later.
3. The Allies, are now Sowing in tears.
4. One soweth, and another reapeth. St John iv:37
5. Sometimes one man Suffers that another may reap the benefits.
6. Our soldiers and sailors are Sowing in tears in order that Europe may reap in joy.
7. The chief Duty of those that stay at home is to Pray.

St Paul's journey into captivity was taught as an 'arrest and scourging' and an 'inner prison'. This message was a particularly pertinent one for Mrs Hayman as her nephew, Captain J. Rollo Hayman RAMC, had been taken prisoner of war in 1914. St Peter's prison experience was also the subject of a lesson, with the result being the writing of a heartfelt prayer for those in captivity. The persecution of British prisoners in German hands was a subject that exercised opinion on the home front at the time. Mrs Hayman's boys learned that 'It is good for the Church to be persecuted for its religion as it helps people to pray more as God helps. It also sets an example of our Lord, who was also persecuted'.

Other Bible stories were couched in military terms. The Parable of the Invitation to the King's Wedding Feast was used to elicit the response from Samuel that people ought to follow the example of General Buller, a recipient of the Victoria Cross during the Zulu War and subsequent leader during the Boer War 'who fought bravely for his country and was a friend to all the soldiers'. Jesus was described as a king changing his headquarters to Bethlehem, then returning to his original HQ on Ascension Day. His 'faithful soldiers' remembered his message before going 'Back to the Trenches'. The story of St George was marshalled in to emphasise that fact that he was an officer in the Roman army and suffered martyrdom himself.

Samuel Ching absorbed both the Christian and the military message of Mrs Hayman's Bible class and eventually joined the Hampshire Regiment after the war. He then worshipped at St Mary the Virgin, Bournemouth, the same church that his old Sunday school teacher attended, until his death in 1972.

As well as continuing to teach her Bible class during the war, Mrs Hayman corresponded with more than thirty of her ex-pupils, continuing to offer spiritual, moral and material support for their war efforts.

Philip T. Bryant was one of Mrs Hayman's Brighton boys. He served on HMS *Queen Elizabeth* and was the pupil upon whom Mrs Hayman seems to have left the deepest impression. His letters to her show a continuing devotion, describing himself as 'your sincere young friend'. He wrote, 'Forgive me if I chatter too much but I forgot myself in talking to you as you understand so much.'[1] He received letters from his mother and Mrs Hayman only, and emphasised the latter's importance in his life: 'I will always bless you for the way you have helped me to keep on the very Narrow Path we have to tread.'[2] He also asked for a personal prayer from her at 10.30 am, Easter Day 1915, so he could feel that spiritual closeness across the waters.

Another of Mrs Hayman's ex-pupils who wrote extensively was Tony 'Chum' Hewitt, a naval recruit serving on board HMS *Russell*. While on leave at Christmas, Hewitt had seen a number of ex-Bible class pupils and complimented Mrs Hayman on the journey she had set them on. 'Your old

Bible class, dear Teacher, is – er – making history, down chin-stays, somebody is blowing, at least they are lining up, going forth nobly to fight!! "Chin stay carried away, Sir."'[3] Hewitt was another who thanked Mrs Hayman for the path she had set him on: 'I am glad you are proud of your Infants, and any old-how, here is one who is proud to be, Your old pupil, Chum.'[4]

Mrs Hayman was an avid sender of parcels. Whilst she could not accompany her boys on their physical journeys, she could make sure that some amusements and comforts could come from her. Tony Hewitt commented on a game of snakes and ladders she had sent in a parcel as being 'very popular'.[5] Evidently, Mrs Hayman had commented on her advancing years to Hewitt, who responded with charm, 'I am like G.W. and really cannot tell a lie, and the last time I saw you I could not help thinking that you had found the secret of perpetual youth.'[6] Kenneth Eady remembered the Brighton class and 'good old St Matthews Church. How well all the boys have done. It's really wonderful what difference a few years makes in the lives of us during these awful times.'[7]

Rex Harris of HMS *Dido* was 'Your Old Bible Class Boy, Rex'.[8] Harold Little was 'Your loving Bible class boy, Harold'.[9] The journey of L. Holland of the 5th Battalion Wiltshire Regiment took him to Mesopotamia and India, expressing happiness at the fact that Mrs Hayman had a new class in Bournemouth, and that he would love to be in her class again. Months later, he asked her to 'Remember me to the Boys of St Mary's Bibles Classes'.[10] For Gunner W.F. Roberts it was the journey away from family that affected him deeply. He wrote of missing his 'dear wife', longing for the 'happy time' when they are reunited saying, 'never mind, everything comes to those that waits, All in God's good time.'[11] He then apologised for not being able to tell her any news, but said, 'there will be a big smash before long I pray God that he will keep me safe for my wife and Baby's sake.'[12] He later wrote, 'Please God I will be able to see all shortly.'[13]

Charles Thomas was another who poured out his innermost heart to Mrs Hayman. He explained how he prayed for his friends in the forces and for a girl: '(I know I can confess to you in confidence) the girl whom I (at my young age) really loved and picked up friendship with her in B'mouth when she was there for her health, her home being in Cheltenham.'[14] He even sent Mrs Hayman a photo of her and wrote of how his friend tried hard to court her but that he 'won her'. The result of Mrs Hayman's parcels and interest in his war journey was that he was 'proud to be considered by you with such friendly interest which I can only repay with a promise to endeavour even more to "stick" to my faith.'[15]

Mrs Hayman also sent forth her boys with a firm dual belief in God and the British nation. Phil Bryant displayed a robust certainty in the rightfulness of the war, and God's purpose for Britain within it: 'I would not be risking my life now if I did not think ours was a just cause.'[16] Furthermore, Britain's position within the world was a God-given one: 'With God's Almighty help we shall all live in England as rulers of the sea again.'[17] He had a strong sense of nationhood pertaining to other countries, echoing the reference in the later Bible classes of sympathy with Belgium: 'Brave little Belgium how well she will be rewarded.'[18] He also believed in divine agency at work in his war experiences, claiming to have been so much 'protected by God's almighty hand … Sometimes I have thought of what might have been our fate and God has indeed been Good in every way. When we have lost ships and men the *Queen Elizabeth* has come through safe and unscathed.'[19]

Bryant's journey took him to the Dardanelles, where he saw action five times. He felt sustained by the Easter message: 'What is there more enchanting than the beautiful glorious lesson of Easter and how we look for it.'[20] Bryant contextualised the war as a fight against evil: 'Yes the fight of nation against nation is little in comparison with a churchman's fight against evil.'[21]

By the autumn of 1915 it was possible to detect a change in the tone of Bryant's letters, an indication of a developing journey of understanding of the nature of war: 'Yes sometimes when the horrors of war are shown in naked light it seems to prove more than ever our own faith and oftimes one thinks that our religion is about the only true thing there is.'[22] He expressed weariness of the fighting and 'incessant killing'. However, the more Bryant's journey into the horrors of war progressed, the greater his journey into the lessons of spirituality and national righteousness he had learned at the Bible class. He wrote, 'The sacrifice is indeed great but it is indeed glorious to know what a cause of right we are fighting in.'[23] He was able to ascribe clear blame for the destruction at the Kaiser's door: 'One man's Covetous nature has plunged the whole world into war and pillage; surely fitting rewards must be paid.'[24] Kenneth Eady, a second lieutenant in the 3/20th Reserve Battalion of the London Regiment, was another who ascribed the destruction firmly at the door of the Germans, expressing the wish to be able to tell Mrs Hayman 'what the Boche and his devilry are like'.[25]

It was also important to Mrs Hayman and her boys to be seen to be doing their duty. Tony Hewitt wrote:

It must be very interesting for you to hear from all your old pupils in all parts of the Globe. Do you remember me saying when you were at Mr Bromley's that your Infants would do you credit. Well good to see, that there are not many of them amongst the slackers, does it?'[26]

As conscription was introduced in 1916, he contended:

It seems hard that we should have come to conscription after all, I should have thought that young fellows who have the nerve to stay at home these days would have the nerve to go anywhere and do anything, but still I suppose they have got nerve, but not what we should call 'guts'.[27]

Similarly, V. Leigh was proud of the commitment to the cause shown by his family. He wrote of his sisters back home, one being a tram conductor the other in the Post Office, 'Don't you think we are a patriotic family three of us on active service and two doing men's work?'[28] For George Marshall it was 'the duty of every Englishman worthy of the name, to take up arms and defend his own country.'[29]

One particularly unpleasant journey experienced by about 200,000 British servicemen was into the hands of the enemy as a prisoner of war. Fortunately for Mrs Hayman's nephew, Lieutenant J.R. Hayman, after having been taken prisoner in 1914 his return journey was a relatively quick one, being one of a party of RAMC personnel and chaplains repatriated as part of a prisoner exchange in the summer of 1915. This elicited contrasting responses from her 'Old Boys', from Tony Hewitt writing that he was sorry to hear the news and that 'we can only send them fodder and hope it will reach them' through to George Marshall, who also expressed personal sympathy but added, 'especially as [the Germans] are not over scrupulous regarding their treatment of the unfortunate prisoners that fall in their clutches.'[30] However, by August, news of the treatment that prisoners of war were receiving had spread and Hewitt wrote, 'It makes one properly wild to hear of the way they treat our prisoners but it certainly looks as if our turn isn't far off.'[31] A. Boreham thought similarly:

> What an awful time your poor nephew must have, fancy those Germans being so wicked after the way we treat our Prisoners. They are allowed everything that is sent to them. I do wish I was put in charge of them. I should get even with them.[32]

One old boy who did find himself a prisoner of war was Private R.E. Davies of the 2nd Wiltshire Regiment. He wrote of receiving lots of parcels and commented that he had heard of the Black Forest in Geography lessons, but never thinking he would get to see it. From there he wrote, 'The time is now 3 o clock and I am sitting in a field now thinking how the world is using my old chums Ben and Arthur Tremlett. What some tales we shall have to tell when we come home which I hope will be soon now.'[33]

Mrs Hayman's work for prisoners went beyond support for her own nephew and students. In 1915 she contacted the Hampshire Prisoners of War Help Committee and was told that they would be 'very pleased to be able to send you the name of a prisoner in Germany who wants a godmother to look after him. It is Pte W. Hall (no.8274), Old English Camp, Sennelager.'[34] This happened to be the same camp in which her nephew had been held. Over the next three years she corresponded regularly with Hall, receiving intermittent replies that thanked her for her kindness and commented on the weather, but were non-committal about conditions in the camp. Hall, like Joseph Garvey (see Chapter 4), spent the entire period from his capture in 1914 through to the end of the war a prisoner. In 1916 he wrote how important it was that 'we are all here but we are not forgotten by friends in the old Country.'[35] However, a year on, despite the generalised comments in the postcards he was able to send Mrs Hayman, it was clear the psychological journey he had been forced to make was not a good one: 'The most needed thing we want is freedom which is half our life and it is getting monotonous after 3 years.'[36]

Mrs Hayman continued her classes right through to her death three decades later. Her obituary appeared in her parish newsletter in March 1944. It referred to:

> the profound respect and deep love felt by all S. Mary's people for Mrs Hayman. Generations of 'her lads' – many of whom are now overseas – still talk and write of those thrilling Sunday afternoons spent at 'Thorncliffe', and to which they owe more than they can ever express in words ... S. Mary's Mothers, too, will never forget her kindly interest in all their doings, and the generous support she always gave to their Christmas festivities and Summer outings in the happier days of peace ... May God rest her gallant soul.[37]

Lillian Hayman set generations of young men on what she saw as the right path on their journey through life. She was held in high esteem by many of those boys into their adulthood and her Christianity was one of a devout faith in her God and her country. Her influence was felt through the first decades of the twentieth century and she gave all she could to those whom she served.

Chapter 12

Maude Royden

'Your sons and your daughters will prophesy'

Whilst many women expressed their Christianity through direct support for the war effort, Maude Royden interpreted her faith differently. Turning her back on her Conservative upbringing and prominent position in the suffrage movement, she became a campaigner for peace. She further raised the profile of women in the established church and was a pioneer in the movement that, a hundred years later, would see the appointment of the first female bishop in the Church of England. (See plate 11.)

Agnes Maude Royden was born in 1876, the daughter of the ship-owning Conservative MP from Liverpool, Sir Thomas Royden – a self-made millionaire. Maude was the youngest of eight children and was born with dislocated hips, finding it impossible to cross her legs. In adult life she played down her lameness. It was this difficulty that first made her think hard about God. She had been brought up to go to church twice on a Sunday and read her Bible, and had learned of a vengeful God. She recalled 'that children who called Elisha "baldhead" should immediately be devoured by two bears was … received by me without a sense of shock.'[1] Her parents taught her that lameness was something sent by God. However, for Maude it gave her a lifelong sympathy for the underdog.

Maude felt that her parents were distant, not having enough time to spend with all eight children, but she found companionship with her siblings. She was educated first at Cheltenham Ladies College from 1893 to 1896, then at Lady Margaret Hall, in Oxford, from 1896 to 1899, at a time when it was still unusual for women to be allowed into university. Indeed, she was the only one of six sisters to receive a formal education. At university she devoted herself to her History studies. Women were tolerated rather than welcomed at lectures, and were not allowed to take degrees.

After a visit to Italy, Maude toyed with the idea of converting to Catholicism. She read the Bible for guidance and was 'considerably surprised' at what she found. 'I suppose most people are, when they read it with a view to acting on the advice they receive. It never occurred to me to do so before.'[2] Her reading of the Bible guided her to show sympathy for the poor. She moved away from the idea of a vengeful God that she understood from the Old Testament to the kindness of Christ in the New Testament. 'To me, Christ is God, and it is to Him that I must look for strength.'[3]

Maude's quest to discover the nature of her own spirituality saw her return to Oxford in 1901 to consult Reverend William Hudson Shaw. Hudson was an Anglican priest and a popular and dynamic lecturer for the University Extension Service, a continuing education service for ordinary citizens. This meeting was to prove of supreme importance for Maude. As well as meeting her spiritual mentor, she had met her soul mate.

Following their Oxford meetings they continued their conversations by post, and shortly afterwards Maude was invited to Shaw's rural parish at South Luffenham, Rutland, to live with him and his wife, Effie. She would undertake the dual roles of parish assistant and companion to Effie while Hudson was away lecturing during the week. Effie saw the love developing between Maude and Hudson but was content that the three-way relationship continued. The love remained platonic right until Effie's death in 1944. At this point, Hudson, then 84, and Maude married. However, the marriage only lasted two months, until Hudson's death.

After graduating in 1899, Maude spent three years working amongst the poor with the Victoria Women's Settlement in Liverpool and then became involved in the women's suffrage movement, becoming a regular speaker for the National Union of Women's Suffrage Societies (NUWSS) from 1908. She was appointed to its executive committee in 1911 and edited its newspaper, *The Common Cause*, from 1913 to 1914. By 1912 she was giving well over 250 speeches a year. The NUWSS was the moderate face of the struggle for women's suffrage, eschewing the more militant tactics of the Women's Social and Political Union (WSPU) led by Emmeline Pankhurst.

In 1912 the Labour Party made support for female suffrage part of its policy for the first time, causing a political split in the women's movement between those who continued to press the Liberal Party for reform and those, like its leader Millicent Fawcett, who supported pro-suffrage Labour candidates against Liberal ones. Maude, the daughter of a former Conservative MP, supported the Labour Party and was one of the speakers at the joint meeting of the NUWSS and the Labour Party held in the Royal Albert Hall in February 1914. Maude considered the Women's movement 'the most profoundly moral movement since the foundation of the Christian Church'.[4]

However, at the outbreak of the First World War, Maude found herself in conflict with many in the NUWSS, which, under Fawcett's guidance, had thrown itself enthusiastically into support for the war effort. Maude expressed disappointment that Christians of different nations were at war against each other: 'I hear of working men who will not shoot down their fellow workers, and Socialists who refuse to fight with Socialists. I hear of no Christians who refuse to shoot down Christians.'[5]

She considered that when Jesus disarmed St Peter in the Garden of Gethsemane, this was symbolic of the disarming of every soldier. She searched the New Testament for any justification for war and found none. This view made her feel isolated from former friends, including the Bishop of London, Arthur Winnington-Ingram, who preached virulently pro-war sermons. Indeed, her own brother, Tom, advised the British Government on the shipping of troops and resources to the Western Front, and her sister, Ethel, helped to establish the Women's Royal Naval Service, the 'Wrens'. This isolation was addressed by Maude joining the coming together of those who found themselves outside the militarist zeitgeist in the Fellowship of Reconciliation (FOR).

Maude spoke at its formation in Cambridge in December 1914. Quoting the gospel of Matthew, she said, 'Christ said to us, "Be ye perfect".' This meant living lives of love and peace, not at some later date when the world's problems had been resolved, but right now. Jesus did not tell his disciples 'that some day, when good was stronger ... it would be their duty to rely on love and put aside earthly weapons of defence. They were to be perfect not in the future, "but now".'[6] The FOR sought to move away from justifying pacifism based on selective biblical texts, onto the fundamental principle of love overcoming evil.

In February 1915 Maude resigned as editor of *Common Cause* and gave up her place on the executive council of the NUWSS, finding her pacifist views increasingly at odds with others in the suffrage movement. She considered militarism and feminism incompatible. She had intended to attend the Women's Peace Congress in The Hague that year but was unable to do so when travel via the North Sea was forbidden.

Maude published her pacifist view in a pamphlet, *The Great Adventure*, in 1915. She argued that as Christ had not remained neutral on the cross, it was wrong for Christians to adopt a position of passive neutrality in the war. For her, the alternative to war was sacrifice, the sacrifice of the British nation as a crucifixion to demonstrate the folly of war. To spread this message beyond the readership of her pamphlet she undertook a peace mission beginning in July 1915, travelling the country in a large horse-drawn caravan with a group of fellow pacifist Quakers, Congregationalists, clergy and lay people. Each day would begin with prayers around the caravan, before the party continued its progress through Derbyshire, Nottinghamshire and Leicestershire towards London. A few clergy and ministers opened churches so the group could hold services. Some converts to pacifism were secured whilst robust discussions took place with sceptics, particularly at open-air meetings where sometimes recruiting sergeants would attend to object to the message that ran counter to their work to increase military enlistment. A visit to the Nottinghamshire mining town of Mansfield resulted in the booing and jeering of prayers at the market cross.

In Hinckley, Leicestershire, two male members of the group had to take refuge in a shop after being attacked in the street. Later in the day a drunken mob advanced to the caravan site. Maude ordered the group to sit in a circle on the ground in silent prayer, practising the policy of non-resistance to violence that she passionately believed in. Their tents were pillaged then torn down and the caravan was engulfed in flames. Not one of the dozen or so pacifists raised a voice or finger in protest and were thus spared physical attack themselves, apart from one drunken man seizing Maude by the throat, then desisting when no one intervened to stop him, and some men in uniform dragging two curates to the burning caravan, but refraining to throw them on it. Eventually, an estimated crowd of 2,000 to 3,000 was present, some of them singing *It's a Long Way to Tipperary* as the caravan burned. Eventually the missioners were put onto the Leicester Express at 3.00 am.

Some of the London press accused the group of being spies financed by Germany, and the *Daily Express* accused Maude of being a 'Peace Crank' and appealed for advance notice of pacifist meetings so they could be publicised in the paper in order for opponents to attend and disrupt.[7]

Despite this, even outside of the NUWSS Maude campaigned for the vote for women through the National Council for Adult Suffrage. When she was challenged that the cause of women's suffrage had been forgotten about during the war, she replied, 'If I forget thee, O Jerusalem, let my right hand forget her cunning' (Psalm 137:5).

In 1916 Maude was appointed to the council of the National Mission for Repentance and Hope. The aim was to return a Britain torn apart by the disruption of war to its core Christian values. However, controversy quickly arose about the precise nature of women's role in the movement. Whilst the idea was that they were initially allowed to speak, as opposed to preach, from Anglican pulpits, this was rescinded by Randall Davidson, the cautious Archbishop of Canterbury.

Maude was not to be deterred. She became an assistant preacher at the Nonconformist City Temple in 1917, the first woman to publicly preach in England. Although an Anglican herself, she was not permitted to preach in the Church of England as a woman. Maude found it astonishing that the churches had ignored that element of the first Pentecost, which St Peter had said had fulfilled the promise of the prophet Joel: 'Your sons *and your daughters* will prophesy' (Joel 2:28, Acts 2:17). For her, nowhere in Jesus's words in the Bible was a difference in spiritual values given for men and women.

In a 1917 speech at Queen's Hall in London Maude used the oft-cited phrase 'The Church [of England] should go forward along the path of progress and be no longer satisfied only to represent the Conservative Party at prayer'.[8] Her deep religious faith led to her establishing her own religious centre, the Guildhouse, in London. Maude was one of very few women to speak from the pulpit. Her sermons became famous and she was invited on tours of the USA, Australia, China and India. She also became a well-known radio voice and her books and pamphlets on women's ordination were widely read. In 1929 she began the official campaign for women priests when she founded the Society for the Ministry of Women, and was later created the first woman Doctor of Divinity.

Maude made several preaching tours across the world from the 1920s to the 1940s and undertook large-scale article writing. At the same time she continued her work for peace, in particular through her 'Peace Army' and the League of Nations. In 1939, however, she renounced pacifism, believing Nazism to be a greater evil than war. After 1945, she was mainly occupied by writing and radio broadcasts on religion. She died in London on 30 July 1956.

Maude Royden was active in the public life of Britain for more than half a century. She was a pioneering Christian, and whilst her view of the application of her faith to the challenges presented by the First World War led her down a very different path to the other women featured in this book, it was nonetheless sincerely held and rigorously applied. Maude challenged the orthodoxies of her time, and it was perhaps her vision of women's place in Christianity that came to hold sway in later decades.

Chapter 13

The Hon. Mrs Edith Lyttleton Gell

'Which will you be, a temptation or an inspiration?'

Whilst many women who rose to prominence during the First World War have retained their place in the public consciousness, Edith Gell, despite being a prolific writer and an extremely well-connected lady involved in a range of public causes, has to a large extent been overlooked by the passage of time. However, her work was taken into war by hundreds of thousands of men, and allowed family members hundreds of miles apart to share prayer and fellowship together. (See plate 12.)

Edith Brodrick (later, Gell) was the daughter of William, 8th Viscount Middleton, later Secretary of State for War, and Augusta Mary Fremantle. Born on 14 June 1860, Edith was brought up in London and educated at home, learning foreign languages, classics, history and music. In addition, 'Religion was presented not as a lesson but a life.'[1] Family prayers were said every morning, and Bible passages and hymns committed to memory, a store of knowledge that would serve Edith well during the war. As a child, she taught in Sunday schools and looked forward to hymn singing and walks in the afternoons.

In 1884 she became Lady of the House at Merton College, Oxford, to support her bachelor uncle, who was warden. It was here that she met Philip Lyttleton Gell, a man 'who touched life at a thousand points and threw himself with enthusiasm into the various forward movements of the day.'[2] They married in 1889, and in 1901 moved to Philip's ancestral home, Hopton Hall, in Derbyshire, an 'ancient spacious house with its historic associations [and] the wonderful beauty of hills and dales and glens and river'.[3] Philip was chairman of many different companies associated with business and administrative matters in British colonies.

Initially, Edith's social work was focused on improving the lives of poorer women in Oxford and London. She was active in establishing the Ladies Oxford Settlement, a charity run by women whose menfolk had a connection with the University of Oxford, about which she wrote to *The Times*:

> The old idea of philanthropists – that one-half of humanity was waiting to be 'done good to' by the other half of humanity – is exploded, and it has been realized that the desire to help can only bear useful fruit when accompanied by a sympathetic understanding of those to whom help is offered. [4]

This help included 'numerous girls' clubs, the classes, the women's meetings, the visiting, the sick-nursing, or, above all, by the welcome accorded to our ladies in homes which have little of home but the name'.

Edith was also active in the work of St Margaret's House, situated in Bethnal Green, in the East End of London. It housed between twelve and sixteen women who tried to engage the poor of the area and help them towards more fulfilled lives. She campaigned for more financial support in order to spread the work into the Isle of Dogs and Stratford. This work was driven by the necessity of improving the moral fabric of the capital's poor.

> We must realize that the womanhood of East London, among who the workers of St Margaret's live, is the root and kernel of our civic life. These women are the mothers of citizens whose determining voice in the council of the State grows daily more insistent ... National righteousness, it has been well said, can never be far in advance of the moral sense of the masses. If we are content to leave the womanhood of our great cities in ignorance and social isolation, the higher standard, the refinement, the lofty idealism which the Universities endeavour to give to the world, cannot be neutralized. For it is the people ultimately, not the aristocracy, either of birth or intellect, who make our laws and direct our administration. As they think, so the nation thinks. It is our responsibility to help them to fell and judge aright. 'To whom much is given, of him shall much be required.'[5]

Edith was appealing for help to work with the mothers who were at the time giving birth to the sons who two decades hence would find themselves in the theatres of war. Thus she used her Oxford University connections in order to spread what she saw and national Christian values to those whom they had not reached.

Edith had a traditional, conservative outlook on the world and expressed this view through many tracts, books and speeches, as well as being active in a wide range of charity and religious groups. She was particularly interested in women's issues, with much of her writing having a moralistic tone. She was active in the Mothers' Union and Union of Women Workers, which were aimed at improving not just the material, but the moral condition of womenfolk.

In much of her work Edith sought to support Philip's interests. This was particularly the case with the settlement of southern Africa. At the beginning of the twentieth century it was thought that females outnumbered males in Britain, and Edith thought that emigration was an answer to this issue of surplus middle-class women who would be unable to find suitable husbands. She was a member of the British Women's Emigration Association and in 1901 became Chair of the South African Emigration Expansion Committee, providing practical advice to female emigrants. Edith would vet the suitability of the potential emigrants for life in Africa and organise initial accommodation in a hostel in Bulawayo. She held a high opinion of the benefits of colonial rule on the native African people and was a staunch Conservative and Unionist in political outlook.

In 1904 a further letter appeared in *The Times*, co-signed by Edith and nine others, including the prominent suffragist and women's rights campaigner Millicent Garrett Fawcett, appealing for funds on behalf of the Women's Horticultural College at Swanley. This body provided training to equip young women for life in the colonies.

We need hardly refer to the value to the Empire of capable Englishwomen in colonial country districts, both in South Africa and in Canada; neither need we emphasize the undue proportion of women now in the mother country or the severe competitive struggle thereby imposed on women workers.[6]

In 1891 Edith published her first book, *The Cloud of Witness*, comprising daily Bible readings with accompanying quotes from great works of literature, based on a weekly theme. As a devoted Anglican, each week's theme was broadly in line with the church calendar. This book was such a success that more than 200,000 copies were sold.

In 1898 came *The More Excellent Way: Words of the Wise on the Life of Love*, an expansion of the sections in *The Cloud of Witness* dealing with Love, Betrothal and Holy Matrimony.

> The varied aspects of LOVE (that central fact of life which, as the title recalls, St Paul placed in the forefront of the Christian virtues) are presented as they have appeared to the Poets and Writers of all ages, and it is the object of the book to show that 'THE MORE EXCELLENT WAY' is most completely realized in Christian marriage.[7]

In 1912 she wrote *The Menace of Secularism*, denouncing plans to disestablish the Church of England in Wales and published further works arguing against women's suffrage. 'Whether we have really gained by dragging women into the political arena is open to doubt.'[8] As befitted a woman of strong opinions, an energetic campaigning style and a thirst for writing, the outbreak of war gave Edith a fresh impetus to both preach and publish. She condemned what she saw as the moral laxity of many women in the years before the war and considered the war to be an opportunity for British womanhood to enter a new era.

> The craving for excitement had grown into a mania. Life no longer seemed worth living without it. Money flowed like water. The Suffragettes, by their most unfortunate methods had aroused a sex-antagonism at first confined to the special question of the Vote, but which re-acted disastrously on the relations between men and women in other respects; while the contrast between the criminal extravagance of the West End of London, and the squalid poverty of the East was such as to arouse the indignation of Overseas visitors when they returned to the Mother Country.[9]

She saw Britain's entry into the war as being 'true to our plighted word' and her first action was to cancel the lavish silver wedding anniversary celebrations she had planned, even though this disappointed many of her friends who were yet to realise the full enormity of the international situation, which Edith saw in biblical terms: 'How was it possible to think of private causes for rejoicing when the mothers of England were already like Rachel of old, weeping for the sons they must surrender to return no more?'[10]

A recruitment meeting in a tent in the grounds of Hopton Hall saw 'one after the other of the boys we had known from childhood shyly stepped forward and offered themselves, and, as we shook hands with them after they were enrolled, it was hard to congratulate them with a steady voice. It meant so much.'[11]

Another area of pressing importance was to increase the domestic production of food, and to this end, Edith, in her work with the Women's Central Agricultural Committee, assisted with the preliminary training of land girls. As a governor of Swanley Horticultural College in Kent, Edith proposed a successful six-week scheme for training dairy maids from urban backgrounds, overcoming initial opposition and scepticism for her colleagues.

At Hopton Hall, her country house, she assembled large weekly parties in her conservatory to knit socks and hood comforters for sailors enduring the bitter cold of the North Sea. She also helped to organise local accommodation for Belgian refugees, although in retrospect considered that they had been made too reliant on the kindness of their hosts. She visited local country houses that had been turned into military hospitals, including Morley Manor, owned by Mrs Lister-Kaye, and considered that such people were displaying 'self-sacrifice and devotion in these humdrum ways'.[12]

Edith was concerned by the attitude of female industrial workers to men at home on leave:

When men returned on leave it was thought that the only thing to do was to give them a good time, and this consisted primarily in drinks on every possible occasion, not to speak of worse evils. The results were naturally deplorable. Weak natures could not stand against the insidious temptations presented; and men who had returned with a certain cachet of nobility from the stoical endurance of the unspeakable squalor and horrors of the front were dragged in the mire during their leave, and went back not strengthened, but degraded.[13]

Therefore she became active in the League of Honour, another organisation that aimed to promote Christian moral behaviour in women working in industry, and gave an account of a meeting she addressed in Mansfield, Nottinghamshire, where young women were given the ideal of how they could best support their menfolk:

> The beautiful picture of the young knight's watch before the altar, the burnished armour at his feet as a preparation for going forth to battle in the name of God and his lady, and of the fair maid fastening her favour in his helm as an inspiration to loyalty and valour, and the thought driven home: 'Which will you be, a temptation or an inspiration?' The thrill of realization passed through the vast assembly like an electric shock; eyes filled with tears and many a vow was registered that never by God's help should word or deed of theirs tarnish the burnished shield of their own true Knight.[14]

Another problem Edith sought to intervene in was the desolation felt by wives and mothers whose men were called up and who did not write home. As president of the Wirksworth branch of the Soldiers' and Sailors' Families Association (SSFA) she spoke to meetings of local women, finding that many of them had little or no idea about the reasons for the war. She undertook to explain the rationale – the promise made to defend Belgian neutrality and the dangers to Britain, claiming, 'They rose to it amazingly, face after face lighted up with the ideals of self-sacrifice, and, having arrived full of despondency, they went out their heads held high exulting in the honour of having a part in so noble a Cause.'[15]

To reinforce this message Edith wrote a play, *The Empire's Honour*, with local people playing the roles of different countries. This displayed in a clearer format the more abstract concepts of the alliance system and the international relations that had led to war. The play was a huge success and was produced around Britain, with hundreds of thousands of spectators seeing it. She ensured her branch of the SSFA sent over a thousand greetings cards to local men at Christmas and Easter, and organised a prayer rota, a 'chain of intercession ... so that from six a.m. to twelve p.m. there was no quarter-of-an-hour in which several were not interceding in their own homes for the living and those perchance in extremis. This was a great comfort to the cottage mother. They said it seemed to bring their boys nearer.'[16]

To give a greater permanence to these links Edith returned to the idea that she had used twenty-three years earlier in *The Cloud of Witness* – a daily Bible quotation, based on a weekly theme and augmented by quotes from literature – to produce *The Happy Warrior*. This was a pocket-sized book of just over a hundred pages with a daily Bible text, this time based on a weekly war theme such as 'The Raising of the Standard', 'On the March' and 'Champions of the Air'. She used her connections to persuade Lord Roberts, who had also provided an introduction to the testaments distributed by the Scripture Gift Mission, to write a foreword. In his words, the pocket-sized booklet would provide 'a golden link between husbands and wives, parents and sons, mothers, sisters and lovers, separated perhaps by thousands of miles, but each day thinking the same thought, praying the same prayer, by the help of *The Happy Warrior*'.[17]

Edith dedicated the book:

TO THE SONS OF THE EMPIRE
WHO
ON LAND AND SEA, BENEATH THE SEA
AND IN THE AIR
RISK THEIR LIVES FOR
IMPERIAL HONOUR, RIGHTEOUSNESS,
AND
LOYALTY TO ALLIES;
TO THE MEMORY OF THOSE HEROES WHO HAVE LAID
DOWN THEIR LIVES FOR
THEIR FRIEND
THESE THOUGHTS ARE DEDICATED BY THE AUTHOR[18]

It became an astounding success, with nearly 400,000 copies printed by 1917. This is another demonstration of the immense hold that Christianity had on the consciousness of the nation. The desire for a book of biblical devotion based on themes of war shows the interplay of these two great issues in the early twentieth century. One of the men who possessed a copy was Lance Corporal Cecil Sargeant of the 7th Battalion, King's Royal Rifle Corps. It had been given to him in December 1915 by a Violet Arkwright, possibly a descendent of Richard Arkwright of the world-famous Cromford Mill, which was a few miles down the road from Hopton Hall. Cecil was killed at the Battle of Arras in 1917 and the book was returned to his family.

In 1920 Edith published *Womanhood at the Cross-Roads*, reflecting on the changed position of women in society due to the war and how the Christian perspective could help society adapt to the changes: 'In every service, the Church, the Army, the Navy, the Civil Service, above all in the far corners of the Empire, their sons and daughters are to be found holding the fort for God and for Britain.'[19]

Unlike Maude Royden, Edith was not enthusiastic about the opportunities the war had afforded women to undertake a variety of roles in society.

The home life of our country is threatened in a thousand ways. The war loosened home bonds in many directions. The educated mother undertook patriotic activities often involving the sacrifice of domesticity, whilst among the wage-earners the absence of the husband and father and consequent loneliness frequently drove the wife to seek distraction and employment outside the home. The result in both cases is the same. The girls just emerging from childhood in 1914 have grown up without the home ideals of their predecessors. They have found interests elsewhere. Their ambition has been stimulated, and the question, 'will the women go back?' is being debated, and a general assumption that woman is free to decide her future in her own interest alone, not in that of the race.[20]

Therefore, she continued to campaign at local and national level for the upholding of traditional values of family life. On Philip's death in 1926, she paid for two stained glass windows to be installed at her local parish church,

St Margaret, Carsington. One was dedicated to him, and all his direct male ancestors, and the other to the females who had married into the Gell line.

When Edith died April 1944, aged eighty-three, the *Derby Daily Telegraph* described her as a 'gifted and prolific writer whose books mainly portrayed life in the Victorian, Edwardian and early Georgian eras'.[21] She had written more than thirty books and had been an active worker for her local church at Carsington, purchasing an organ as well as the land for a new graveyard. She had been active in the local, regional and national Mothers' Union, being in great demand as a speaker throughout the country. In addition, she had held an annual 'quiet day' during Lent at Hopton Hall for all associated with the work of the church. Like Mrs Hayman down on the south coast, she had also conducted a Sunday school in her home.

Even in death it was Edith's desire for hard work and moral behaviour to be rewarded. In her will she stated:

> It was the special desire of my husband and myself that whoever succeeded the Hopton Hall property should adopt some hardworking profession and justify his existence in the world. I look forward to the estate forming a centre for all that is good and progressive in the future as in the past.[22]

Edith Gell brought her strong-willed and campaigning nature to her efforts in the First World War. This was allied firmly to ideals of family, nation and empire. She worked tirelessly for the many causes she espoused and it could truly be said of her that she fought her good fight with all her considerable might.

Chapter 14

Edith Cavell

'But this I would say, standing as I do in front of God and eternity: I realise that patriotism is not enough. I must have no hatred or bitterness toward anyone'

The story of Edith Cavell has been high in the public consciousness in Britain and beyond since her execution at the hands of a German firing squad in October 1915. Her statue stands in St Martin's Place near Trafalgar Square in London, and her name adorns many hospitals and nursing homes. Whilst this chapter will serve to remind those who are already aware of her story of the essential facts, and introduce her remarkable story to a new audience, it will also highlight the centrality of her Christian faith in her actions, with a particular focus on her engagement with the words of the Bible throughout her life.

Edith's father, the Reverend Frederick Cavell, was parson of Swardeston, near Norwich, Norfolk. He was married to Louisa, and Edith Louisa was the eldest of their four children, born on 4 December 1865. Edith's childhood days began with family prayers in the morning and ended with the call for vespers in the evening. Her father ran a strict Victorian Sunday, with toys, needlework and even secular books locked away until Monday. But his generosity was shown in that when a fine roast dinner had been prepared, he would tell his servants, in the language of the Bible, to 'go out quickly into the streets and the lanes of the city, and bring hither the poor, and the maimed, and the halt, and the blind ... that my house may be filled' (Luke 14:21).[1] This attitude of serving those less fortunate was one taken to heart by Edith during her career.

Edith developed a love of poetry and was sent to study at Miss Margaret Gibson's School for Young Ladies in Peterborough before obtaining a position as a governess for a lawyer in Brussels, where she stayed for five years. She returned to Norfolk in 1895 to care for her ailing father, a move that inspired her to develop a new career as a nurse. Inspiration for this move was also found in the Bible. In her personal Bible, now housed in the Norwich Public Library, Edith had marked out 1 Thessalonians, 5:24: 'Faithful is he that calleth you, who will also do it.' In the margin she had written, 'Oct 11/95 Amen'. Amongst other portions of scripture marked out by her at this time was the prophetic John 17:21: 'But all these things will they do unto you for my name's sake.' Next to this Edith had written, 'Be prepared to be treated as Christ was.' She also marked out Psalm 18: 'God girdeth me with strength.'

Edith became a probationer nurse at the London Hospital on Whitechapel Road and rose through the ranks to become temporary matron of a hospital in Manchester. She was invited to return to Brussels in 1907 by Dr Antoine Depage to become director and teacher for a new nursing school, L'École Belge d'Infirmières Diplômées, (the Berkendael Medical Institute) on the Rue de la Culture. By 1910, she had launched the nursing journal *L'infirmière*, and by 1911 she was a training nurse for three hospitals, twenty-four schools, and thirteen kindergartens in Belgium.

Her reputation grew for strict discipline tinged with kindness. In July 1914, as war broke out across Europe, Edith was on holiday in Norfolk. As thousands of others fled the Continent to the safety of Britain, 48-year-old Edith travelled the other way, landing in Belgium on the day before Britain entered the war. One of her first acts was to help several German nurses return home safely by accompanying them to the Gare du Nord in Brussels.

On 19 August 1914, Brussels was captured by German forces. Edith gained a different perspective on the period that has become known as the 'rape of Belgium'. Writing of her feelings for the German troops she saw, some of whom were too tired to eat after incessant marching, she said, 'We were divided between pity for these poor fellows far away from their country and their people … and hatred of a cruel and vindictive foe bringing ruin and desolation on hundreds of happy homes in a prosperous and peaceful land.'[2] Edith and other English nurses in the city were offered safe conduct to neutral Holland, although most refused.

Edith continued to direct her nursing home in Brussels. But she soon began to flout the rules laid down by the German occupiers. Any Belgian male aged over eighteen leaving the hospital was meant to report to the German military police to be sent to forced labour camps in Germany. British and French soldiers were meant to be handed to the authorities to be held as prisoners of war. However, Edith agreed to take in wounded Allied soldiers, but when such a patient left Edith's hospital, they were told to report to the police or the home of a Mme X, where safe passage to the front or a neutral country would be found. The choice was left to the patient and Edith and her staff were able to honestly report to the authorities that they had directed them to the police. Edith became part of an extensive Belgian underground network, although she was not aware of its full existence and only dealt with a handful of people later arrested by the Germans.

Among those involved in the network was Prince Reginald de Croy, who produced fake documents at his Château de Bellignies near Mons. From there French and British soldiers were conducted by various guides, including Louise Thuliez, to the houses of Cavell, Louis Séverin and others in Brussels, and furnished by them with money to reach the Dutch frontier and with guides obtained through Philippe Baucq.

The German authorities became suspicious of the comings and goings at the hospital, including a loud rendition of *God Save the King* at Christmas 1914. In March 1915, Edith took ten of her nurses to Antwerp to care for wounded soldiers there. As she arrived she knelt on the ground and recited Psalm 23. On her return to Brussels, realisation grew that the hospital was under close observation by the Germans. However, the number of wounded Allied soldiers arriving was increasing and Edith could not find it in her heart to turn any away, despite the obvious danger to herself.

In June 1915, mysterious strangers arrived at the hospital asking if they could rent the premises once the hospital moved to new quarters, and asked to conduct a detailed investigation of the building. One of the nurses noted they had German army issue shoes. Edith's work carried on. She was eventually arrested on 5 August 1915, along with more than thirty Belgian and French citizens involved in the subterfuge, most of them unknown personally to Edith. She was taken to the prison of St Gilles to await trial. She was held there for ten weeks, the last two in solitary confinement. She made three depositions to the German police, admitting that she had been instrumental in conveying about sixty British and fifteen French soldiers and about 100 French and Belgians of military age to the frontier and had sheltered most of them in her hospital.

In all, about 200 soldiers had made it safely out of German hands due to Edith organising safe conduct. She had given each some money to aid their escape, much of it raised from Britain to help the work of the hospital, and some of it out of her own pocket.

During Edith's imprisonment, trial and the time she spent awaiting execution, she had three books with her to give comfort and strength: the Bible, her prayer book and *The Imitation of Christ*, by Thomas à Kempis, a devotional book written in the early fifteenth century. Edith spent many hours annotating and underlining Kempis's interpretation of different biblical texts. This book was returned to her family and an edition of it was printed in 1920, complete with the annotations she had made therein during those agonising months of 1915 and an introduction by the Dean of Westminster.[3] It is through these annotations that we can find another dimension of the nature and quality of Edith Cavell's Christian faith.

To prepare herself for the probable death sentence, she highlighted, 'Into Thy hands I commend my spirit (Luke 23:46), for Thou has redeemed me, O Lord, Thou God of Truth.'

Edith found passages that seemed to make sense of her impending death: 'Vanity it is, to wish to live long, and to be careless to live well' and 'O God who are the truth make me one with Thee in everlasting charity'.

She felt that her devotions during a time of great trial drew her closer to God: 'Neither is it any such great thing if a man be devout and fervent when he feeleth no affliction; but if in time of adversity he bear himself patiently there is hope then of great proficiency in grace.'

She recognised the supremacy of God's will in seeking respite from the troubles of wartime: 'Thou that rulest the power of the sea and stillest the violent motion of its waves, arise and help me' (Psalm 88), 'Scatter the nations that desire war' (Psalm 68:30), and 'There is no other hope of refuge for me, save in Thee, O Lord my God' (Psalm 71).

Her court martial began on 7 October 1915 and Edith openly admitted the charges against her. She said she had been doing her duty to her country. She did not consider herself a spy. In freely admitting her guilt, she was following the precepts that she had marked out in the *Imitation of Christ*: 'O

Plate 1. Philip Bryant, a Christian in khaki who felt God's presence at all times. (*Courtesy of Jonathan Greaves*)

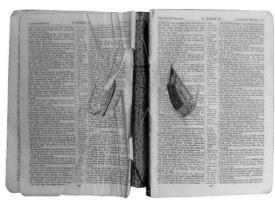

Plate 2. J.V. Salisbury's Bible, complete with the piece of shrapnel that could have killed him but for the Bible's presence in his pocket. (*Liddle Collection, University of Leeds*)

Plate 3. Joseph Garvey, in prison uniform during his four years of captivity. (*Courtesy of Graeme Garvey*)

Plate 4. David Jones, who partially exorcised his war demons through works of poetry. (*The Estate of David Jones*)

Plate 5. The Leaning Virgin of Albert Cathedral, as seen by Lewis Valentine in October 1916. (*TAHO / Wikimedia Commons*)

Plate 6. The saddest duty of army chaplains was the conducting and recording of the burials of their men. (*Wikimedia Commons*)

Plate 7. *The Last General Absolution of the Munsters at Rue du Bois*, by Fortunio Matania, depicting Francis Gleeson ministering to his men before the Battle of Aubers Ridge. (*Wikimedia Commons*)

Plate 8. Reverend John Esselmont Adams, architect of one of the most poignant moments of the 1914 Christmas Truce. (*Liddle Collection, University of Leeds*)

Plate 9. For many young women, such as those in the Chavasse and Cadbury families, nursing training enabled them to get closer to the front. (*Wikimedia Commons*)

Plate 10. Lilian Hayman, who shaped the lives of many of her Bible boys in Brighton and Bournemouth. (*Courtesy of Norman Ching*)

Plate 11. Maude Royden, the pacifist daughter of a Conservative MP and the first woman to preach at the City Temple. (*Wikimedia Commons*)

Plate 12. The Hon. Edith Gell, writer of *The Happy Warrior*, a book treasured by tens of thousands of people during the war. (*Courtesy of Brian Gell*)

Plate 13. Edith Cavell's execution was used as anti-German propaganda both in Britain and the then-neutral USA. (*Wikimedia Commons*)

Plate 14. Louise Thuliez, outside her German prison cell. (*Author's collection*)

Plate 15. Martin Niemöller, U-boat captain and later prisoner of the Nazis. (*Author's collection*)

Plate 16. Pastor Pieter-Josef Dergent, tortured and executed by German troops during the 1914 Rape of Belgium. (*Author's Collection*)

Plate 17. Alvin York, conscientious objector turned battle hero. (*Wikimedia Commons*)

Plate 18. Howard Marten, pictured at Dyce Quarry, near Aberdeen, while engaged on the Home Office Work Scheme. (*Liddle Collection, University of Leeds*)

Plate 19. Laurence Cadbury in his Friends' Ambulance Unit uniform. (*Courtesy of Cadbury Research Archive, University of Birmingham*)

Plate 20. The memorial window to the Huntriss brothers at Mattersey Church, Nottinghamshire. Many hundreds of young men were commemorated through biblical imagery and verse. (*Dawn Broom, 2015*)

Plate 21. The Liverpool VC Memorial, depicting Noel Chavasse and a stretcher bearer attending a wounded soldier. The statue was unveiled in 2008 and is now permanently located in Abercromby Square at the University of Liverpool. (*Dawn Broom, 2015*)

Plate 22. The Brocklesby family, of Conisbrough, Yorkshire. Phil is on the right on the back row, with Bert next to him in civvies. (*Liddle Collection, University of Leeds*)

Plate 23. Many communities commemorated their fallen with memorials placed in the parish churchyard, such as this example in Dilwyn, Herefordshire. (*Dawn Broom, 2014*)

God, who art the truth, make me one with thee in everlasting charity', 'No man speaks securely, but he that holds his peace willingly', and 'It is more just that thou shouldest accuse thyself, and excuse thy brother'. Next to the latter Edith had written, 'St Gilles'.

For Edith it was not a case of avoiding conviction and probable execution, but of pleasing God rather than mankind. Two further passages highlighted read:

It is no small prudence to keep silence in an evil time, and inwardly turn thyself to Me, and not to be troubled by the judgement of men. Let not thy peace be in the tongues of men; for whether they interpret well or ill of thee thou art not therefore another man.

My son, cast thy heart firmly on the Lord, and fear not the judgement of men, when conscience testifieth of thy dutifulness and innocency.

The court decreed that she should be one of six people, including Louise Thuliez, handed down the death sentence on 11 October. Edith now had less than a day left to live.

She turned to her *Imitation of Christ* and heavily marked the following passage, writing, 'St Gilles 11 Oct':

I indeed labour in the sweat of my brows. I am racked with grief of heart, I am burdened with sins, I am troubled with temptations, I am entangled and oppressed with many evil passions and there is none to help me, none to deliver and save me, but Thou O Lord God my Saviour, to whom I commit myself and all that is mine, that Thou mayest keep watch over me, and bring me safe to life everlasting.

Edith's final visitor the night before her execution was the Reverend Horace Gahan, the chaplain in charge of Christ Church in Brussels, where Edith had worshipped during the past year. He reported her final meeting to Brand Whitlock, the American ambassador to Belgium who had made an unsuccessful attempt to intercede for mercy on Edith's behalf:

On Monday evening, October 11, I was admitted by special passport from the German authorities to the prison of St Gilles, where

Miss Edith Cavell had been confined for ten weeks. The final sentence had been given early that afternoon.

To my astonishment and relief I found my friend perfectly calm and resigned. But this could not lessen the tenderness and intensity of feeling on either part during that last interview of almost an hour.

Her first words to me were upon a matter concerning herself personally, but the solemn asservation which accompanied them was made expressly in the light of God and eternity. She then added that she wished all her friends to know that she willingly gave her life for her country, and said, 'I have no fear nor shrinking. I have seen death so often that it is not strange or fearful to me.' She further said:

'I thank God for this ten weeks' quiet before the end. Life has always been hurried and full of difficulty. This time of rest has been a great mercy. They have all been very kind to me here. But this I would say, standing as I do in front of God and eternity: I realise that patriotism is not enough. I must have no hatred or bitterness toward anyone.'[4]

Gahan then performed the communion service with Edith, saying the Lord's Prayer in unison then both reciting the words of her favourite hymn, *Abide With Me*:

> *I fear no foe, with Thee at hand to bless;*
> *Ills have no weight, and tears no bitterness.*
> *Where is death's sting? Where, grave thy victory?*
> *I triumph still if Thou abide with me.*
> *Hold Thou Thy cross before my closing eyes;*
> *Shine through the gloom and point me to the skies;*
> *Heaven's morning breaks, and earth's vain shadows flee,*
> *In life, in death, O Lord, abide with me.*

Gahan then recorded, 'We sat quietly talking until it was time for me to go. She gave me parting messages for relations and friends. She spoke of her soul's needs at the moment, and she received the assurance of God's Word as only the Christian can do.

'Then I said "Good-bye", and she smiled and said, "We shall meet again."'[5]

At 5.00 am the next day, Edith was taken from her cell and driven to the place of execution. She made one last entry in her prayer book:

Died at 7 a.m. on Oct 12th 1915
With Love to My Mother
E. Cavell

Her final words to the German Lutheran prison chaplain, Paul Le Seur, were recorded as, 'Ask Father Gahan to tell my loved ones later on that my soul, as I believe, is safe, and that I am glad to die for my country.' [6]

She was then tied to a post alongside Philippe Baucq. Two firing squads, each of eight men, fired at their victims from six paces. As the shots rang out through the morning air, one bullet pierced Edith's skull and another tore a large hole in her heart. Her body was buried in a rough grave close by. However, in 1919 it was brought back in ceremony to Britain, and she was given a memorial service on 15 May at Westminster Abbey before being taken by train to Norwich to be buried in the grounds of the cathedral. Her grave was visited by the king and queen.

Craftsmen from her native Swardeston gave their services to produce a beautiful stained glass window above the altar of the parish church where her father had served. The following Bible quotes appear on the window: 'But he was wounded for our transgressions' (Isaiah 53:5), 'Greater love hath no man than this, that a man lay down his life for his friends' (John 15:13), and 'He was bruised for our iniquities' (Isaiah 53:5).

Edith's execution created outrage around the world. It was used in Britain to drive recruitment for the army. Her picture was hung in schoolrooms and a new recruitment poster exclaimed, 'Murdered by the Huns! Enlist and Help Stop Such Atrocities!' Her waxwork became the most popular attraction at Madame Tussauds. Eventually, a number of streets and hospitals were named in Edith's honour. Her execution was one of two major events of 1915, the other being the sinking of the *Lusitania*, which helped turn American public opinion firmly behind the Allies. (See plate 13.)

In 1919, an edition of her copy of *The Imitation of Christ*, was published. Herbert Ryle had written in the introduction that 'memories are short: and the younger generation will quickly grow up, and will not have heard of who she was, or what she did or how she suffered.'[7] However, the erection of a statue in the centre of London in 1920 meant that tens of thousands of people pass by her likeness every day, and annual services held both there and at her grave in Norwich mean that recognition of her suffering and sacrifice has extended beyond the span of human memory, and will continue to do so for many decades, if not centuries, to come.

Edith's Cavell saved the lives of many whilst sacrificing her own. Her statement that 'patriotism is not enough' emphasised her love of her country, but her greater love of God. Her strong Anglican beliefs propelled her to help all those who were in need of it, both German and Allied soldiers. She lived her life by her Christian upbringing and her continued devotion to her Bible and prayer book. At her time of deepest spiritual need she was comforted by them and the devotional book *The Imitation of Christ*. Like many others in this book, the war's trials and tribulations led to a deepening of Christian faith, although it was cruelly cut short.

Part IV

Christians from Other Nations

'And there's another country, I've heard of long ago, Most dear to them that love her, most great to them that know'

The First World War can be seen as ushering in a new world order in political, economic and social terms, but also in terms of the Christian faith. Ordinary young men in the British, German, French, Russian and Belgian armies saw the war in religious terms. In many cases they were motivated by high ideals, such as the righteousness of the defence of Belgium, and from the identification of the cause of their nation with the will of God. Russian soldiers fought under the banner of 'Faith, Tsar and Fatherland', until that triumvirate was replaced in 1917 by the rather more practical Bolshevik 'Peace, Bread and Land'.

The First World War was a religious crusade for millions. Overwhelmingly, Christian nations fought each other in what many saw as a spiritual conflict. Philip Jenkins wrote, 'Religion is essential to understanding the war, to understanding why people went to war, what they hoped to achieve through war, and why they stayed at war.'[1] Both nations where there was an official state church, such as Britain, Germany, Russia and Austria-Hungary, and those secular republics such as the USA, France and Italy, all used Christian imagery and rhetoric to promote their war aims. Whether or not one thinks this is justifiable from a Christian perspective, the fact that they chose to do so demonstrates the resonance Christianity had for millions across the continent of Europe and beyond. Pictures of Christ's suffering, of angels such as that allegedly seen at Mons, and of saints such as the warrior-like St George and St Michael were used in propaganda, and images of religious devastation, like the mutilation of the cathedral at Albert already alluded to in the account of Lewis Valentine's war, were used to reinforce the idea of the war as a religious struggle.

Americans such as Alvin York who had doubts about killing were acting in the context of their nation's theologians, expressing sentiments such as that which claimed that Jesus 'would take bayonet and grenade and bomb and rifle' or that the sterilisation of the German people should be undertaken.[2] Elite and educated opinion in Germany saw the war as a spiritual event, an opportunity for the nation to undertake God's role on earth. Germany's big push of 1918 was codenamed 'Michael', after that saint.

In the decades that followed the First World War, western Europe underwent a period of secularisation. In 1914, the World Christian Database suggested there were 560 million Christians in the world, 68 per cent of whom lived in Europe and 14 per cent in North America worshipping under various Protestant, Catholic and Orthodox banners. However, after 1917 the 25 per cent of the world's Christians who lived in Russia faced active persecution for pursuing their faith.[3] In the Middle East, ancient Christian communities went into near-terminal decline. On a more positive note for the future of worldwide Christianity, the war heralded the start of the explosion of Christian faith in Africa, one that is still in a period of growth into the first quarter of the twenty-first century.

It was within that context of both sides in the conflict claiming Christianity as a justification for war that the actions of the four characters we meet in this section – Louise Thuliez, Martin Niemöller, Pastor Pieter-Jozef Dergent and Alvin York – were enacted.

The 'rape of Belgium' in August and September of 1914 received much coverage in a British press keen to emphasise the righteousness of Britain's war aims. A series of war crimes committed against civilians and property shocked the public into providing relief for Belgian civilians and provided an extra impetus to army recruitment. In 1914, Belgium had the sixth-largest economy in the world, but the dismantling of industry and the deportation of 100,000 workers to Germany to support the war economy meant it never recovered from this shock.

Whilst the destruction of the university library in Louvain / Leuven, and the mass execution of the prominent citizens of Aerschot / Aarschot have received continued coverage, the martyrdom of one seemingly unremarkable Belgian priest from the village of Gelrode has, over the decades, been largely forgotten outside of his own area. The execution of Pastor Pieter-Jozef

Dergent also made the headlines in Britain in early 1915, and his remarkable story is told here.

America had only entered the war in April 1917 after a sustained propaganda campaign by Britain in particular, including highlighting the case of Pastor Dergent. In addition, acts such as the sinking of the *Lusitania* and the execution of Edith Cavell sought to make the moral case for America's intervention for the Allied cause. President Woodrow Wilson had issued a proclamation of American neutrality. But it was the German campaign of unrestricted submarine warfare in 1917 that finally convinced America that her interests were in line with those of the Allies. Not all Americans were convinced of the need for war. One of them was Alvin York. However, by the end of 1918 he had received the Medal of Honor for one of the most remarkable acts of courage in combat seen during the war.

France nearly fell in 1914 as German troops reached the river Marne on the outskirts of Paris. Fierce resistance in September 1914 pushed them back to the river Aisne, partially establishing the line of the Western Front, and an occupation of parts of north-eastern France for four more years. As far as Christianity was concerned, the status of the Catholic Church in France was a contested one, with Republicans opposing its influence in society and Monarchists benefitting from its support for the return of a monarchy to France. In the decade before the war, Catholic schools had been closed and the Church and State were separated by law in 1905. In some ways this benefitted Catholicism in France as it was able to speak with a voice independent of government influence. French Catholics showed, like Christians in Britain, Belgium and Germany, that service to their nation was not incompatible with their service to God. Marshal Foch, who had commanded French forces at the Marne and who rose to become Commander-in-Chief of the Allied armies by the spring of 1918, was a devout Catholic. Louise Thuliez was also one such Christian whose personal bravery in smuggling Allied soldiers across the German front line saw her sentenced to death, but then imprisoned for over three years, her faith remaining strong.

Germany's role in the outbreak of the war has been a matter for intense historical debate ever since the Treaty of Versailles of 1919 assigned the entire War Guilt to them. The historiography has swung between toleration and blame, but for those individual Germans of a Christian faith, many did what they saw as their duty to their god and their Kaiser in a similar way to how British men of the same generation did their duty to their god and their king. Kaiser Wilhelm himself was head of the German Lutheran Church, of which Martin Niemöller was an ardent member.

Here are the stories of four remarkable people who lived lives of sacrifice and honour. I trust the reader will find some inspiration in the telling of their tales from a Christian perspective.

Chapter 15

Louise Thuliez

'For every cross is given the corresponding strength to bear it'

Following her birth in 1881, Louise Thuliez grew up in Mauberge, France, close to the Belgian border. She recalled receiving a very patriotic education at a time when the memory of the Franco-Prussian War was still fresh in the public consciousness. Indeed, the map of France in a geography textbook showed the provinces of Alsace and Lorraine, taken during that war, as coloured in black, showing that many in France could not accept their loss.

Brought up in a devout Catholic household, Louise's brother trained as a priest, whilst Louise qualified as teacher, holding a post in Lille. On the outbreak of war in July 1914, Louise was on holiday in Saint-Waast-la-Vallée, in northern France. She felt it her duty to volunteer immediately for work in the Red Cross Hospital there, but her application was rejected. Her brother prophetically told her that God would have a task marked out for her in the war, and that she would be given a chance to serve.

By late August 1914, English, Scottish and Irish troops were retreating through Saint-Waast-la-Vallée following the French defeat at the Battle of Charleroi. Belgian refugees were also crossing the French border to escape the 'rape of Belgium'. British troops were quartered in the village, which now contained only about sixty of its original 800 inhabitants.

Early on 24 August, most of the British wounded were taken by ambulance to the rear, except for six men for whom there was not room. It was expected that an ambulance would return for them, but none arrived. At this time, due to the near evacuation of the village, there was a shortage of food. Louise gained permission from the mayor to break open a locked and deserted bakery to make some bread, challenging some of her own countrymen when she insisted that the first priority was to feed the British troops.

At 8.00 am on 24 August, a company of Uhlans (German cavalry) was spotted on a hill overlooking the village. By 9.00 am German planes were seen overhead, so at 10.00 am Louise took the decision to have the six remaining British soldiers taken to the house of a friend, Henriette Moriamé. At 12.00 noon the feared Prussian Death's Head Hussars entered Saint-Waast and began to ransack private dwellings and pillage the shops.

As the uniforms of the six Britons had been laid out to dry in the sun, the men were soon discovered and questioned by the Germans. Having satisfied themselves, by removing their bandages, that the men were genuinely injured, the Germans left them in the care of the ladies in the house. As the day wore on, the German army made its way through the village, occasionally bringing with them hostages taken in Belgium.

Once the village was under occupation, Louise and Henriette hung a makeshift Red Cross flag from a window to indicate that wounded troops were in the house. Apart from an occasional desultory check, no effort was made by the German authorities to remove the men into captivity. A French Red Cross official who visited in September 1914 told the women to keep the men at the house rather than voluntarily hand them over to the Germans. This was at a similar time to when Joe Garvey had been sent to an overcrowded prisoner of war camp in Poland, so rounding up extra prisoners does not seem to have been a priority. Food was provided for the men by local farmers, and gradually they recovered their strength.

This provided a new dilemma for Louise and Henriette as there was now no justification to keep the men in the house. On 23 October an order was given that all remaining French and Allied soldiers in German-occupied territory were to give themselves up. This left her in even more of a predicament. She did not want to have the men handed over to the Germans, but to keep them in the house would risk retribution for the whole village. Therefore it was resolved that the men should be removed from the village.

A safe house in a remote part of the countryside was found for the men by a local nobleman, Prince Reginald de Croy, and they were given civilian clothing. When they reached the house, they found an English soldier who had already been hiding there for two months. A decision was made to attempt to get all seven men back to the front. En route they met up with other, larger, collections of fugitives until eventually the group numbered about forty.

Orders were given by Captain Preston (one of two men of the group to hold a commission) for the men to give themselves up. However, the two officers – Captain Preston and a Lieutenant Bushell of the Queen's Bays – considered it their duty as officers to attempt to escape. On 28 December 1914, they told Louise of a possibility of escaping to neutral Holland. This opportunity was afforded through a priest, Monsieur l'Abbé de Longueville, who was arranging for another man to cross the border in order to join up with the French army. Louise travelled to Brussels to make the arrangements and then came back into France to escort Captain Preston and Lieutenant Bushell into Brussels. They carried long batons of bread in order to look like local civilians and false passports were provided for them in Mons. From there they progressed through Brussels and Holland before reaching England and active service again.

Although Louise's duty was done as far as these two men were concerned, she did not consider it the end of the matter of helping fugitive British and French soldiers. Many more were still hiding out in the nearby Forest of Mormal area. Many of the people involved in the escape plans were priests, due to their connections within the communities. One bonus for Louise was that on establishing her headquarters at the house of a Canon Flament, she had the happiness of hearing Mass every day and described it as like having a private chaplain. By 1915, Louise was in contact with Edith Cavell, and would frequently deposit soldiers at her Brussels nursing home for Edith to send them on the next stage of their journey. These journeys to Brussels were undertaken at night, with the men walking close to hedgerows so they could throw themselves into a ditch to hide.

In time the serving soldiers were joined by local French youths who wished to escape from German control and join their country's army. Again, the strength of the Catholic Church in this part of France was put to good use. Monsieur l'Abbé Lothigier organised a group of youths who wanted to leave. As Louise could not attract too much attention by visiting his presbytery too often, she suggested that he come to her to hear her confessions so that they could discuss the details of the operation without being overheard.

Louise made contact with a Mademoiselle L'Hotellier, who had been hiding sixty wounded Allied soldiers in her position as Superintendent of the General Hospital in Cambrai. She had somehow managed to conceal their presence from many of the hospital staff and the other patients whilst contriving to find the extra food needed to keep them alive. However, the Germans were becoming increasingly vigilant and Louise's initial attempts to help one of these men escape across the line were in vain. Another important contact of Louise's was the Princess Marie de Croy, who resided at the Château de Bellignies with her brother Reginald and her grandmother. It was here that Captain Preston had found shelter in October 1914 and where subsequently many other soldiers being assisted to escape found overnight refuge during their journey. They were housed in the great hall of the chateau, but on one occasion, having been unofficially warned of an imminent German search, Louise and the princess had to house fourteen men in a narrow passageway in the chateau's round tower.

At that time, life in occupied France was different from life in Belgium. As all French men were liable for conscription, any found by the Germans were considered civil prisoners, whereas in Belgium many man carried on in their civilian jobs. It was therefore easier for escapees to merge into the crowd in Belgium rather than France. In addition, travel was easier in Belgium as a public tramway and railway system was maintained. However, the Germans were employing police dogs, road blocks and barbed and live wire to try to stop the movement across the border.

There was much resistance in Belgium to German occupation. A number of underground newspapers were produced, including the *Mot du Soldat* by two Jesuit priests, Monsieurs Meaul and Pirsoul. A further act of defiance by the Belgians was seen by Louise on 21 July 1915 – Belgian Independence Day. The flying of the national flag had been banned, but Louise saw three young girls appear on a balcony and stand in a line. They were attired consecutively in dresses of black, yellow and red.

As the numbers of men seeking to escape was increasing, German surveillance was becoming stricter, and Louise was obliged to undertake more journeys all the way to Brussels. On these occasions she would hand the men over to the care of Edith Cavell at her nursing home on 149 Rue de la Culture, and sometimes to a small café-hotel in the Rue Haute. Louise used various pseudonyms to remain anonymous in Brussels, including Jeanne Martin, Marie Mouton and Madame Lejeune. As well as fugitive soldiers, arrangements were made for the transfer of mechanics and metalworkers across the border into Belgium as their skills were of great use in keeping the Allies supplied with munitions. However, on 31 July 1915, while meeting architect Phillipe Baucq at his Brussels home, Louise and Phillipe were arrested during a German raid. She was taken to the prison of St Gilles in the city and locked in a cell while a search of Baucq's house revealed a huge amount of incriminating evidence against them and many others involved in helping Allied soldiers across the Dutch border. From this evidence further arrests, including that of Edith Cavell, were made in the following week.

The prison had a fortress-like aspect, with cells measuring 4 by 2 metres. When in communal areas, Louise was made to wear a 'cagoule' – a veil with two holes cut for the eyes. She was allowed thirty minutes' exercise per day (see plate 14). When attending the prison's chapel, Louise noticed that the altar was placed several metres above the floor, and each prisoner was placed in a standing stall, which prevented them having sight of other detainees. Interrogations were conducted by two German lieutenants, Bergen and Pinckoff, who played the prisoners off against each other, pretending that one had made a full confession of the facts to encourage the others to do the same. Louise managed to convince them that she had guided the men across the Franco-Belgian border alone, thus saving her friend and confidante Henriette Moriamé from arrest. Henriette then entered a convent, dying in September 1918, having only once corresponded with Louise during her time in prison due to the disapproval of her superiors. Louise later considered that Henriette entering the convent was another sacrifice made by French and Belgian patriots during the war as she was voluntarily giving up her freedom of movement for the protection of a convent.

Accused alongside thirty-four others, Louise's trial began on 7 October 1915 at the Senate building. When asked why she had performed her actions, she answered, 'Because I am a French-woman.'[1] She was accused of high treason, with the prosecutor demanding the death sentence for her and seven others, including Phillipe Baucq and Edith Cavell. Court proceedings were conducted in German, with translations being made for the prisoners and no access to their defence counsels being permitted. On hearing the demand of the death sentence by the court, she remarked, 'For every cross is given the corresponding strength to bear it.'[2]

On 11 October the prisoners were assembled in the central hall of St Gilles prison. After five names, the word 'todestraffe', meaning 'death penalty', was read out. Those five names were Phillipe Baucq, Louise Thuliez, Edith Cavell, Louis Severin and Jeanne de Belville. Louise later described feeling a great calm and relief at that moment thanks to her Catholic faith and her belief in the afterlife. She thought of those dear to her who had died, including her parents, and that, as a Catholic, she firmly believed that she would soon be meeting them again. The Countess de Belleville told Louise that she considered the death sentence for them God's judgement, whereas Louise thought it a sacrifice for their country that would balance out their other human imperfections.

The five were then returned to their individual cells, but Louise and the countess were allowed to join together in one cell. They were joined by the prison chaplain, a Father Leyendecker, who suggested they submit an expression of regret for their actions and a formal appeal for mercy, but at this point they were not of a mind to do so. The next morning, 12 October, they were reading their prayer books in their cell when Louise felt an overwhelming rush of anguish on behalf of Edith Cavell. She had already been executed that morning. Unbeknown to Louise, the orders for her own execution were for the morning of 13 October.

Louise continued to receive Holy Communion and have confessionals while awaiting the death penalty. On 17 October she asked the prison chaplain if he would tell her in the evening if she were to be shot in the morning, which he agreed to do. Finally, on 27 October, she was informed that a reprieve had been granted after the intervention of the Marquis de Villobar, the Spanish ambassador in Brussels, who had gained an intercession from his king, Alphonse XIII. Further appeals had been made directly to Kaiser Wilhelm II by Pope Benedict XV and indirectly from President Woodrow Wilson of the then neutral USA.

Louise was then transferred back to Cambrai, in northern France, where her prison conditions were considerably worse than those in Brussels had been. There she was accused of the 'crimes' she had committed on the French side of the border, but despite being found guilty, word came through that the Kaiser's clemency had been extended to these cases too. By the end of

January 1916, Louise had been moved to a prison at Siegburg, in Germany, to begin nearly three monotonous years of incarceration. Medical care there was inadequate and many of the female prisoners died, one in Louise's arms as she comforted her, and another whose husband had also died in prison the previous week, leaving a 4-year-old boy as an orphan. As in the prisoner of war camp inhabited by Joe Garvey, typhus spread and trenches were dug near the exercise yard to bury the victims.

Louise's experience of the staff running the prison led her to conclude that the natures of German women were insincere and lacking in kind-heartedness and moral courage. Louise copied down the inscription that she saw when entering Siegburg, one that to her was a distortion of the true meaning of Christianity:

You are now a prisoner. Your barred window, your bolted door, the colour of your clothes, all bear witness that you have forfeited your liberty. God did not wish you to continue to defy Him by sinning against His laws and the law of men. He had brought you here so that you may expiate the crimes of your life.

So, incline yourself under the all-powerful hand of God, incline yourself under the iron laws of this house. If you will not obey of your own will, your will shall be broken and bent. But if you receive humbly the punishment that is inflicted on you the fruit of your submission will be a chastened heart and a peace conscience. God has willed it so.[3]

For Louise, the repentant sinner was always pardoned by God, and for society to withhold this pardon was a crime.

She undertook small acts of private protest, including sewing buttons deliberately loose on military uniforms so they would fall off at the first hint of pressure. Religious neutrality was not permitted in the prison, so each Sunday all prisoners attended either a Catholic or Protestant service. As in St Gilles, each worshipper was kept in an isolated stall so only the tops of the heads of the others were visible above the partitions. This amused Louise and reminded her of a picture she had seen of St Francis of Assisi speaking to the fishes. The services were held in German and despite requests for a French or Belgian priest, Louise was unable to make confession or hear the words of consolation and hope that she craved. However, patriotic sentiment was shown each 14 July, when threads of red, white and blue material were worn on their uniforms. Louise also wrote a letter of protest to the German Minister for Home Affairs against political prisoners like herself being forced to undertake munitions work.

As prison discipline relaxed during the latter half of 1918, it became clear to Louise that the war was nearing its end. Again, like Joe Garvey, Louise heard of acts of mutiny by German sailors that included freeing prisoners. On 7 November, four days before the official armistice, the doors of Siegburg were thrown open and Louise witnessed at first hand some acts of the short-lived German revolution, including the tearing of decorations from the breasts of officers by their men. The male and female prisoners from Siegburg were put on a train and taken to Cologne. From there Louise travelled to Louvain and eventually arrived back in Lille, to find her flat had been pillaged. Louise wept as she compared the devastated French landscape with the Germany she had just left where factories still stood intact.

In 1919, Louise had the Legion d'Honneur and the Croix de Guerre conferred on her by Georges Clemenceau, President of the French Republic. He cited that she was:

Model of the purest patriotism, she rendered signal services to the Allied Armies in the invaded regions. Spent herself in caring for the wounded, and in the midst of the gravest danger, probed herself to be actuated by heroic courage and complete disregard for personal safety. Victim of her devotion to our country, France, she was condemned to death by the Germans. This sentence was later commuted into one of transportation with hard labour.

Louise Thuliez continually placed herself in danger. Like many others in this book, her faith was allied to a fierce patriotism that led her to refuse to allow herself to submit morally to her captors. Her faith remained strong throughout the war and she continued her teaching after it.

She wrote her memoirs in the early 1930s and they were translated into English in 1934. During the Second World War she was active in the French resistance, helping more English and French soldiers to safety and receiving the Order of the British Empire. She died in 1966.

Chapter 16

Martin Niemöller

'We saw that situations could arise in war in which it was utterly impossible to preserve a clear conscience'

Few German Christians have the worldwide reputation and respect accorded to Martin Niemöller. As author of the famous Niemöller Prayer, his later life became a symbol of peace and reconciliation from the destruction caused by the Second World War. Less well known, however, is his role as a U-boat officer in the First World War. It was during this time that the faith of his childhood received the first of many challenges it would encounter in the course of his long and remarkable life. (See plate 15.)

Martin Niemöller was born on 14 January 1892 in Lippstadt, Westphalia, Germany. His father, Heinrich, was a Lutheran pastor who viewed Kaiser Wilhelm with loyalty, not just as Emperor of Germany, but also as head of the German Protestant Evangelical Church. Martin Niemöller remembered his family Bible – richly illustrated, almost a metre high and a metre broad, and filled with steel engravings. The stories of Jesus so caught the young boy's attention that Christ always seemed to him a close friend.

In 1900 the family moved to Elberfield, a town in the industrial Rhineland area. Martin attended the grammar school, studying Greek, French, Mathematics and Physics, and becoming 'Vorturner', or demonstrator, in school gymnastic displays, just as Joe Garvey had done.

Martin was given the opportunity to visit England as a guest of a Dr Lumb and his family in London in 1908. Here, on the Sabbath, he was made to attend church twice and was forbidden from playing the piano. He would read Shakespeare out loud in order to improve his understanding of English. His visit lasted six weeks and he took the chance to visit St Paul's Cathedral, the Tower of London, the Houses of Parliament, Westminster Abbey and Hampton Court Palace.

At the age of seventeen all young German men became liable for conscription, therefore it was no surprise when a letter arrived in March 1910 ordering him to report to the Flensburg-Mürwik Naval Training College. He was now a member of the German Imperial Navy. The navy was experiencing a period of rapid expansion as both Germany and Britain sought to outdo each other in terms of superiority in a naval arms race. After a year Martin was promoted to midshipman and in 1913 became torpedo officer on the *Thüringen*.

Martin had a double reason for allegiance to the Kaiser, as commander-in-chief of the German Navy as well as head of the Lutheran Church in Germany. On the outbreak of war in 1914, Martin's ship spent the next year taking part in occasional raids on the British coast. However, this was a relatively uneventful period for him and he found the routine of keeping watch tedious and 'dreamed of submarines, of destroyers, of airships.'[1] In addition to warships, the German Navy became the first to successfully deploy submarines, 375 of which had been built by 1918. It was in this new form of vessel that Martin's immediate future lay.

In 1915, his wish was granted as he was assigned to become a second lieutenant on SM U-73, planting mines in front of Port Said. U-73 flew a French flag to fool the British into not firing on her and proceeded to torpedo three British ships. In August 1917, Martin Niemöller became first officer on SM U-151, attacking shipping on the Bay of Biscay and the Straits of Gibraltar, setting a record of sinking 55,000 tons of Allied shipping in 115 days. In May 1918, Martin became commander of SM UC-67 and was awarded the Iron Cross (First Class) for his service in the war.

Throughout the war, Martin sought to reconcile his experiences with his biblical upbringing. When the U-boat he was serving on during Christmas 1916 broke down, he spent the time it was being repaired reading the Christmas Gospel story in his Confirmation Bible. On 25 January 1917, his U-boat had to fire on a French ship trying to rescue survivors of another torpedoed ship. Martin recalled discussing the incident with his comrades:

The whole complex problem of war presented itself to us and we realised from this single experience of ours something of the tragedy involved ... we saw that situations could arise in war in which it was utterly impossible to preserve a clear conscience. Assuming we survived, the question of whether our conscience survived with us depended on whether we believed in the forgiveness of sins ...That 25 January was the turning point of my life, because it opened my eyes to the utter impossibility of a moral universe.[2]

Martin's faith was challenged further by an incident that occurred on 6 July 1918. His U-boat received three direct hits from an Allied convoy and he had to dive his stricken vessel, leaking water, down to 130 feet below sea level and wait until nightfall to emerge again. The fate of the ship's company hung in the balance and Martin pondered weighty matters:

Is there peace anywhere ... And we are, as ever, faced by the eternal questions: life, the universe and God? These questions are not prompted by curiosity – they force themselves on us. All we know is that we have not found the answers to them.[3]

Martin's final wartime act was to return his vessel to the naval port at Kiel following the signing of the armistice in November 1918. However, he mistakenly took the wrong route and ended up going through mine-infested waters near Corfu, something he only realised afterwards. Referring to this as a miracle, he later wrote, 'I felt certain that some new task awaited me. Why otherwise would God Himself have taken over our helm?'[4]

Following Germany's defeat in 1918, Martin was instructed to tow two U-boats to Britain as part of the surrender of the Germany Navy under the terms of the armistice. He argued that as he had not personally signed the armistice, he was under no obligation to obey that particular order.

As he watched the structures that had provided permanence in Germany collapse around him, Martin became disillusioned with the new democratic government in Germany and resigned his naval commission. On Easter Sunday 1919, he married his fiancée, Else Bremer. After a brief, unsuccessful career as a farmer, he entered university to study to become a Lutheran pastor, like his father. His motivation was to use the Gospel to bring meaning and order to a broken German society on the brink of revolution. He wrote:

I had been taught as a child that belief in Christ as our Lord and Saviour and diligent attention to God's Word can transform men and give them freedom and strength. That lesson I had never forgotten, for my own experiences had proved it to be true. I now became convinced that the best and most effective help I could give to my fellow countrymen in the national calamity would be to share that knowledge with them. That, I believed, would be a truer form of service than withdrawing to the depths of the country in order to farm.[5]

He became a battalion commander in the Freikorps, a paramilitary body formed to put down revolutionary uprisings. Martin was ordained in June 1924 and served as curate, superintendent and pastor of Protestant churches in Germany. In the 1924 elections he voted for Hitler's fledging Nazi party due to his policies of autonomous worship for those of Christian faith and Martin's belief that Germany needed a strong leader to promote national unity and restore the honour that had been lost by the defeat of 1918. Martin had inherited conservative political views from his father and as an anti-Communist briefly welcomed Hitler's accession to power in Germany in 1933 as he thought it would herald a national revival.

However, in 1934 he was one of a group of pastors who founded the Confessional Church, which opposed the Nazification of German Protestant churches, and in 1936 he publicly opposed the Aryan Paragraph, which excluded non-Aryans from many political and social rights, as being incompatible with the Christian value of charity. Despite this, Martin still maintained the theological position that one of the reasons for Jewish suffering through the years was that Christ had been crucified by the Jews.

Martin's opposition to the Nazis eventually led to his arrest and imprisonment in Sachsenhausen and Dachau concentration camps from 1938 to 1945. He expressed bitter regret at having taken Hitler's word that Christianity would be protected in Germany and that there would be no mass pogroms of Jews. He was eventually liberated from Dachau by American troops. In 1945 he was a signatory to the Stuttgart Declaration of Guilt, acknowledging that the German Church should have done much more to resist the Nazis.

In 1946, Martin wrote his famous confessional, *First they came …*

First they came for the Socialists, and I did not speak out – Because I was not a Socialist.

Then they came for the Trade Unionists, and I did not speak out – Because I was not a Trade Unionist.

Then they came for the Jews, and I did not speak out – Because I was not a Jew.

Then they came for me – and there was no one left to speak for me.

In 1947 he undertook a world tour to express collective German guilt for Nazi persecution and crimes against humanity. This made him unpopular in the nation that he had served with such distinction in the First World War. However, he continued to blame the political weakness of Weimar Germany for Hitler's rise to power and condemned the division of Germany into East and West by the victorious Allies.

By the mid-1950s, Martin had become a pacifist and worked with the World Council of Churches to promote international peace and reconciliation. He died in 1984 aged 92.

Martin Niemöller was a man whose faith was intrinsically tied up with his German patriotism. As an officer in the Kaiser's navy, as a pastor and member of the Freikorps, as a supporter of the Nazis and later as a vociferous opponent of Hitler, and finally an advocate of world peace and reconciliation, his Christian faith guided and informed his remarkable life. The complexity and contradictions of the various positions he took are to some extent a reflection of the challenges of developing a Christian faith in a country that experienced such extremes in the twentieth century.

Chapter 17

Pastor Pieter-Jozef Dergent

'A simple village pastor, but a great priest'

Pieter-Jozef Dergent was a rural Catholic priest from the Leuven region of Belgium (see plate 16). He had not set out to achieve greatness or fame, but to quietly and humbly serve his parishioners. However, the events surrounding the German invasion of Belgium in August 1914 meant that his name became known around the world as a symbol of the brutality with which some German troops were alleged to have treated the native population. Like Edith Cavell, his death was portrayed as martyrdom and used as propaganda against Germany. But his life and death reveal a man of simple but steadfast Christian faith.

Most of what is known about Pastor Dergent is the result of interviews and analysis carried out by the Belgian theologian Monsignor Karel Cruysberghs in the late 1940s. It appears that Karel had known Pastor Dergent as a young man, and considered his sacrifice as worthy of future sainthood. However, he was careful to weigh up and cross-reference the evidence he was given to produce an account of integrity in his booklet *Pastoor Pieter-Jozef Dergent: Een Priester-Martelaar* in 1949.

Pieter-Josef Dergent was born in Geel on Ascension Day, 1870. His father was a tailor and his mother came from a farming family. The family did not benefit from robust health, with his father being constantly short of breath and his brother, Alfons, who also became a priest, dying in 1904 of tuberculosis. 'Jef', as he was known to his friends attended Geel College from 1881 but did not have a reputation as a brilliant student. On progressing to the Catholic seminary at Mechelen, his academic studies flourished, and he was considered by his fellow students as jovial, devout and strong willed.

Jef was consecrated as a priest in August 1893, serving in Bierbeek, Retie and Lichtaart in the next two decades. Tall and broadly built, but suffering from chronic bronchitis, he built a reputation as a hard worker, venturing out in all weathers to minister to his parishioners. At Lichtaart he engaged in the hobby of photography with some friends, but they would not trust him with the negative plates as he would drop them. This trait caused laughter between the friends. Jef loved relaxation, had a positive outlook and was generous with his time and possessions, and could not bear to see people suffer without offering them help. Karel Cruysberghs described him as an optimistic companion, but full of willpower, also being firm and occasionally stubborn. He took care over the preparation of his sermons, which were without literary embellishments, but his people loved to hear him speak. In Reite people talked about how Jef would spend an hour in the afternoon in the closed church, praying on his own.

Jef became priest at Gelrode, a village near the town of Aarschot, in November 1913. He was considered by his parishioners as a man of the people, who took care of children and the infirm. He set up a Gregorian singing choir and was holding harvest time rehearsals in the church. Cruysberghs considered that there would have been a Christian revival in Gelrode had the war not intervened.

On 19 August 1914, German troops invaded Aarschot. At 5.30 pm matters took an ugly turn when in the confusion of possible shooting from remnants of the Belgian army and civilian partisans, Major General Stenger of the 8th Infantry Brigade appeared on a balcony and was shot through the chest. Some reports claimed that he had been shot by one of his own soldiers due to his unpopularity. Whatever the precise details, the effect was a series of brutal reprisals on Belgian citizens. (After the war Stenger was tried for war crimes but was found not guilty.)

Seventy-five civilians were shot on the Leuven-Aarschot road, then another twenty-nine in the town, including Mayor Tielemans. Priests were considered by the Germans to be dangerous partisans, capable of inspiring resistance from the Belgian people. Four priests hid in a well for three days and then left Aarschot in disguise on the night of 23 August. The dean of the town was held prisoner as a partisan.

The village of Gelrode was also occupied on 19 August, and according to the eyewitness account of Dr Jacobson, the German soldiers seemed tense.[1] They were obsessed by the thought of partisans everywhere. An Aarschot man who had fled to Gelrode was shot in the stomach. On 20 August, seven people were reported as having been executed next to the cemetery without any form of trial. Jef's church was now being used as a prison.

When the Germans searched Jef's house, old gun cartridges had been found in a storage room. These had been the property of his predecessor, a keen shot. Jef was kept under arrest in a room in his house and then released on 20 August. However, he was now under suspicion of subversion. Three men had been wounded in the initial fighting and had remained without access to medical care as their situation deteriorated. It was decided by a group of villagers, led by Jef, to transport them to Aarschot in an attempt to save their lives. Despite some opposition from the men's families due to the huge risk of being seen travelling across the countryside in such a fraught situation, Jef stubbornly pushed through his plan. At 8.00 am on 26 August he left Gelrode on a cart, with a driver and the wounded men. They managed to reach the Damien Institute, home of the Fathers of the Sacred Hearts, which was being used as a Red Cross field hospital. Jef was advised by the father superior to stay there for his own safety, but he considered it his duty to return to Gelrode to hear the confessions of his parishioners.

At 11.00 am Jef and the driver set off back to Gelrode, but this time they were arrested on crossing the Market Square in Aarschot and both men were imprisoned in the city hall until 5.00 pm the following day. It is alleged that at some point during this incarceration, some German troops barged into the room in which they were being held and offered the men some wine, saying, 'Have a good drink because later tomorrow you're finished.'[2]

Cruysberghs recounts evidence that Jef was stamped on by a German cavalry officer and then handed to a group of soldiers at the church at Aarschot, which was housing nearly 3,000 prisoners rounded up from surrounding parishes. Jef was kept outside the church, and as a group of civilians who had been arrested and marched from Gelrode to Aarschot were approaching, they witnessed him with his arms held high facing the wall at the bottom of the clock tower next to the church door. The Vervoort family testified that they heard a German soldier ask Jef 'Will you renounce your faith?' His response was to raise two fingers of his right hand and say, 'I swear before God and the saints that I will not renounce my faith.'[3] He was then beaten and stoned. Further witnesses reported seeing Jef crumpled on the ground, with German troops beating his feet with the butts of their rifles and urinating on him. Again he was asked, 'Will you renounce your faith?' This time the question was accompanied by showing him a handful of bullets. His replied, 'Never as long as I live … Death I do not fear.'[4] Another witness reported him saying, 'Anything but that – I will die for that gladly.'[5]

After a while the Germans grew tired of the horrible spectacle they had created. As some of the civilians were allowed out of the church to relieve themselves, the guards found a new level of degradation, ordering the people to urinate on the priest. This was, to Cruysberghs, the grossest but clearest symbol of disrespect. 'The Catholics are told to foul their priest of whom they can think no harm.'[6]

Jef's lips were seen still moving, as if in prayer. Just after 7.00 pm, as darkness started to fall, soldiers were seen leading him away with his hands raised in the air. He was taken to a house called the Blykershuis, about 200 yards distance from the church, near a river bridge. He was led behind it, and then killed with what Father Verstreken, who was present in Aarschot, claimed were two rifle shots. His body, lying on its back, was initially left by the house. Blood was running from his eyes. Jef's body was thrown into the river Denier, and was found naked two days afterwards 5 kilometres from Aarschot and retrieved by Red Cross volunteers. The corpse was identified by his watch inside his tunic, which was floating a little distance away, inscribed, 'J Dergent, onderpastoor te Lichtaart'. It was thought that the Germans had tried to cover up the murder by stripping the body.

He was buried at first not far from the spot where he was found, and then on 14 November the body was removed to the church of Gelrode, in the presence of Cardinal Mercier, Archbishop of Mechelen. The good shepherd had returned to his flock, according to Cruysberghs. In January 1915, Cardinal Mercier wrote a long pastoral letter to his occupied people and in it he made reference to Jef:

In my diocese alone I know that thirteen priests or religious were put to death. One of these, the parish priest of Gelrode, suffered, I believe, a veritable martyrdom. I made a pilgrimage to his grave, and, amid the little flock which so lately he had been feeding with the zeal of an apostle, there did I pray to him that from the height of Heaven he would guard his parish, his diocese, his country.[7]

Father Verstreken gave an account to the British press that included details of Jef's hands and feet being bound with copper wire.[8] Verstreken had been with Jef two days before Gelrode had fallen to the Germans, and had been shown where he had hidden the parish treasures for safekeeping. He had subsequently fled to England and edited a newspaper for Belgian refugees.

Jef's ordeal was widely reported in the British and American press. For example, the *Western Daily Press* of 7 January 1915, under the headline 'German Vandals: Atrocities in Belgium: Terrible Story of Cruelty' carried numerous reports of atrocities committed across the country, including details of Jef's fate, stating that 'a number of captured inhabitants were ordered to bedaub him in the filthiest manner.'[9] His example was used by Lilian Hayman as a lesson to her boys' Bible class in Bournemouth on 28 January 1915 in comparing his betrayal with that of Jesus by Judas Iscariot.[10]

The investigation carried out by Jef's friend, Monsignor Cruysbergh, over three decades later attempted to circumvent much of the contemporary emotive response to the killing. He pointed out that many of the witnesses he spoke to were not churchgoers, and therefore had less reason to bias. He left his file of evidence in the library at Mechelen and only included what he considered to be verifiable facts. Cruysberghs also pointed out that he wrote not from a spirit of hatred or revenge, but of love and truth. He compared the actions of the German soldiers who committed the atrocity to those of the Roman soldiers who crucified Christ at Calvary, who 'knew not what they did.'[11] He felt he owed it to his friend to have all doubts and contradictions eradicated so that his true martyrdom would be known and appropriate recognition be given to it by the Catholic Church, possibly in the form of beatification. To that end, as well as interviewing eyewitnesses and combing official archives for documentary evidence, Jef's body was exhumed in 1948 to carry out a forensic investigation into his death. This established that he had indeed been shot twice in the head as well as through his vertebrae. His body was then reinterred at a special ceremony in Gelrode churchyard on 4 September 1949. Today the village school in Gelrode is named VBS Pastor Dergent and stands on the street named after him.

Pieter-Jozef Dergent remained steadfast in the maintenance of what he saw as his duty as a parish priest to care for those in need. Regardless of the threat to his personal safety in the context of German occupation of his homeland, he insisted on taking injured men to hospital. When arrested and brutalised, he refused to renounce his faith and died a terrible death at the hands of his captors. He may have been a simple village pastor, but he showed personal courage of immense magnitude and rightly became a symbol of Belgian resistance during the war, and latterly of the Catholic piety so deeply rooted in many areas of that country.

Chapter 18

Alvin York

'It surely must have been divine power that brought me out. No other power under heaven could save a man in a place like that'

A lvin York was one of America's most decorated soldiers of the First World War (see plate 17). However, upon conscription in 1917, he had originally registered as a conscientious objector, and it was only after persuasion based on the Bible that he changed his stance. Had that not been the case, it is doubtful that what was later referred to as the most remarkable act by a private soldier in the war, would have taken place.

Alvin Cullum York was born in a two-room log cabin on 13 December 1887 in Pall Mall, Nashville, Tennessee. He was the third of eleven children born to William and Eliza York. The family earned money by blacksmithing and farm labouring, and all their clothes were home-made. Alvin attended school for only nine months and withdrew from education because William York wanted his sons to help him work the family farm and hunt small game to feed the family.

As a boy, Alvin would spend his Saturdays at shooting matches, one part of which was a long-range turkey shoot. Each man or boy would pay a dime per shot to fire at a turkey tied by a 2-foot cord to a pole. The first person to shoot the turkey claimed it as his prize. Another event saw a turkey tethered behind a log so that only its head was intermittently visible. The trick here was to react as soon as it was in sight and fire. It was skills learned at these shooting matches that were to prove invaluable to Alvin a decade later.

Despite his mother's devout Christianity the young Alvin developed a taste for hard liquor following the death of his father in 1911 and took part in many saloon bar brawls and was also a keen gambler. He was arrested frequently, but during this period he still attended church regularly, and often led the hymn singing.

Alvin's conversion to a deeper and more personal faith began on 1 January 1915, when he arrived home drunk to find his mother waiting up for him. She asked him when he was going to grow up to be a real man like his father and grandfather. This hit home, with Alvin deciding to:

give up smoking, drinking, gambling, cussing and brawling ... I am a great deal like Paul, the things I once loved I now hate ... I found out the truth of what the Bible says: 'There is more rejoicing over one sinner that repenteth than over ninety-nine just persons that need no repentance.'[1]

He became Second Elder at the local congregation of the Church of Christ in Christian Union, a sect that had been formed in 1909 in a split from the Christian Union, which itself had split from the Methodist Episcopal Church over the violence of the American Civil War and was committed to a pacifist doctrine. The church maintained that God spoke directly to mankind through the Bible, and that the Bible contains no errors as its writers were guided by the Holy Spirit when writing it. It contained all mankind needed to know about God. This was to prove significant in altering Alvin's view of the war.

Alvin was drafted into the American army in June 1917 aged twenty-nine, but this was not easy for him due to the pacifism of the Church of Christ in Christian Union. For Alvin:

I was not a Sunday Christian. I believed in the Bible. And I tried in my own way to live up to it ... I had to accept the Bible as the inspired word of God. I did. And the Bible said, 'Thou shalt not kill.' That was so definite a child could understand it. There was no way around or out of it.[2]

However, Alvin's application to register as a conscientious objector was refused as the church was not recognized as a legitimate Christian sect. He was sent to the 328th Infantry Regiment at Camp Gordon, Georgia in November 1917. At the camp, Alvin had a long conversation with two senior officers, Captain Edward Danforth and Major Gonzalo Buxton. They asked him why he had objected to going to war. This led to an exchange of Bible quotations about fighting and war:

'Because I belong to a church that disbelieves in fighting and killing.'

'What sort of church creed do you have that tells you this?'

'The only creed is the Bible, which I have done accepted as the inspired word of God and final authority for all men.'

'What do you find in the Bible that's against war?'

'The Bible says: "Thou shalt not kill."'

'Do you accept everything in the Bible – every sentence; every word – as completely as you accept the sixth commandment?'

'Yes sir, I do.'

The two officers opened their Bibles and began to quote, with Alvin responding with quotes of his own:

'He that hath no sword, let him sell his cloak and buy one' (Luke 22:36).

'If a man smite you on one cheek, turn the other to him' (Luke 6:29).

'Render unto Caesar the things that are Caesar's and to God the things that are God's' (Mark 12:17).

'If my kingdom were of this world, then would my servants fight?' (John 18:16).[3]

Buxton asked Alvin if the Jesus who had driven the money changers out of the temple would stand around when the helpless Belgian people were overrun and driven from their homes.

The trio read and discussed the Bible for an hour, including Peter being told to put up his sword on the arrest of Christ, the Sermon on the Mount, including the reference to Blessed are the Peacemakers, and Ezekiel 33 about heeding the warning trumpet and taking up the sword.

Alvin was granted ten days' home leave to consider his position. He came back convinced that God wanted him to fight and would keep him safe. He sailed to France and on 8 October 1918, the third major life-changing event, following his conversion to Christ and his conversion to the army, occurred. This action took place during the United States-led portion of the broader Meuse-Argonne Offensive in France, masterminded by Marshal Ferdinand

Foch to breach the Hindenburg Line and make the opposing German forces surrender.

A party of eighteen soldiers was sent to take command of the Decauville railway line. However, due to misreading their map in the fog they ended up behind enemy lines. A brief fight resulted, which led to the surrender of some twenty or so Germans to the eighteen-strong party. The enemy then realised that the American contingent was smaller than they had first thought and opened fire, having first shouted at their own men in German to lie down. Nine Americans were killed, leaving Corporal Alvin York as the most senior man left. Alvin recalled, 'Thousands of bullets kicked up the dust all around us … The air was just plumb full of death.'[4] As the survivors lay down, German guns tried to pick them off. But every time an enemy solider raised his head above the trench, Alvin picked him off with his pistol, just as he had done at the turkey shoots in his youth. During the assault, six German soldiers in a trench near Alvin charged him with fixed bayonets. Alvin had fired all the rounds in his M1917 Enfield rifle, but drew his .45 Colt automatic pistol and shot all six soldiers before they could reach him.

Eventually the German machine-gun nest was taken, and they surrendered. Thirty-two machine guns were captured and 132 German soldiers taken prisoner by a handful of Americans led by Alvin. He escorted the prisoners right through the enemy front line, threatening to shoot the German commanding officer unless he gave clear orders to the soldiers to hold fire as they passed through. Alvin carried on through his own lines and right through to Divisional HQ, where he reported to his divisional commander.

He was promptly promoted to sergeant, and received the Distinguished Service Cross. A few months later, an investigation resulted in an upgrade of his DSC to the Medal of Honor, which was presented to him by the commanding general of the American Expeditionary Force, General John J. Pershing. The French Republic awarded him the Croix de Guerre and the Légion d'Honneur. Italy awarded him its Croce di Guerra al Merito and Montenegro its War Medal. He eventually received nearly fifty decorations. His Medal of Honor citation read:

After his platoon suffered heavy casualties and 3 other non-commissioned officers had become casualties, Cpl. York assumed command. Fearlessly leading 7 men, he charged with great daring a machine gun nest which was pouring deadly and incessant fire upon his platoon. In this heroic feat the machine gun nest was taken, together with 4 officers and 128 men and several guns.[5]

Alvin regarded his remarkable action as being watched over by God, whilst Marshal Ferdinand Foch, Commander of the Allied Powers on the Continent, called the action 'The greatest achievement accomplished by a common soldier in all the armies of Europe.'[6]

On returning to his company late that night he recorded 'I'm a-telling you the hand of God must have been in that fight. It surely must have been divine power that brought me out. No other power under heaven could save a man in a place like that.'[7]

On his return to America in May 1919, Alvin was invited to stay at the Waldorf Astoria, and attended a formal banquet held in his honour. He toured the subway system in a special car before continuing to Washington, where the House of Representatives gave him a standing ovation and he met Secretary of War Newton D. Baker, and the President's secretary, Joe Tumulty, as President Wilson was still in Paris. Alvin proceeded to Fort Oglethorpe, Georgia, where he was discharged from the service, and then to Tennessee for more celebrations. He had been home for barely a week when, on June 7 1919, he married his childhood sweetheart, Gracie Loretta Williams.

Alvin subsequently turned down many promotional opportunities for companies eager to use his heroism and fame, but did much to promote charitable and civic causes. He did accept the gift of a 400-acre farm from the Nashville Rotary Society. This venture lost him money and by 1921 the man who had shown such courage in wartime was in debt, a debt publicly reported. However, this publicity saw an appeal that saved him from bankruptcy.

He founded the Alvin C. York Foundation to promote educational opportunities for the poor in Tennessee. To support economic development, he campaigned for the Tennessee government to build a road to service his native region, succeeding when a highway through the mountains was completed in the mid-1920s and named Alvin C. York Highway.

In 1940, in order to finance an interdenominational Bible school, York accepted the latest of many offers to have his life story made into a film. *Sergeant York*, with Gary Cooper in the starring role, was released in 1941. Alvin visited the White House to promote the film and received praise from President Roosevelt. It formed part of the winning of American hearts and minds in preparation for entering the Second World War in December 1941.

During the Second World War, Alvin attempted to re-enlist in the army, but was refused on the grounds of age and medical condition. His value was recognised and he was commissioned a major in the Army Signal Corps. Alvin toured training camps and participated in bond drives in support of the war effort, usually paying his own travel expenses. He also raised funds for war-related charities, including the Red Cross.

In later years, the former conscientious objector stated that he would be willing to press the nuclear button against Russia if nations came to war. He died on 2 September 1964. His wife then sold most of the farm to the State of Tennessee and it was converted into a visitor attraction, the Sgt. Alvin C. York State Historic Park.

Alvin York's war experiences were based on a sincere and literal interpretation of the Bible. From a disordered lifestyle to that of a sincere Christian, from a position of conscientious objection to that of brave soldier, his beliefs and actions were shaped by his Bible-based faith. From poverty to fame, he never lost sight of his faith and lived a life of physical and moral courage.

Part V

Conscientious Objection in the First World War

'When peace, like a river, attendeth my way, when sorrows like sea billows roll'

The Military Service Act of 1916, whilst aimed at conscripting men into the armed services, included exemption clauses for certain groups of people. This included absolute exemption on the grounds of religious or moral objection to war. This allowance was in some part due to the campaigning of the pacifist No-Conscription Fellowship, set up in 1915.

Over 16,000 men made that claim. They were required to attend a tribunal – a legal panel of leading local citizens and always containing a military representative – to have the sincerity of their claims assessed. However, despite the laudable aim of the conscience clause, in practice the tribunals showed little sympathy to any point of view opposed to the war, in part driven by the desperate need to fill the ranks of the hundreds of thousands who had already been killed or seriously wounded by 1916.

Conscientious objectors came from all walks of life, and varied widely in their ability to cope with often rude and aggressive interviewers. Some didn't get a chance to say a word, others embarked on a well-prepared argument. Whatever they said, the result was the same: only a handful received full exemption, and many were denied any form of exemption at all. Most tribunal members found it difficult to understand why a man would not accept alternative work of national importance, such as civilian work in certain key industries, or medical work in the Friends' Ambulance Unit (FAU) or the Royal Army Medical Corps (RAMC).

Some conscientious objectors were 'absolutists', opposed to conscription as well as war, upholders of civil liberty and the freedom of the individual. Absolutists believed that any alternative service supported the war effort and in effect supported the immoral practice of conscription as well. The tribunals had the power to give these men complete and unconditional exemption. Two of the men we meet in this section, Howard Marten and Francis Meynell, fell into this category and both pushed their claims to the ultimate level of facing death for their beliefs.

Some were 'alternativists', prepared to undertake alternative civilian work not under any military control. Tribunals had power to exempt them from military service on condition that they actually did this work. The FAU, set up in 1914, offered this kind of service to men who, like Laurence Cadbury and Corder Catchpool, felt it their duty to stand alongside the rest of their generation in experiencing the horrors of warfare, whilst being opposed on religious grounds to propagating that war.

'Non-combatants' were prepared to accept call-up into the army, but not to be trained to use weapons, or indeed have anything to do with weapons at all. Tribunals had the power to put these men on the military register on this basis. These men often joined the newly formed Non-Combatant Corps, sarcastically termed the 'No Courage Corps', undertaking labouring tasks behind the front lines, or sometimes they joined the Royal Army Medical Corps after attendance at a tribunal. Lewis Valentine (Chapter 5) had already joined the RAMC without recourse to facing a tribunal due to the foresight shown by the setting up of the Welsh Students Company.

Out of 820 men imprisoned in Britain for maintaining an absolutist position by 1917, 126 were Quakers, fourteen were Anglican, twenty-one were Congregationalists, twenty-one were Methodists and nine were Jews. The tribunals often did not use their powers with much judgement or sympathy. Not only was unconditional exemption rarely granted, but they also frequently allocated absolutists or alternativists to non-combatant duties. In many cases applications were turned down altogether, which meant that the men were liable for call-up as ordinary soldiers. These unwilling conscripts could be arrested and handed over to the military; if they disobeyed military orders they would be court-martialled and sent to prison.

Conscientious objectors faced these unpleasant consequences with responses as varied as themselves. Some were sent hundreds of miles from home to undertake their civilian work and put on a soldier's pay, so there could be seen to be some equality of sacrifice with those in the armed forces.

Some were brutalised in military prisons, whilst a handful, including Howard Marten, were sentenced to death. Francis Meynell inflicted unpleasant consequences on himself in order to prove the sincerity of his case. In all, seventy objectors died either in military or civilian prisons, mainly due to the treatment they received, a percentage death toll not dissimilar to those who served in the military.

Whilst conscientious objectors often faced ridicule, ostracism and violence, in the main they stuck to their position to the extent where such victimisation was not enacted in the Second World War. They had fought a fight to establish their position, and whatever was felt about the justification for their conclusions, it was much harder to argue that they were not sincerely held.

Chapter 19

Francis Meynell

'A man not yet enlisted is bound in conscience to examine the justice of a war, nor can he in conscience enlist while in doubt concerning its justice'

Francis Meynell was a man who took his objection to war to its logical extreme of total and utter resistance to what he saw as the military machine. He was hours from death, until his stubbornness defeated the authorities and so a career in the written word was allowed to flourish.

Born in May 1891, Francis's long and varied career included publishing, politics, journalism and public relations. His mother was the celebrated poet Alice Meynell, whose own father had been a close friend of Charles Dickens, and his father was the journalist and publisher Wilfrid Meynell. They had established a literary, journalistic and mostly Catholic circle. Francis's mother had converted to Catholicism at a young age and his father had done so at the age of eighteen. Alice had been educated in Latin, Greek, Italian, French and German but Wilfrid had had little schooling. His father could cite generations of Quaker ancestry, including William Tuke, who had set up the first human lunatic asylum in 1790, and Samuel Tuke, who had worked alongside William Wilberforce on slavery abolition. A more remote ancestor, another William Tuke, had been imprisoned for his opposition to the Militia Act of 1668, a fact in which Francis expressed pride.

Wilfrid had moved to London aged eighteen and would never pass a beggar without leaving a small gift. Wilfrid and Alice met when he read a poem written by her and he arranged to be introduced to her. The marriage produced seven surviving children, four girls and three boys, of which Francis was the youngest. Francis was named after the poet Francis Thompson, who took on the role of his godfather. Thompson had been a penniless, failed medical student, often sleeping on London's Embankment, when he had sent a poem to the magazine *Merry England*, published by Francis's father. Thompson was a frequent visitor to the Meynell household and he wrote a special poem for Francis, referring to him as a 'young poet wayfarer', which the boy found thrilling.

Francis recalled his parents and their friends spending many days reading literary proofs as the young Francis would sit under the table while reading and reciting Gray's *Elegy*. Francis was educated first at the school of the Convent of Our Lady of Sion in Bayswater and then at a small boarding school in Hove. He later recalled being taught a very nationalistic view of England in relation to the Boer War, buying a toy called 'one in the eye for Kruger', where a button could be flicked at a picture of the face of the president of the Boer Republic. This was confiscated by his Liberal and pacifist mother.

Francis learnt the dates of the kings and queens of England and all his times tables up to the unusual multiple of nineteen. His religious education included such questions as 'Would you prefer to be burnt at the stake or frozen to death?' Francis took his first communion aged seven and learnt many prayers and litanies off by heart.

His next school was St Anthony's, at Eastbourne, where he developed a keenness for cricket. He wrote to the Yorkshire and England all-rounder George Hirst during his benefit year of 1904, enclosing half a crown and asking for advice on how to make the ball swerve. He was thrilled to receive a reply from the great man, which included his signature twice, one to swap with his friends.

Aged eleven, Francis began to experience doubts about his faith. At confession he queried whether a really good God would consign people to Hell. The verdict from the confessor was that he was suffering from spiritual pride and needed to say ten *Hail Marys* as a penance. He asked his mother the same question and was told the Catholic view that if there were a Hell, God would not keep people there for eternity.

From St Anthony's he moved on to Downside, the Benedictine school in Somerset. Francis recalled further spiritual challenges, including questioning the headmaster over the requirement during evening prayers to say 'I desire to be dissolved and to be with Christ'. It was his view that no one really wanted to be dissolved. By the next term the phrase had been removed from the school prayer book. Following in the footsteps of his parents, and as a precursor to one of his future careers, Francis became editor of *The Raven*, the Downside school magazine. He persuaded his eminent literary mother to contribute an article comparing English and Irish landscapes. Francis had his first paid writing commission at this time, bringing up to date *A Short Catechism of English History*, which had originally ended in 1870. However, the unedited insertion of the question 'What great statesman attempted to do justice to Ireland in 1885?' with the answer 'William Gladstone' led to the directors of the publishing firm, Burns & Oates, having to withdraw the book from circulation after protests from many of its Unionist purchasers.

Francis continued his interest in sport, reaching the first elevens at cricket, football and hockey, although the cricket bat he was 'given' by the school for scoring a fifty for the first team resulted in a bill being sent to his father! He was also showing the political awareness and activism that would become so influential in his decisions in the First World War by persuading the school library to start taking *The Tribune*, a Liberal-supporting daily newspaper. In 1906 he proposed a motion to the debating society that 'we welcome with joy the election of the first Labour MPs', the motion receiving only a seconder but no other supporter.

In 1909 Francis was taken to Rome to witness the beatification of Joan of Arc by Pope Pius X by an older lady friend of his, a Mrs Cryan. Having failed the entrance interview for a place at Balliol College, Oxford, Francis expressed a preference for attending Trinity College, Dublin. This was partly due to the fact that he preferred the more modern focus of the English Literature course, but it also meant that he could lodge with Mrs Cryan's family, thus saving considerable expense. Francis became a member of the Society of St Vincent de Paul, visiting the large section of the Dublin population who lived in poverty to 'dispense platitudes or religious comfort along with totally inadequate gifts of money or food or medicine.'[1]

Francis's friendship circle in Dublin included Thomas MacDonagh and James Connolly, later to become two of the fifteen men to be executed in 1916 for their roles in the leadership of the Easter Rising. Later in life he reflected that it had taken him many decades to overcome their deaths, described as 'the wanton and cold-blooded execution by my country'.[2] Francis also felt personal angst after falling in love with Mrs Cryan's daughter Edith, and being banished from the house and forbidden from seeing her further. He left Dublin after two years, before taking his degree, and went to work at the publishing firm of Burns & Oates, then owned by his father.

Francis began to move in fashionable literary circles and was invited to many dances as an eligible young bachelor, including one given by the eminent author H.G. Wells. Ezra Pound was a companion of Francis, as was the Home Secretary, Reginald McKenna. Like Maude Royden, Francis's mother and sisters were active suffragists. Francis, however, tended to favour the more militant approach of the suffragettes and during one rally outside the Houses of Parliament in November 1911 he was arrested for tipping a policeman off the plinth of the statue of Richard Coeur de Lion. He was arrested and taken forcibly to Scotland Yard, with his protestations of being friends with the Home Secretary failing to persuade the police to loosen their grip on him. Francis was fined £5 by the magistrate, a sum equivalent to about £400 in the money of 2015.

In March 1912, Francis attended a meeting held at the Queen's Hall convened by West End traders to call for tougher punishments for the actions of the suffragettes who were disrupting commerce. He repeatedly rose to speak out against the resolutions, and was asked by the chairman whom he was representing. Francis answered that he worked for Burns & Oates, receiving howls of derision. He returned to work the next day expecting disciplinary actions from the Tory directors of the firm, but instead was visited by two ladies who had admired his stand and gave him a £500 commission to have books printed to send to poor Catholic communities, the largest order received by Burns & Oates up to that date.

Francis was keen on discussing politics with his mother. She believed that communism was in accordance with the teaching of Christ, and he had been greatly moved by scenes of extreme poverty he had seen both in his university days in Dublin and during his young adulthood in London. In 1913 he was introduced to George Lansbury, who had recently resigned as a Labour MP to campaign for women's suffrage. Lansbury was to become one of the greatest influences in Francis's life. At the time Lansbury had taken over as chairman of the *Daily Herald* newspaper and then bought it outright when it went bankrupt. Francis, still aged only twenty-two and with a full-time job at Burns & Oates, was appointed general manager by Lansbury. The first major campaign of the newspaper was in support of the great strike in Dublin, where employers were attempting to remove trade unionism from their workplaces. Francis organised two large meetings at the Royal Albert Hall, the second of which being addressed by James Larkin, the great Irish trade union leader.

When war came in August 1914, Francis saw it as a clash of two imperial powers at the expense of the common man. However, his parents, to his great disappointment, accepted the propaganda of the time and reluctantly supported the war. Francis had fallen in love with Hilda Saxe, a concert pianist five years his senior, and they were married the month that war broke out. As Hilda was an agnostic and Francis a Roman Catholic, he performed an unofficial 'baptism' on her with a sprinkling of water and a few words. They had a daughter, Cynthia, whose birth was announced in the *Herald*, 'born into a family wherein rebel and artistic and literary traditions are so happily blended.' She had also been born into a world of 'capitalists, diplomats and repressors of life generally' but it was hoped that this would soon change.[3]

Francis became friends with Siegfried Sassoon, who lived nearby. Francis's sister Viola lent her cottage to D.H. Lawrence and his wife for six months, during which the author and Francis became well acquainted. Francis joined the No-Conscription Fellowship and became friendly with its founders, Fenner Brockway and Clifford Allen, as well as prominent supporter Bertrand Russell. In order to save the embarrassment to his parents of his anti-war activities, particularly in association with his employment at Burns & Oates, a wealthy patron helped Francis to set up the Pelican Press. One of the first accomplishments of this publisher was to produce *The C.O.'s Hansard*, a weekly round-up of parliamentary business relating the issue of conscientious objection.

Francis and his friend Stanley Morison, who had succeeded him as manager at Burns & Oates, established a group in 1916 that reflected their Catholic, socialist and pacifist outlook, the Guild of the Pope's Peace. However, its membership numbered only seven, including two priests. It promoted Pope Benedict XV's appeals for an immediate end to the war and a negotiated peace, publishing *Prayers for Peace* through the Oxford University Press. In 2009 MI5 released documents relating to suspected communist activities in Britain from 1916 to 1949. Francis had been one of those under surveillance, as the Guild of the Pope's Peace was thought to be undermining the war effort as well as being seen as pro-German due to its Catholic beliefs. The English Catholic Church hierarchy opposed the Pope's anti-war message, a position that started to encourage Francis away from his faith and towards what would eventually become a position of 'conscientious agnosticism'.

The repression of the Easter Rising in Dublin in 1916, and the subsequent execution of men known personally to Francis, including Thomas MacDonagh, James Connolly and Sir Roger Casement, caused him to become even firmer in his opposition to the actions of the British state, and when his conscription papers arrived in the summer of 1916, it was perhaps inevitable that he would register as a conscientious objector. Francis's case was heard at the Marylebone Tribunal in August. He cited an emotional objection to the thought of killing and inflicting pain, a religious objection as the Pope had denounced the war, and a political objection as a socialist who saw the war as a fight between two imperialist systems. Francis's defence referred to the sinking of the *Lusitania* and the execution of the leaders of the Easter Rising as examples of military actions he would refuse to undertake. He also quoted Gury-Ballerini's work of Catholic theology: 'A man not yet enlisted is bound in conscience to examine the justice of a war, nor can he in conscience enlist while in doubt concerning its justice.'[4]

Francis pointed out that there were Catholics in both the Allied armies and those of the 'other side' who had perfectly honestly come to totally different conclusions. However, the chairman of the tribunal quoted Christ's words from Matthew 22:21, to 'Render unto Caesar the things which are Caesar's'. Francis's reply was that his conscience was not a material possession that the law could claim, but a matter for God.[5] He argued that Catholics of the past that had refused to swear an oath of allegiance to Queen Elizabeth had set their private judgement against that of the state. Francis's objection was absolute, refusing to undertake non-combatant service, work on the land or anything under the compulsion of the Military Service Act.

The chairman accepted the sincerity of Francis's case, but considered his conclusions erroneous. Francis pointed out that the job of the tribunal was not to judge his beliefs, merely to assess whether they were sincerely held. Despite this he was ordered to do non-combatant service, but was told he had the right of appeal. His reply was that he would resist all the way to the death penalty, referring to those like Howard Marten and Bert Brocklesby (whom we meet in Chapters 20 and 23 respectively), who had been sentenced, then reprieved, in France. At his appeal, heard in September 1916, Francis produced letters from the novelist H.G. Wells and the former Conservative government minister Lord Lytton confirming the sincerity of his views. However, the appeal was turned down and Francis handed himself in to the military authorities in January 1917. The case was reported in *The Herald*:

> Last week our friend and comrade Francis Meynell was before the appeal tribunal at Spring Gardens, London. He made a splendid and courageous stand for his claim to full and unconditional exemption. The tribunal was scrupulously fair and gave his case a full seventy minutes' discussion and consideration; but, while agreeing that he had proved his conscientious objection to all service, refused him exemption and ordered him to find work of national importance within twenty-eight days and further promised to consider an application for the right of appeal to the Central Tribunal. The case of our comrade illustrates the absurdity of the position with regard to the Military Service Act. This act professedly gives the conscientious objector the right to claim exemption from military service on his being able to prove that he is possessed of a conscience to the satisfaction of the tribunals, but it leaves to the tribunals a discretion by which they can attach such conditions to their certificates of exemption as to make it impossible for out-and-out C.O.s to accept their exemption. Two thousand two hundred and sixty men have been arrested under the Conscription Acts; 1,266 have been court-martialled and 147 released.[6]

Francis handed himself in to the military authorities in January 1917 and was taken to Hounslow Barracks. Bravely, he decided on a hunger and thirst strike. Having seen the suffragettes endure force-feeding, he reckoned that his shunning of fluids in a crowded army guardhouse would go unnoticed until the authorities would either have to let him die or release him. Francis also combined his Christianity with his publishing skills to have bound in vellum a 1635 Douai Bible that he possessed, but leaving enough room in the board for cavities in which he could hide thin paper and pencils. He was locked in a guardroom with a handful of other objectors, with two half-hour periods of exercise per day and frequent visits from Hilda. By the end of a week of starving and thirsting, his mouth, tongue and throat were parched and painful, and sleep was fitful.

To weaken his body's strength, he would march vigorously during exercise periods, and walk up and down in the guardroom at other times. Francis wore no coat against a biting wind and rubbed snow on his head. On the ninth day of fasting he chewed down two morphine tablets to enable some sleep. He could no longer speak to Hilda when she visited due to the dryness of his tongue. He took an ice-cold bath to further shock his body and on the twelfth day he finally collapsed and was taken to a military hospital, where he was diagnosed as being too far gone for force-feeding. He was told that if he agreed to eat and drink he would be discharged from the army unconditionally. He agreed and took a spoonful of milk, 'the sweetest drink of my life'. [7]

Francis was discharged from the army in February as 'unlikely to become an efficient soldier' and received a further letter telling him he did not qualify for an army pension![8] After a recuperative holiday in Cornwall, he resumed his work at the *Herald* and the Pelican Press. His anti-war propaganda continued, most notably after a visit from Bertrand Russell and Siegfried Sassoon. The latter, a decorated war hero, had come out against the war and was refusing to rejoin his regiment. The Pelican Press printed his denunciation of the way the war was being conducted and he was later invited to join the *Herald* as literary editor. Francis also oversaw the paper's support for the Bolshevik Revolution in Russia from 1917 onwards and published the alleged secret treaties the Tsar had made with the British Government to carve up parts of Europe after the war.

After the war Francis Meynell had a rich and varied career, as a publisher, introducing new typefaces into Britain and setting up the Nonesuch Press, and as a designer of utility clothes and adviser on rationing in the Second World War, amongst many other roles. The former rebel who had nearly starved himself to death in 1917 and who had been under surveillance for his subversive activities in the First World War was awarded a knighthood at the end of the Second World War for his contributions to public life.

Francis Meynell was spurred by his conscience, his faith in the Catholic Church and his politics. Despite his wealth of society connections, he was willing to sacrifice his life for his beliefs, undergoing twelve days of torment to get his point across. The man of many words found that when his words were ignored, his actions were not. His strength of character and sincerity of belief could never be in doubt again.

Chapter 20

Howard Marten

'I had a sense of representing something outside my own self, supported by a strength stronger than frail humanity'

Howard Marten was one of thousands of men who found themselves presented with a stark choice in January 1916. They could either obey the new Military Service Act compelling all men from the ages of 18 to 41 to register for military service, or they could stick to a belief, be that a religious, political or humanitarian one, that war was wrong and that they could take no part in the slaughter. Howard was one of 16,000 who chose the latter, and his belief in God took him to dark places and the precipice of death during the subsequent two years.

In later years he wrote his reminiscences in the hope that people might 'gather some deeper insight into the way in which the Divine Providence leads us over the rough and stony places of life [and] to show that somewhere in the hearts of all men the Divine Light still shines.'[1]

Howard Cruttenden Marten was an only child, born in Pinner, Middlesex in 1884. He grew up attending churches of many different Protestant denominations, including the Congregational Church, but it was not until after the war that he was to declare an allegiance to the Quaker Church. A bank clerk at the outbreak of war, he was convinced that war was not justifiable and was willing to stand his ground in the face of moral and physical pressure.

Howard's case was heard at the Hendon Tribunal on 13 March 1916, one of the tribunal members being an Anglican clergyman. Whilst they both agreed that the 'war was due to the evil tendency in man', they could not agree on the way to meet the current demands. Howard argued that he thought it possible that one day war could be abolished if humans attuned themselves to the spirit of Christian ideals. This was despite him being challenged on the biblical prophecy that there would always be 'wars and rumours of wars'.[2] Howard was granted exemption from combatant status only. However, his position was an absolute refusal to undertake any form of work under military control, the absolutist position. This was in contrast to others who were, like Lewis Valentine, willing to serve in a non-fighting capacity in the Non-Combatant Corps or the Royal Army Medical Corps.

Howard appealed, and his case was heard at the Guildhall, Westminster, on 23 March 1916. The appeal was dismissed and a policeman called to arrest him on 15 April, at a time when he was out cutting the grass at the local Quaker burial ground. Howard had already taken the precaution of leaving his job at the Capital and Counties Bank branch at Piccadilly, receiving a letter of appreciation from eight of his colleagues and a pipe as a leaving gift. Two days later he was sent to the local magistrates' court, fined £2 and placed under military escort. Howard was then taken to Mill Hill Barracks and ordered to sign Army Attestation papers, which he refused to do. He was given an army uniform, but refused to put it on. However, he did allow a non-commissioned officer to dress him without offering physical resistance.

Howard was taken to Felixstowe, then Harwich. The army was attempting to make a soldier of him yet, but he refused to obey more orders, including drilling. He was handcuffed, along with five others, and made to stand facing a wall for hours on end before being sentenced to solitary confinement with bread and water for three days. During this first punishment his faith sustained him through an uncomfortable period. In addition he received letters of support from many prominent individuals, including Maude Royden. Thus Howard knew that he had a large network of supporters sympathising with his plight.

> The walls were of stone, while the concrete floor, without bed boards made the place cold at night and even during the daytime. There was no stool or chair of any kind, while at night my overcoat and blanket were taken outside. The best device I could adopt was to take off my tunic and sit on it ... I was permitted to have my Bible and read and re-read the Gospel of John and several of the epistles.[3]

As it became clear that Howard and other conscientious objectors would not succumb to military orders in England, the decision was taken to raise the stakes and move the men to Le Havre. As Europe was a theatre of conflict, it followed that any act of disobedience would be a court martial office, potentially resulting in the death penalty. Howard's answer was to turn to God: 'During the afternoon those of us in the Guard Room held a Meeting for Worship after the manner of Friends and never perhaps had we experienced a time when the need of Divine Help and Guidance was more felt.'[4]

Sixteen other men were in the party that left for France: Cornelius Barritt, Bernard Bonner, H.F. Brewster, F.C. Bromberger, Alfred Evans, Jack Foister, G.E. Hicks, J.B. Lief, Adam Priestley, Oscar Ricketts, John Ring, Harry Scullard, Frank Shackleton, Harry Stanton, Harry Wilson and Rendell Wyatt. Howard commented, recognising the integrity of men of all faiths and none, 'Among our numbers were Friends (Quakers), members of the Church of England, Free Churchmen, a Roman Catholic, an International Bible Student with others who adopted the less orthodox but equally sincere faith of Socialism.'[5]

Once in Le Havre, shovels and wheel handles were placed in Howard's hands and he was set to work. When the soldiers let go of him he stopped working. Howard wrote of the sympathy shown by the soldiers detailed to try to make him work, giving him extra rations and being impressed by the sincerity of his stance. However, this was not enough to prevent the military authorities continuing attempts to force him to comply and he was sent to Boulogne to face a court martial. Once again, the fellowship of faith sustained him:

As night came on, we had got into friendly converse with our escort and after making a meal from the rations brought with us, we expanded into song. We had two copies of the *Fellowship Hymn Book* in our possession and went steadily through all the old favourites. Our Welshman was in great form and took a leading part in rendering many well-known hymns. He also gave us solos and we shall all of us long remember his rich voice in *Jesu, Lover of my Soul* ... This, in spite of the unknown future, it was an evening of happiness and promise and one that I shall always retain very vividly among my collection of memory pictures.[6]

On arrival at Boulogne Howard was taken to the Field Barracks, placed in handcuffs and locked in a cell. Initially he recorded his food and drink ration as, 'Breakfast 1 pint Tea (no milk or sugar) and 4 biscuits, Dinner 1 tin of Bully Beef. Tea – 1 pint of tea'. The beef was subsequently removed, so he was surviving on just four biscuits per day. Again, for Howard, the most important thing to him was to be allowed his Bible:

We were allowed to retain an extra change of underclothing, our small kit (i.e. soap, comb, shaving tackle and 'housewife') and a few handkerchiefs. Some of the warders responsible for searching us were more lenient than others and, although all were allowed to retain Bibles, a few of us were able to keep other books which proved a solace in the days ahead. Besides a Bible, therefore, I was also able to retain possession of a Fellowship Hymn Book and a little book of Quotations called *Life's Compass*.[7]

Howard was taken to be interviewed and told the panel that 'War is contrary to the Spirit and Teaching of Christ.' In one act of humanity, Lord Kitchener gave permission for a visit by the Reverend Dr. F.B. Meyer, a leading Nonconformist minister. However, this did not mean that the army would give up on Howard's case. On 2 June 1916 he was court-martialled. The case broke down on a technicality and he was called for a retrial on 7 June, being brought out from a rat-infested cell he was sharing with eleven other men, including one suffering from dysentery. A further wait then had to be endured before 24 June, when the first sentences were to be announced. Howard and three others were taken to the parade ground at Henriville, with Howard himself being the first ordered to step forward.

The sentence was handed down: 'to suffer death by being shot'.

I have often been asked what my sensations were at that moment and have found it difficult to recollect very clearly. I think I may say that for the time being I had lost the sense of 'personality' and, standing there on the parade ground, I had a sense of representing something outside my own self, supported by a strength stronger than frail humanity. However, in a few moments it was evident that this whole had not been said and the officer went on to tell that 'this sentence had been confirmed by the Commander-in-Chief but afterwards commuted by him to one of 'penal servitude for ten years'.[8]

Initially, Howard was taken to Hard Labour Camp at Rouen, where he was visited by Rowntree Gillett, who had been granted special permission by the War Office to act as an informal Quaker chaplain. They sang a few hymns together and read from the Bible. Subsequently he was taken to Winchester Gaol, where he was surprised to find out that his case had been raised in Parliament on 26 June. Some MPs had spoken in his defence, demanding his immediate repatriation to Britain, whilst others had questioned why he had not been shot after a court martial as any other soldier would have been.

Howard was now on safer ground, as his sentence was transferred from military to civil authority to enforce.

On the evening of my arrival at Winchester, I received two visitors in my cell. The first was the 'schoolmaster' who, after asking me a few questions, departed, leaving behind him a Bible, a prayer-book with hymns (Ancient and Modern) and a Church of England devotional book called *The Narrow Way*. Or, as one CO afterwards expressed it, *The VERY narrow Way*. This last, after weeks of petitioning, I was able to exchange for a copy of *The Pilgrim's Progress* ... and lastly I was presented with a card evidently designed for the spiritual welfare of prisoners. On one side of this were printed 'Things a Christian Ought to Know' and on the other, 'Psalms, Prayers and Hymns for Morning and Evening Use'. Among the latter was a paraphrase of the 23rd Psalm with the very obvious omission of the verse, 'Thou preparest a table before me in the presence of mine enemies'. Much of the advice given against running into all manner of temptation seemed rather superfluous under the circumstances![9]

Howard was glad of this visit as the second visit from the prison chaplain was lacking in Christian understanding:

My other visitor was the prison chaplain who held what to me were strange notions as to the manner of exercising his office. He seemed undecided as to whether I ought to have been shot or whether that was too good for me and that it was fitter I should linger in a prison cell. We had a vigorous discussion, but when I challenged him with the truth of the 'Light Within' he would hear no more, told me I 'worshipped my own mind' and bounced out of the cell, emphasising his final word by violently slamming the door of the cell.[10]

However, it was this chaplain's services he had to attend while at Winchester, and Howard only enjoyed the singing portions of them. In August 1916 he was transferred briefly to Wormwood Scrubs, 'having no work to perform and no books except Bible, Hymn and Prayer Books,' and thence to Aberdeen to do 'work of national importance under civilian control'.[11] This work of national importance was to take place at Dyce Quarry Camp, which had been specifically set up by the Home Office as a solution to those men, like Howard, who had refused to have anything to do with the military machine (see plate 18). Serving under Home Office regulations was more acceptable than serving under those of the War Office to some objectors like Howard. Compared to Winchester and Wormwood Scrubs, it allowed for a relatively free life. Men were permitted to frequent local pubs, or in Howard's case, to go to the Friends' Meeting House in Aberdeen at weekends. Conditions still remained poor and several MPs visited to examine them and raise concerns in Parliament. Among these MPs was the future Prime Minister, Ramsay McDonald. This led to the closure of the camp in October 1916, so Howard was transferred to Wakefield Prison and then Dartmoor Prison in March 1917.

A year later the authorities allowed his release in order for him to undertake directed work in the London Office of the Friends' War Victims Relief Committee. Howard was finally discharged from the Home Office scheme in April 1919, ending more than three years of compulsion and imprisonment for his faith. In later life, Howard had a successful business career and was active in the Fellowship of Reconciliation, the leading conscientious objection movement of the 1930s and 1940s. He died in 1981, leaving his massive archive, including a 159-page typed account of his war experience, to the Liddle Collection at the University of Leeds.

Howard Marten experienced years of trial, tribulation and rejection. He never wavered from his belief that the war was morally and spiritually wrong and was willing to endure imprisonment and even death for his ideals. His spiritual journey led him from an undefined nonconformist faith to that of the more devout pacifism of the Quaker movement.

Chapter 21

Laurence Cadbury and Corder Catchpool

'But I too am enlisted, not merely for three years or the duration of the war, under a Captain who also calls for adventure and sacrifice in His name'

L aurence John Cadbury was born into a world of wealth and privilege in 1889. His father was George Cadbury, head of the world-famous chocolate firm. The large Cadbury family was brought up in the Quaker tradition. There were five children from George's first marriage, and Laurence was the eldest of a further six from his second marriage, to Elizabeth Taylor. Laurence attended Leighton Park School, a Quaker establishment, and studied economics at Trinity College, Cambridge, graduating in 1911. In the spring of 1913, he travelled through North America. Laurence was a keen engineer and was fascinated by cars at a time when they were a rare sight on British roads. He was particularly attached to his own car, which he named the *Beetle*.

One of the principle tenets of Quakerism was the philosophy of non-violence. Applied to the situation the country found itself in during the summer of 1914, for many Quakers this meant a refusal to support any part of a war effort. However, for Laurence, as for his brother Bertie, this was an unsatisfactory position. Their positions in society as well as their personal beliefs meant they felt compelled to undertake action of some kind.

Thomas Corder Pettifer Catchpool found himself in a similar situation to Laurence. Born in Leicester on 15 July 1883, Corder had attended the Quaker Sidcot School in Somerset and Bootham School in York, and, like Laurence, had trained to be an engineer. A keen walker and mountaineer, August 1914 had found him in the Swiss Alps but as he managed to make his way back to England, the sight of the suffering of the invaded people of France made him convinced that he had to find a way of allying his Quaker pacifist beliefs with doing something to alleviate their situation. He later wrote:

> the horror of it seemed more than I could bear. Believing that war is contrary to the will of God, as revealed in the life and teaching of Jesus Christ ... I was unable to enlist or bear arms ...Within a few days however, I had experienced a call to take up ambulance work.[1]

The idea of a Friends' Ambulance Unit had been first publicly mooted in the pages of *The Friend* on 21 August 1914 by Philip Noel-Baker. He appealed to those who wanted to render some service beyond that possible on the home front and suggested that there would soon not be an adequate number of people involved in ambulance work on the front line. Therefore he suggested that a group of friends form an ambulance corps, numbering forty-eight individuals, to go to Belgium to work in war relief. He appealed for subscriptions to enable those without private means to be able to do so. Noel-Baker emphasised that the group would work under the auspices of the neutral Red Cross, and that whilst members would be placing themselves at personal risk, they would be saving many lives and alleviating great suffering among the victims of war. Despite some criticism from fellow Quakers that ambulance work was focused on treating wounded soldiers, and therefore supporting the military machine, Noel-Baker was able to recruit enough men for what became the Friends' Ambulance Unit (FAU).

Both Laurence Cadbury and Corder Catchpool were among those early recruits (see plate 19). Laurence's official FAU record shows that he enlisted with the unit on 7 September 1914, serving right through until 2 March 1919. Initially, the FAU consisted of a group of forty-three men, supported by a donation of £100. By the end of the war there were 600 men on the Western Front alone and the unit had received more than £136,000 in voluntary contributions. All its members were unpaid, with many of them having the private means to enable them to take on the work, and it was managed by the Joint War Committee of the British Red Cross Society and the Order of St John of Jerusalem.

After an initial period at a training camp at Jordans, Buckinghamshire, the first party of FAU men left for Dunkirk on 31 October 1914. Laurence took his Vauxhall car, the *Beetle*, over with him. The men were, according to an official history of the FAU published after the war:

> not content to remain passive with folded hands in the midst of the conflict, because of their religious views, upbringing, or conscientious objection to war ... they desired to stand beside their companions and friends who went to fight, and share their dangers, their self-renunciation, devotion and sacrifice ... they were impressed with the inadequacy of the means and agencies then existing for dealing with the miseries and desolations of war.[2]

Their first experience of war work came almost immediately, when they treated 3,000 wounded soldiers who had been evacuated to sheds in Dunkirk Railway Station and left there without medical help. The unit set up its headquarters in the Hotel du Kursaal, Malo-les-Bains – a seaside suburb of Dunkirk, about a mile from the town centre. It was divided into civilian divisions, hospitals, ambulance trains and ambulance convoys, in which Laurence Cadbury and Corder Catchpool worked. The ambulance convoys, known as Sections Sanitaires Anglaises (SSAs), were made up of twenty ambulances, with a further two in reserve. Each section was staffed by fifty-six men, led by an officer in charge or 'chef-adjoint', a sous chef and an assistant responsible for the administration of the convoy. Although there were at first several numbered convoys, the ambulance convoys were eventually reduced to three, known as SSA 13, 14, and 19.

Laurence Cadbury was chef-adjoint of SSA 13 until September 1916, when he, with some reluctance, was sent to headquarters at Malo to carry out administrative work as Officer in Charge of the Transport Section of the unit. From then, he refers to his job as 'OC Cars'; this involved negotiating with officers in the French army to find work for the unit, attaching sections to a new division when its old division moved, organising the repair and maintenance of convoy cars, recruiting and training drivers, appointing heads of sections, and driving to visit the sections stationed in the field in the *Beetle*.

At first, the unit took whatever relief work it could find. The Belgian army had suffered significant losses at Yser and their medical sources were straining to cope. Therefore, Noel–Baker approached the chairman of the Joint War Committee, the Hon. Arthur Stanley MP, who allowed the First Anglo–Belgian Ambulance Unit to proceed to the war zone. But as it grew, it was joined to the French army and a more formal structure developed.

The unit then volunteered to help the medical staff of a division of the French army (the 87th Territorial) at Woesten, near Ypres. Several stations were established in the Ypres region, and the unit also undertook civilian relief work, treating wounded and gassed civilians during fighting at Ypres and opening a hospital at Sacré Coeur, Ypres. Another hospital, the Queen Alexandra, was opened at Malo in November 1914, which was staffed by eight of the unit's nurses; other hospitals included Château Elisabeth, Poperinghe, taken over by the FAU on 14 January, which moved to Ferme de Rycke, known as 'The Farm', Watten, in July 1915. The unit treated victims of a typhoid epidemic in the Ypres district and casualties from the Second Battle of Ypres, as well as from the German advance towards Hazebrouck in April 1918.

Initially, the volunteers found the work rewarding. In November 1914 Corder was able to write, 'the need for help is so urgent that I have never tasted purer happiness than during the past week.'[3] He had met several old Sidcot boys, although of a younger generation to himself, and he felt himself to be a father figure to them as they went around lifting stretchers, speaking French to the wounded and dispensing cigarettes and chocolate.

Laurence spent Christmas 1914 in high spirits, with dancing and songs organised in the unit. He also seems to have overlooked the traditional Quaker aversion to alcohol, enjoying bottled beer, whisky and port. He also managed to attend a midnight Mass in Poperinghe alongside soldiers of the French Eighth Army. Laurence described the sound of the big guns and rifle fire being heard in pauses between the hymns. He wrote to his father of the sermon, calling for the desire for peace to take precedence over that for victory, and how 'the soldiers stood silently in prayer while the low rumble of the guns echoed through the Church; it was very impressive.'[4]

Corder was at the same service and admired the Catholic decorations of the 'Manger and Babe, Virgin and Magi, and Cherubs floating around'.[5] He noted how the soldiers knelt before the crèche, above which were hung the flags of the Allies. Corder himself knelt and 'thought of Christ and the flags, and that perhaps He is nearer to the trenches than one thinks in one's moments of anguish at the horrors of war, nearer to the German trenches and nearer to our trenches.'[6]

Laurence had heard of soldiers of either side organising frequent informal truces and he thought it would be 'a very amusing conclusion' to the war if the combatants would pair off like MPs, 'went on strike and refused to fight any more.'[7] He wrote of the difficulties refugees faced in a war zone and of an outbreak of typhoid in early 1915 due to a lack of drainage and water supply. He put forward the case for inoculations, despite it being opposed by 'some beastly cranks (antivivisectionists or other objectionable persons, who in the piping times of peace can be tolerated, but now want corking) that advise men not be inoculated for conscientious reasons'.[8]

By the spring of 1915 the FAU was well-established and organised, with more than thirty cars and spare drivers, fitters and repairers. At times they worked alongside members of the American Red Cross and the British Red Cross. Although Laurence expressed admiration for some of the latter, those who had been turned down by the army and those too old for military service, he thought the majority of them cowards, preferring work far behind the front line. 'Why should they be paid 35/- a week, run no risks to speak of, live like fighting cocks, and yet be looked on as heroes to a certain extent, while better men are getting a rotten time as Tommies?'[9]

For Corder, the tragedy of the war came to the fore, reflecting that:

It is grand the way men give all ... gladly to serve their country, in a cause they believe to be right [but] with all the sublimity of their sacrifice, are dupes; we, dupes, all the world, dupes of the handfuls of charlatans who make wars, exploiting, trading upon, those nobler traits of human nature. 'Your country needs you', cry armament manufacturers, Junker, Chauvinist, well knowing that at that cry millions of hearts that beat true and honest will begin to beat proudly and courageously, and millions of men will march out to slay their brothers.[10]

The FAU set up its own hospital in France, the Queen Alexandra in Malo, where Laurence's sister, Millie, worked. She became engaged, then married, to Bill Greeves, another FAU member. Laurence's younger brother, Bertie, served in the Royal Navy on HMS *Zarefah* and HMS *Sagitta,* then joined the Royal Naval Air Service as a flight sub lieutenant, based at the Great Yarmouth Air Station after training.

Corder found time to reflect on the religiosity of the area in which the FAU was serving. He noted the large number of convents and monasteries and that a high proportion of young girls seriously considered becoming nuns. He had frequent conversations about Quakerism, and the pacifist view of the war and was 'surprised at the amount of sympathy and interest generally expressed'.[11] He was pleased to see a French nurse kindly treating a wounded German, and when she was asked if he liked nursing him, she replied, '*Il est blessé; que voulez vous?*' For Corder, 'The reply should be shouted over Europe.'[12] He also noted that with the expansion of the previously secularist French army, each corps now had a number of chaplains, Protestant as well as Catholic. Corder assisted a Protestant *aumônier* with a service for troops.

Following the excitement of the early part of the war and the First Battle of Ypres, work grew increasingly monotonous for both men, with a greater degree of administrative work due to their senior positions, Corder being an adjutant.

Membership of the FAU had been voluntary, so until the introduction of conscription in 1916 it was difficult to plan ahead as men could join or leave at will. However, once conscientious objectors began to choose FAU service as an alternative to armed combat, it became possible to formalise involvement with an initial six-month service, followed by rolling periods of three months. The conscience clause in the Military Service Act of 1916 caused problems between Laurence and his comrades in the FAU, particularly Corder Catchpool. By the summer of 1916, Laurence had 'been having a terrible time'.[13] The best that could be said about a series of problems to resolve was that it kept Laurence's mind 'from becoming too desperately depressed at the idea of two or three more years utterly wasted in this infernal war'.[14] There were debates within the FAU as to the morality of imprisoning men in Britain who had refused to join the army due to a stated conscientious objection. For Laurence:

I don't object to conscience, not even over-manured ones, so long as they only prompt people to self-regarding actions, but when they start seriously and adversely affecting other people, I consider it time to remind their owners that there are other considerations besides their own particular and peculiar individualities to be borne in mind, that there are other people in the world, and that their welfare should at least be given a thought ... A zealot is in a position to be envied anyway, untroubled with doubts and perplexities, in his single mindedness only seeing one side of a question, content to subordinate everything else to his one master purpose.[15]

A particular problem for Laurence was that a petition had been circulated within the FAU stating that the signatories would withdraw their war work and return home unless the government desisted in jailing conscientious objectors. He saw this as the work of a small minority of volunteers, but that those volunteers had blackened the name of the FAU in the eyes of the authorities on the Western Front. On the home front, he wrote approvingly of 'Mother ... taking in hand the job of counteraction the effects of the blighters in the Society [of Friends] who have been advocating the employment of strike methods in regard to compulsion, and bleating about their precious, pampered and over-sensitive consciences.[16]

One of the men who did return home was 'T.C.P.C., [Corder Catchpool] with whom I have been closely associated so long, and who is such a thoroughly genuine old man'.[17]

Corder too had noticed a change in the ethos of the FAU, with some men having chosen to join the army (and some, like Laurence, giving it serious consideration). He had already expressed disillusionment that he was 'getting soul-sick of the work out here the last four months of mending motor-cars instead of men'.[18] By December 1915 he was beginning to feel like a part of a large war machine and was becoming aware of the pressure being heaped on fellow Quakers at home for continuing to resist the calls to enlist.

Laurence was not a man to parade his conscience, and had little respect for those who kept 'a careful guard against any suppression of their own individual eccentricities in conforming to any regulation uniformity'. But accepted that 'in such a heterogeneous collection of super-fatted consciences, a percentage of intractable and unreasonable cranks is unavoidable.'[19]

These doubts about the value role in the FAU did not prevent Laurence from receiving the Croix de Guerre from the French government. The awarding ceremony took place against the backdrop of enemy strafing and included men from the Royal Naval Air Service, Royal Marine Artillery and some French officers. *La Marseillaise* was played for each recipient, and the French general who awarded Laurence his cross managed to prick him with the medal's pin! He watched in amusement as 'all the right people had undergone that moment of intense nervousness when they wondered whether their decoration would be attached merely to their tunics or to their persons as well.'[20] This award may well have reassured Laurence that his reputation would be enhanced after the war, and would sit alongside the Distinguished Service Cross that his brother Bertie had been awarded in 1916.

The Military Service Act polarised the splits in the Quaker movement that had been expressed at the original formation of the FAU in 1914. The unit was disowned by the Friends' Service Committee. It was receiving large numbers of applicants who preferred membership of the FAU to military service. For Corder, this was only one step away from compulsion. He had joined on an entirely voluntary basis. Now men were being coerced into joining. In addition, men released from services undertaking work done by the FAU were being transferred to fighting units. Corder and Laurence had been granted certificates of absolute exemption, but were being joined by men who exemption from military service was conditional on that very membership. This was, for Corder, both illogical and immoral. Therefore, after long consideration he took the only course of action that seemed right to him. In May 1916 he resigned as an adjutant and saw his absolute exemption certificate withdrawn.

Corder had to appear at both a local and appeal tribunal. This gave him the opportunity to eloquently state his position:

Conscience does not primarily object and refuse, but commands. It commands loyalty to the voice of God in the heart … I have little desire for my own safety and comfort, when hundreds of thousands of my fellowmen of all nations are laying down their lives. Most strong young men to whom the ideal makes an appeal are possessed by a passion for adventure and sacrifice in a noble cause. I am no exception: I understand

and honour those, my comrades, who have enlisted in the army to fight, as they believe for right ...

But I too am enlisted, not merely for three years or the duration of the war, under a Captain who also calls for adventure and sacrifice in His name: whose commands to me are unmistakeable, not only to act towards enemies in a very different spirit, and to overcome them redemptively with very different weapons from those which are being used on the battlefields to-day; but also to proclaim His commands and to win recruits to His cause ... I cannot undertake 'alternative service' under the Conscription Act for this would imply a bargain with militarism which I believe to be utterly wrong.[21]

Therefore, whilst acknowledging the integrity of the positions taken by others of his generation, Corder found himself moving in the opposite direction to Laurence Cadbury. The Military Service Act had forced his hand out of the FAU and into the tribunal system. For Laurence, it nearly sent him the other way, into the army.

Laurence Cadbury was far from being an absolutist conscientious objector. On a number of occasions during the war he expressed an interest in entering regular service. His papers contain an uncompleted application for a temporary commission in the Royal Fleet Auxiliary (RFA), posted to him as far back as March 1915. A couple of weeks later he received a letter from his friend Norman Birkett, who in 1945 was to serve as the British judge at the Nuremburg War Trials, written in the style of a court case:

May I please your Lordship ...
a) The work you are now doing is without question very valuable, and as far as 'doing your bit' is concerned, you couldn't do anything else of more value to the State ...
b) As far as public life is concerned, you can hold your head with the best. For after all you have been in the thick of it from the beginning, and not like some officers who have been safely in the country all the time, and who have yet received admiration from all and sundry.[22]

Whilst recognising the status that might be gained by an army commission, Birkett summarised, 'My Lord, I am of opinion that you ought to stick to the Unit and not join the RFA.'

In March 1918 Laurence received another letter, this time from Sir George Newman, chairman of the FAU, which also pleaded for him to remain with the unit, saying that he would see far less action in the regular army than with the FAU. In addition, Newman reminded Laurence of his indispensability and of the 'generally bracing effect you have on the Unit: you are a very cheerful dog'.[23] On the reverse of this letter Laurence had listed the pros and cons of staying with the FAU. One of the reasons for considering leaving was the future 'shame of not being a combatant'. Despite his Croix de Guerre, Laurence evidently felt that he would be stigmatised in years to come for his sincerely held stance in the war. This demonstrates that Laurence persistently examined his conscience and reviewed his position in the light of unfolding events. He did not take a position and rigidly stick to it, just as his friend Corder Catchpool reviewed and changed his position. For Laurence this led to further honours and recognition. For Corder it meant imprisonment and ill health.

Corder had returned to England to study international relations at Woodbrooke Settlement in Birmingham and was one of seven men whose arrests were reported in the local press in January 1917.[24] From there the men were taken to barracks at Worcester, where Corder wrote, 'My Friends at the front give their lives in one way – I must give mine in another. I want these experiences to make me fitter for a life dedicated to the service of God and men.'[25] The men were ordered to put on a military uniform, refused, were court-martialled and sentenced to 112 days' hard labour, this being served at Wormwood Scrubs. On their release, the cycle of refusal to obey military orders, court martial and imprisonment was repeatedly undergone. However, Corder drew strength from placing himself in the tradition of Quaker resistance, stating at his third court martial in October 1917:

Two and a half centuries ago our Quaker ancestors were filling the dungeons of the land, dying often of exhaustion in prison before they reached the age of thirty, giving their young lives to the cause of religious freedom … We are suffering imprisonment today, and are prepared to suffer death ... to help in shaping a new world from which the dark clouds of war shall have rolled away for ever.[26]

At his fourth court martial, Corder made the point of wearing his Mons ribbon, awarded to those who had seen action in the very earliest stages of the war, as it symbolised for him the work he had done helping the wounded and dying. In all, Corder appeared before four court martials and served three years' imprisonment, finally being released in 1919, his health temporarily broken by pneumonia.

Before his return to civilian life, in December 1918 Laurence received a confidential letter from the Home Office informing him that his name was to be submitted for an Order of the British Empire (OBE) for his work in the war. This award was announced in the New Year's honours list of 1919 with the investiture taking place on 25 February. Among the letters of congratulations he received was one from the commanding officer of the American Red Cross in Belgium:

> In spite of the amount of joking we do when we are around you I think all of us appreciate the mighty good work, which you have done, and the serious purpose that has been in all your shooting about with the *Beetle*.[27]

Following the war Laurence Cadbury became a director of the Bank of England, served in a British Economic Mission to Moscow on behalf of the British Government during the Second World War, helping to keep the supply lines open to Britain's new allies. Eventually, in 1944, he succeeded his brother Edward as head of the famous chocolate company.

Corder Catchpool continued to work for peace and reconciliation, moving to Germany to undertake relief work. During the Second World War he campaigned against the Allied bombing of Germany and was suspected by MI5 of being involved in subversive activities due to this position.

Both Laurence Cadbury and Corder Catchpool were initially drawn to serve the Belgian and French people in the early stages of the war. Their Quaker faith led them to believe that taking up arms against a fellow man was wrong. However, as that faith laid a great emphasis on the freedom of thought of the individual, both men continually reviewed their positions as both the nature of the work of the FAU, and the political climate in Britain, changed its emphasis to a more military outlook. For Laurence, this meant wrestling with his conscience as to whether he should stand alongside his countrymen in the great sacrifices being made. For Corder, it meant standing alongside those who resisted being told by the government to be part of the mass slaughter being enacted on various fronts. That two men from the same faith, starting out on the same path in the war, should come to such different conclusions demonstrates not only the different ways in which faith could be interpreted in the war, but the central importance of that faith in modulating those responses.

Part VI

Families in War

'Alas! for homes, where sorrow, Like night must ever brood'

One fact that differentiates the generation who experienced the First World War from their descendants a hundred years on is that of typical family size. Many parents saw three, four, five or more sons go to war, with daughters serving in hospitals, industry and elsewhere.

Mary Riley of St Helens, Lancashire, lost four sons in the war, the other returning home suffering from shell shock and dying of tuberculosis in 1922. She walked the streets of her home town knocking on doors to collect pennies for the local war memorial, which now stands in Victoria Square.

The Souls family of Great Rissington, Gloucestershire, lost five sons. Alf and Arthur Souls were identical twins. Born an hour apart, they died five days apart. Fred Souls was never found but his mother Annie kept a candle burning in her window in the hope that he would return. Annie got a shilling a week for each dead son and a letter from Prime Minister Herbert Asquith in 1916 conveying the 'sympathy of the King and Queen for Mrs Souls in her great sorrow' after three of the boys had been killed. Asquith himself had a son who was killed in the war. The painfulness of the memories saw family papers later burned by Annie.

The Beechey family of Lincolnshire saw eight sons go to war, with five of them killed and a sixth left permanently disabled by a sniper's bullet. Like Annie Souls, Amy Beechey thought little of the official recognition of her sacrifice. Having been reduced from the vicarage of Priesthorpe to a two-up, two-down house in Lincoln on the death of her vicar husband, in April 1918 she was presented to King George and Queen Mary, who honoured her for her sacrifice. She replied, 'It was no sacrifice, Ma'am. I did not give them willingly.'

Some families had members who took very different directions in the war. We have already met Laurence Cadbury, who agonised over how his war service in the Friends' Ambulance Unit would look when set aside that of his brother. The war also caused a rift between Tom Attlee, who served two years in prison as a conscientious objector, and his brother Clement, who served as an officer in the South Lancashire Regiment at Gallipoli and later became Deputy Prime Minister in the Second World War, and arguably Britain's greatest ever peacetime prime minister from 1945 to 1951.

The Pope family of Dorset has, to the knowledge of the author, the most numerous and extensive war record of any family in the war, with ten sons, four daughters and three sons-in-law all engaged in war service of some kind. The Huntriss family of Mattersey, Nottinghamshire, represents the thousands of young men commemorated on war memorials in parish churches up and down the country. Usually bearing the names of young junior officers of public school education, these commemorate young men who, had the war not intervened, would have been the flower of their generation. As it was, Charlotte Huntriss lost everyone and chose to remember her trio of sons with a memorial window that is breathtaking in its beauty and setting (see plate 20).

Here we meet two families whose contribution to the war was exceptional. The Chavasse family of Liverpool, descended from French Huguenot ancestors, served in army chaplaincy, medicine, nursing and combat, with a slew of gallantry awards. One son, Noel, stands apart as the only man to be awarded two Victoria Crosses in the war. The Brocklesby family of Conisbrough, near Doncaster, again undertook a variety of roles, with two of their number coming close to death; one at the Battle of the Somme in 1916, the other condemned for his absolute objection to military service.

All these families were motivated by a sense of duty to varying degrees to their country, their god and each other. I trust their stories will provide reflection and inspiration for the reader.

Chapter 22

The Chavasse Family

'What should we do in such sorrow as this, if we could not rest on the character of God, on his love, and wisdom and righteousness

The family of Francis Chavasse achieved exceptional feats in the twentieth century. Francis himself instigated the building of Liverpool's Anglican Cathedral, now the longest cathedral in the world. One of his sons, Noel, became the only man to be awarded a double Victoria Cross during the First World War, and his twin daughters, May and Marjorie, became the first British twins to live to the age of 100 in 1986. In addition, three other sons served in the war and the family made a huge contribution to theological and medical life in Britain for many decades.

Francis Chavasse was born at Sutton Coldfield, Warwickshire, on 27 September 1846. The name Chavasse is of French Huguenot origin. His father, a surgeon, had planned for him to attend Chesterfield Grammar School, but he was educated privately due to a range of health problems. In 1865 Francis went up to Corpus Christi College, Oxford, and developed his views towards an evangelistic outlook whilst maintaining good relationships with those with high church views. He was awarded a first class degree in Law and Modern History in 1869.

Francis was ordained into the priesthood in 1870 and became curate at St Paul's at Preston, Lancashire. He was known as the 'Ministering Angel' for his insistence on visiting the sick during an epidemic. In 1873 he moved on to St John's, Upper Holloway, London, where he served as vicar for five years before returning to Oxford as rector of the evangelical St Peter-le-Bailey. *The Times* reported, 'He had a genius for pastoral work, and his parish became an important centre for those who preferred the simpler services and the more individual teaching of Evangelical Churchmanship.'[1]

In 1881 Francis married Edith Maude, younger daughter of Canon Joseph Maude, Vicar of Chirk, Denbighshire. They had seven children: four sons and three daughters. In 1889 he was appointed principal of Wycliffe Hall, Oxford, where he showed sympathy for a wide range of views beyond his evangelical ones.

In 1899, the octogenarian Bishop of Liverpool, J.C. Ryle, gave notice that he intended to retire on 1 March 1900. The Prime Minister, the Marquis of Salisbury, chose Francis to succeed him. Francis expressed some doubts about his ability to fulfil such a demanding and high profile role:

> A man with my feeble body, average ability and temperament can hardly be intended by God for such a diocese. God is blessing Wycliffe, and ought I to leave it at present? Can I not do more good by training bishops than becoming one?[2]

However, he overcame his doubts and was consecrated on 31 May 1900. His obituary stated that 'Liverpool welcomed him with acclamation and remained enthusiastically loyal to him.'[3]

As Liverpool had only become a bishopric in 1880, it lacked a cathedral. Despite some opposition from his own clergy that an expensive building was unnecessary, Francis argued that the building of a fine church would be 'a visible witness to God in the midst of a great city'.[4] At a public meeting to launch the scheme, he put forward the vision that, 'We must build for posterity, we must take a leaf out of the book of our noble forefathers, who have handed down to us those great Cathedrals which are among the greatest heritages of the English nation.'[5] Work began in 1904 under the direction of the 23-year-old Giles Gilbert Scott, whose other architectural achievements were to include Waterloo Bridge, Battersea Power Station and the red telephone box.

However, the onset of war in 1914 meant that men and materials were diverted to the war effort, and Francis did not see the progress he had hoped for in the building of the cathedral. He retired from his post in 1923, moving to Oxford, where he founded St Peter's Hall, an institution that allowed men of modest means to attend the university. Francis died aged eighty-one in 1929 and was buried beneath in the precinct of Liverpool Cathedral.

The eldest child of the Chavasse family was Dorothea, followed by Christopher, who was born twenty minutes before Noel on 9 November 1884, in Oxford. In many ways the boys' early lives followed the same trajectory. They both attended Magdalen College School, Oxford, from 1896 to 1900, and then Liverpool College from 1900 to 1904. From there they were both accepted into Trinity College, Oxford, and both competed in rugby and athletics. Both were selected to compete in the British team at the 1908 Summer Olympics in London, both in the 400 metres, and both being eliminated on the preliminary heats.

Whilst Noel chose a career in medicine, Christopher decided to follow his father into a pastoral role. He was ordained a deacon on 20 February 1910 and became curate of St Helens in Lancashire, which fell under his father's Liverpool diocese. He also played rugby league for the town team and formed a Harriers running club for young men. With Noel's assistance he formed a 'Rough Lads' Club', hiring premises to provide football and boxing opportunities. At the time, playing in the Rugby League meant that an individual would be barred from playing Rugby Union. Christopher forewent the opportunity to possibly play the latter code for Lancashire so he could identify himself with the team representing the town of St Helens, nicknamed 'The Saints'. When he was challenged as to why he was identifying himself with a sport played and watched by people with coarse manners and language, a 'company of sinners', he replied, 'Not sinners, the "Saints".'[6]

In 1914, Christopher became the first of the family to enlist, into the Army Chaplains' Department, and left for France in late August, being appointed chaplain to Number 10 General Hospital at St Nazaire. Like Francis Gleeson (see Chapter 7) he frequently wrote to the families of those he had ministered to in their final hours. For example, he wrote to the mother of Gunner Frank Wilkinson of Hull that:

He was wonderfully good, patient and brave … There was always a smile from him whenever I came to see him … He was a very good boy, and as he told me once, never forgot his prayers and was trusting in our Lord Jesus Christ … On October 1st came the sudden collapse … I was immediately fetched to his side in the morning, and had just time to whisper a prayer in his ear, and to feel him squeeze my hands ... and very peacefully passed away at 2.15 pm.[7]

Christopher also had to act as chaplain at the execution of a soldier, which affected him deeply and he had long conversations on the issue during meetings with Noel.

On 15 August 1916, Christopher was promoted from Chaplain to the Forces 4th Class (equivalent to captain) to Chaplain to the Forces 3rd Class (equivalent to major) and by 30 September 1918, he was promoted to Chaplain to the Forces 2nd Class (equivalent to lieutenant colonel).

Christopher was awarded the Military Cross for outstanding and consistent devotion to duty and his men. His citation, published in *The London Gazette* dating 25 August 1917, read:

> For conspicuous gallantry and devotion to duty. His fearlessness and untiring efforts in attending to the wounded were magnificent. Although continually under fire, he volunteered on every possible occasion to search for and bring in the wounded. No danger appeared to be too great for him to face, and he inspired others to greater effort by his splendid example.[8]

He was also awarded the French Croix de Guerre, 'for distinguished services rendered during the course of the campaign'.[9]

After the war, Christopher married Beatrice Willink in 1919, having three sons, Noel, Michael and John. He rose through the ranks of the Church of England, emulating his father in achieving the status of bishop, taking over the see of Rochester in 1940, serving until 1960. He continued the evangelistic tone set by Francis, chairing the Archbishops' Commission on Evangelism in 1943 and supporting the crusade of Billy Graham in 1955. He founded a church school in Rochester and was awarded the OBE in 1936.

Having followed the same educational path as he elder twin, Noel Chavasse graduated with first class honours in 1907 and stayed on at Oxford to study medicine. He also took a keen interest in the work of Grafton Street Industrial School in Liverpool, where he ran a Bible class, attended annual camps and otherwise supported boys from disadvantaged backgrounds.

In January 1909, he joined the Oxford University Officers' Training Corps Medical Unit. By the following May, he was promoted to lance sergeant. Noel finished his studies at Oxford in July 1909 and returned to Liverpool. He was admitted to the Royal College of Surgeons in 1910, having studied pathology and bacteriology at the Rotunda Hospital in Dublin.

In 1912, Noel was registered as a doctor with the General Medical Council, having been awarded Liverpool University's premier medical prize, and became a house surgeon at the Royal Southern Hospital, Liverpool. In 1913, Noel applied for and was accepted by the Royal Army Medical Corps and attached to the Territorial Army in the 10th Battalion of the King's (Liverpool Regiment), the Liverpool Scottish, as surgeon lieutenant.

Noel was preparing for a two-week summer camp with the battalion and signed the leave book at the Southern Hospital on 2 August 1914. However, he was never to return to his position. On 4 August 1914, Britain declared war on Germany, and on 9 October 1914, orders were received for the battalion to move to Tunbridge Wells in Kent, prior to moving overseas. Noel finally arrived in Le Havre on 2 November. He quickly got to work ensuring that he could proactively better the health of the men of the Liverpool Scottish, as well as tending to their wounds.

Noel was concerned at the possible effects of winter on his men, so treated the wounded with an anti-tetanus serum. This idea soon spread through the rest of the army, with millions of doses being used over the next four years. Many of the medical problems Noel had to treat were caused by conditions in the trenches, and the pervasive mud concerned Noel as it often meant it was impossible to observe good medical practice in keeping his hands clean when administering treatment. He also noticed the new phenomenon of trench foot. This proved a debilitating condition, not only for the individuals concerned but for the battalion as a whole. The ranks of the Liverpool Scottish were reduced from 829 men and twenty-six officers in November 1914, to 370 in total by January 1915, with just thirty-two of those losses being battle casualties.[10] Men of all ranks were also afflicted by lice. Noel sought to alleviate this and other problems by requesting his sister Dorothea post him singlets and socks for their physical comfort, and books, magazines and games for their entertainment.

As well as the physical needs of the men, Noel was also concerned about their moral and spiritual provision. Some of the battalion were billeted in a Belgian Catholic church and 'the men were very good and reverent, and I have not heard any swearing in the Church.'[11] He wrote of how the village carried on with their High Mass as the men slept in straw around the church. However, Noel had been unable to attend a Holy Communion between his departure from Liverpool in August 1914 and Christmas of the same year. He requested hymn sheets from home so he could conduct his own church parades in the absence of a chaplain. In his own dressing station he hung sacred pictures and wrote, in March 1915, 'I ask God daily to give me courage and patience for naturally I am not overburdened with either.'[12]

By August he had bought some hymn sheets and organised a choir in the battalion. Noel's opinion of religious provision in the army was mixed. Whilst he probably agreed with the analysis he heard that Christopher was bound to be a bishop one day, he found one Presbyterian chaplain a 'washout', who only worked on a Sunday, and personally disliked another.[13] This was a yawning gap to someone as keenly aware of the need for a strong rock on which to have a foundation in such terrible times, 'When they go into danger, our men … want a Fatherly God to keep an eye on them (and they seem to feel in their bones that there is such a person too) …'[14] Therefore, Noel used his Anglican prayer book at the burial services of many of the men of the Liverpool Scottish. He also took on some of the roles sometimes performed by army chaplains in writing lengthy comforting letters to the families of those he had treated.

The Liverpool Scottish was to play a key role in attack at Hooge on 14 June 1915. Noel later informed his father of various services that took place the day before: a Holy Communion for 130 Anglicans; eighty men attending a Presbyterian Communion; and fifty at a Roman Catholic Mass. The attack took a huge toll on the battalion, with only 130 men returning to camp out of 550. For his tireless work in treating the wounded and continually going into dangerous territory to search for more, Noel was awarded the Military Cross. The exact citation was lost in the confusion of wartime. He was eventually chosen to receive his award in person from King George V on 7 June 1916. In August 1915 he was promoted to captain.

During periods of leave Noel was able to return home and meet up with other family members who were supporting the war effort. His younger brother Bernard had served with the RAMC in Egypt and Gallipoli before proceeding to the Western Front, and his youngest brother, Aidan, had gained a commission with the King's (Liverpool Regiment). Marjorie was working as an assistant at the Beaconwood Auxiliary Hospital in Worcestershire, whilst May had progressed from there to serve in the Liverpool Hospital in France from 1915 through to 1918, being mentioned in despatches by Sir Douglas Haig. Like Christopher and Noel, Bernard too was to receive the Military Cross, in 1918.

On 7 August 1916, the Liverpool Scottish was involved in an assault on Guillemont, on the Somme. Battered by German shelling then exposed to heavy machine-gun fire, out of the twenty officers who attacked, five were killed, five were missing and seven were wounded. Of the 600 men, sixty nine were killed, twenty-seven were missing and 167 were wounded.

During the action, Noel was wounded by two small shell splinters in his back, but he continued his work, leading men into no-man's-land to bring in the wounded. After a short period of sick leave, Noel rejoined his battalion and continued to risk his life on a regular basis out in the thick of the action. His father heard informally through Lord Derby that he had been recommended for the Victoria Cross, along with gallantry awards for his stretcher bearers. Noel's award was confirmed in *The London Gazette* of 26 October 1916. The citation read:

During an attack he tended the wounded in the open all day, under heavy fire, frequently in view of the enemy. During the ensuing night he searched for wounded on the ground in front of the enemy's lines for four hours. Next day he took one stretcher bearer to the advanced trenches, and, under heavy fire, carried an urgent case for 500 yards into safety, being wounded in the side by a shell splinter during the journey. The same night he took up a party of trusty volunteers, rescued three wounded men from a shell hole twenty-five yards from the enemy's trench, buried the bodies of two officers and collected many identity discs, although fired on by bombs and machine guns. Altogether he saved the lives of some twenty badly wounded men, besides the ordinary cases which passed through his hands. His courage and self-sacrifice were beyond praise.[15]

The family was overwhelmed with congratulations and praise. However, this was not enough to prevent Noel becoming prey to army politics and he found himself transferred back to a smaller hospital away from the front. He had criticised the effectiveness of the RAMC's Field Ambulance Service, finding it was too slow to react and arrive where it was needed. His second criticism was of the treatment of venereal disease among troops. Numbers succumbing to such diseases had reached alarming proportions, with up to 15,000 men being affected at any one time.[16] By 1918 there were twenty hospitals in the United Kingdom entirely given over to its treatment.

The docking of pay and withholding of leave had not proved successful in combating the epidemic, so in 1915 the *Maisons de Tolerance* scheme was introduced, whereby a street was permitted as being in bounds for troops, with prostitutes allowed to ply their trade as long as they accepted hygiene advice from the British medical authorities. For Noel, so dedicated at maintaining the health and well-being of his men in any way possible, this was an issue of morality, not health; officers should set an example and not acquiesce in immoral practices.

By Christmas 1916, Noel had been transferred back to the Liverpool Scottish, and on 5 February 1917 he went again to Buckingham Palace to receive his Victoria Cross. The youngest Chavasse brother, Aidan, was transferred to the 17th Kings, a Pals battalion where his brother Bernard was medical officer. Although all four brothers had so far survived the war, the summer of 1917 and the Third Battle of Ypres (Passchendaele) was to prove a tragic one for the Chavasse family. On 1 July, at Observatory Ridge, about 5 miles from Ypres and a mile from Hooge, Lieutenant Aidan Chavasse and eight men were out on a raiding party when they met a German patrol. In the fighting, Aidan was wounded. When the party returned, Aidan was missing. Although his brother Bernard and some others went out to try to bring him back, he was never found.

For the Liverpool Scottish, the main offensive started at 3.50 am on 31 July. They had managed to break through the wire and achieve their main objectives by 7.45 am. Noel had moved his aid post forward with the attack and set it up in a captured German dugout at Setques Farm. However, he had been injured in the head by a shell splinter as he stood up and waved to indicate the position of the aid post. It is possible he suffered a fractured skull in this incident. After being dressed at the Wieltje dugout, Noel returned, despite advice to stay put, to his aid post. His stretcher bearers had been busy and Noel too was very busy until dusk. As night fell, Noel went out into the devastated landscape to look for survivors. It was raining again by this time.

Early the following day, Noel found a German captive who was a medic and the two of them worked hard to treat wounded men in the impossible conditions of mud, blood and water. Noel went to the door of the dugout to call in the next man when a shell flew past him and down the stairs, killing the man who was waiting to be carried away by the field ambulance. At about 3.00 am in the morning of 2 August, another shell entered the aid post as Noel slept. Everyone in the aid post was either killed or seriously wounded. Noel had received four or five wounds, the worst being a gaping abdominal wound from which he bled profusely. He managed to crawl up the stairs and out to another dugout, from where help was summoned.

Noel was sent to Casualty Clearing Station No. 32 at Brandhoek, which specialised in abdominal wounds. He was operated on immediately and after all the shell splinters had been removed he was patched up. He regained consciousness but died peacefully at 1.00 pm on 4 August 1917. Word reached Francis on 9 August.

The *Liverpool Echo* printed a letter from a Private Broomhall, who had been with Noel:

I last saw him attending to the wounded just after we had reached our objective on the 31st. His head was then bound up and covered with blood. Nevertheless he carried on, and later received another wound which apparently has proved fatal. Poor chap! A magnificent man! Absolutely without fear even in the most awful circumstances – how awful it would be impossible to describe.[17]

The Bishop wrote to Bernard, informing him of Noel's death:

You will have heard by this time that our dearest Noel has been called away ... Our hearts are almost broken, for oh! how we loved him ... again and again, we keep praising and thanking God for having given us such a son. We know he is with Christ, and that one day – perhaps soon – we shall see him again. What should we do in such sorrow as this, if we could not rest on the character of God, on his love, and wisdom and righteousness ...[18]

Noel was buried on 5 August. The whole battalion paraded and every medical officer at the hospital attended the funeral. King George V sent a personal message of condolence to Francis. Obituaries appeared in all the local press, the *British Medical Journal* and the national press. The *Daily Mail* had a picture of Noel. Christopher, being Noel's twin, was deeply affected. He had a sense that Noel had gone, even though he was 80 miles away at the time. Gladys, Noel's fiancée, was distraught. Back in Liverpool, a memorial service, ostensibly for the local men who had died at Passchendaele, was held on 29 August at 3.00 pm at St Nicholas' Church on the Mersey waterfront. The partly built cathedral wasn't big enough to hold everyone. The singing was accompanied by the sounds of a violent storm outside.

The *Liverpool Courier* wrote that:

It may be said that he fully lived up that standard of British pluck and bravery of which the great distinction of the Victoria Cross is the symbol ... It is not too much to say that a large number of men in the fighting line owe the fact they are alive today to his magnificent bravery and heroic self-sacrifice.[19]

The war continued, with Bernard's Military Cross being gazetted on 29 September. Early in September a letter arrived at the Bishop's Palace from Lord Derby that made the bishop break down in tears. It read:

I signed something last night which gave me the most mixed feelings of deep regret and great pleasure and that was the submission to His Majesty that a Bar should be granted to the Victoria Cross gained by your son. There is no doubt whatsoever that this will be approved and while it cannot in any way diminish your sorrow, still from the point of view of those who are your friends, it is a great pleasure to think that your son in laying down his life laid it down on behalf of his fellow countrymen, and that it is recognized, not only by those who knew him, but by the King and Country as a whole. In all the records of Victoria Crosses given I do not think there is one that will appeal to the British Public more than the record for which this Bar is to be given, and as I said at the beginning of my letter, it was a great pleasure to think that this recognition of his services is thus recorded.[20]

This award was announced in *The London Gazette* on 14 September 1917. The citation read:

Though severely wounded early in the action whilst carrying a wounded soldier to the dressing station, he refused to leave his post, and for two days, not only continued to perform his duties, but in addition, went out repeatedly under heavy fire to search for and attend to the wounded who were lying out. During these searches, although practically without food during this period, worn with fatigue and faint with his wound, he assisted to carry a number of badly wounded men over heavy and difficult ground. By his extraordinary energy and inspiring example was instrumental in rescuing many wounded who would have otherwise undoubtedly succumbed under the bad weather conditions. This devoted and gallant officer subsequently died of his wounds.[21]

Christopher described the long-lasting sense of loss of his twin and close companion:

I still mourn my Noel every day of my life, and have done so for forty-four years ... I seem still to think over things with Noel, and to feel he might walk into the room any minute. And sometimes I wake in the morning, feeling I have been with him in my sleep – and I believe that our spirits have been together.[22]

Noel is buried in Brandhoek's New Military Cemetery in Belgium. His grave is the only headstone in the world to have two Victoria Crosses engraved on it. The inscription, from John 15:13, *Greater love hath no man than this, that a man lay down his life for his friends*, was selected by Francis.

The Chavasse family left a huge imprint on the twentieth century. From Francis's vision that Liverpool should have a cathedral to reflect its importance as a British city, through the pastoral and educational legacy left by Christopher, the medical career of Bernard and the nursing contributions made by May and Marjorie, the former through both world wars, the lives of thousands of people were saved and materially improved by the work done by the family over many decades. Aidan had little chance to fulfil his potential before his early death. However, it is in the depth of devotion to his men, to his duty and to the ideals of his solid and sincere Christian faith that Noel showed to become the only person to be awarded a double Victoria Cross in the war, that the name of Chavasse will shine for evermore. (See plate 21.)

Chapter 23

The Brocklesby Family

'It is very difficult to understand how conscience drives men in exactly
opposite directions'

John Brocklesby was a grocer in the West Riding pit village of
Conisbrough. In addition to his business he served as a Justice of the
Peace, overseer of the poor and chairman of the parish council. At the
outbreak of the First World War, John and his wife Hannah had four grown-
up sons: George, aged twenty-seven; Bert (John Hubert), aged twenty-five;
Phil, aged twenty-one; and Harold, aged seventeen (see plate 22).

As well as his business and life of public service, John was a Methodist
lay preacher and attended the imposing chapel that had been built in
Conisbrough in 1877. It is possible that Bert inherited his fundamentalist
and literal outlook on life from his mother, who thought that the use of
pain-killing drugs was unnatural, as well as that fighting of any kind was a
shameful practice. Bert was taught that the Bible was the word of God and
he grew up dreaming of one day becoming a missionary. As a young man he
joined the Mission Band, which sought to convert people in the village to
Christianity, and he was the organist at the Methodist chapel.

Bert taught in the Methodist Sunday school, was a pupil-teacher at the
local school from the age of twelve, and in 1907 he left Conisbrough to attend
the Methodist College in London to undertake a teacher training course. He
returned to Yorkshire to take up a vacancy at a nearby school and assumed
the role of choirmaster at the chapel, where he caught the eye of a chorister
named Annie Wainwright.

When war broke out Bert was on a cycling holiday with his brother Harold
and a friend from college, Maurice Oliver. On reading the newspapers calling
for volunteers to join up, Bert resolved that 'However many might volunteer
yet I would not. God had called me to work for his kingdom. God had not put

me on earth to go destroying his own children.'[1] The rest of the Brocklesby family took a different view of their Christian duty during wartime. John was elected as chairman of Conisbrough's War Fund Committee, Hannah served on the Ladies' Committee for Soldiers' Relief and George assisted the recruiting sergeant in the hall next to the family's shop, later taking over the role when the sergeant left on active service.

In the light of this familial commitment to the war, along with the persistent recruitment campaigns of the time, Bert began to question whether his literal interpretation of the biblical commandment of 'Thou Shalt not Kill' was the correct position to take. Inspired by a story of the founder of Methodism, John Wesley, casting lots to decide on an important matter of personal morality in 1737, Bert decided to do something similar, tossing a coin repeatedly and getting a result of around twelve throws to one in favour of not enlisting.

However, rather than keeping this decision a matter of private conscience, for Bert it was a case of proclaiming the case against war. Using his position as a lay preacher, he spoke at the chapel one January evening in 1915, choosing as his text Romans 12:19-21, 'Dearly beloved, avenge not yourselves, but rather give place unto wrath: for it is written, Vengeance is mine; I will repay, saith the Lord.' Bert backed up this argument by citing that the Catholic Archbishop of Westminster, Cardinal Bourne, had commented that as Christians were fighting on all sides of the conflict, it was the job of those Christians to pray for a prompt end to the war. He also used the images conjured up by Dr Alfred Salter in his 1914 pamphlet, *Faith of a Pacifist*:

Look! Christ in khaki, out in France thrusting his bayonet into the body of a German workman ... See! The Son of God with a machine gun, ambushing a column of German infantry ... Hark! The Man of Sorrows in a cavalry charge ... No! No! That picture is an impossible one – and we all know it.[2]

This sermon caused a negative reaction in the Methodist community. Some considered Bert guilty of cowardice for speaking out against the war, whilst others resented the quoting of a Catholic archbishop in a Nonconformist chapel.

With George already busy in recruitment work and youngest brother Harold an officer in the University of Sheffield Training Corps, Phil Brocklesby had the difficult decision to make of whether to follow the rest of the family in actively supporting the war, in this case by enlisting, or to follow the path of his elder brother and hero, Bert, in opposing it. He was torn between taking on what he saw as his share of the responsibility currently being shouldered by others of his generation in fighting the Germans, and the fact that he had no strong anti-German or pro-war feelings himself. He decided on the former course of action and was enlisted by his brother, with his father as Justice of the Peace hearing his oath. He then went to nearby Pontefract to join the York and Lancaster Regiment, the Barnsley Pals.

By August 1915, Phil was in France. He was soon to witness friends he had made in the army being shot by snipers and began to have doubts about the righteousness of the war. Harold was involved in the Battle of Loos, finding himself lying in a shallow trench at the edge of the line of advance, being both shelled by his own artillery and shot at by the Germans. He too saw close comrades killed, an experience described in a local newspaper as 'a series of thrilling experiences'.[3] All four fellow officers in Harold's company were killed.

In October Phil was selected as a candidate for a commission and returned to England for officer training. However, things were not looking so positive for Bert. The Military Service Act had become law at the end of January 1916 and Bert, having claimed the conscience clause, was soon up before a tribunal in nearby Doncaster. The *Doncaster Gazette* reported:

A single elementary school teacher at Conisbrough applied for exemption on conscientious grounds to taking part in combatant service. On his appeal form he stated that he felt war was incompatible with Christian principles therefore he could not conscientiously take part therein.

The clerk stated that he had received a letter from [the] applicant's father stating that though he did not hold his son's views, after very careful conversation with him, he was fully persuaded he was sincere in his conviction. He did not think that he could engage in the operation of war without violating his conscience. Two of his sons held commissions in the army and the third an appointment under the military authorities.[4]

Bert was then given a series of scenarios and asked if would not fight in those circumstances. These included the enemy reaching Conisbrough Castle or another man knocking out his tooth. Bert argued these were hypothetical. When asked if he would use a revolver if six men were threatening him with open sword and bayonet, he stated that the Sixth Commandment was 'Thou shalt not kill' and therefore he would consider it better to be killed than to take another man's life.

It emerged there were around forty-five local members of the No Conscription Fellowship and that Bert would not undertake munitions work or minesweeping, and claimed:

I am ready to die for my principles. I am standing up for freedom of conscience of all Englishmen. You cannot bring evidence to prove conscientious objection. The only way to prove it is to be ready to suffer for it and if necessary die for it. As there are thousands of men who have been ready to sacrifice their lives for their country it would be a pity if some were not prepared to sacrifice them for a higher principle.[5]

Like other absolutists, Bert was granted exemption from combatant service as the tribunal accepted his case that he had a conscientious objection to taking life. They did not, however, accept his points about not wishing to be part of a wider war effort that was still aimed at killing people, so he was recommended for non-combatant service. Bert appealed, but one of the tribunal members was a political opponent of John Brocklesby who had publicly stated his intention to push Bert as far as he would go. The appeal was turned down but a local Methodist business owner, William Wilson, offered him the chance to work in his wool mill, thus becoming an essential worker. Bert politely refused this opportunity.

John Brocklesby doggedly refused to condemn his son's position. He was told that he should turn him out of the house and that Bert was in danger of being shot for sticking to his beliefs. John's reply was that he would rather Bert be shot for his beliefs than abandon them.

In May 1916 a policeman came to arrest Bert. He was taken to Doncaster Magistrates' Court and thence to Pontefract Barracks, the same place Phil had reported to the previous year. Unlike the welcome accorded to a new recruit, Bert was placed into a cramped room with a latrine in the corner that was flowing out onto the floor. He had taken his Teacher's Bible, which served as a makeshift pillow. The major in charge of Bert quickly decided that he belonged in Richmond Castle and so he was put on a train to Darlington and thence to the Norman castle, which was reminiscent of the one in his home village of Conisbrough. One section of the castle had been allocated as a training ground for the Non-Combatant Corps. There were eight cells ready to house those who refused to obey the military orders of the officers of the corps.

At Richmond Bert was given a series of tests. He agreed to peel potatoes under orders as they were to be eaten by his fellow conscientious objectors, but when he found out that they had been eaten by the officers he refused to peel any the following day. Things became more serious when he refused to appear on drill parade. He was challenged by a captain and stated that his idea of Christianity was not taking part in a war. Bert was placed in one of the cells, measuring 6 by 9 feet. The cells were meant to be solitary, but a hole left over from a previous heating system meant that Bert could peer through to make contact with Norman Gaudie, a fellow conscientious objector. The hole was big enough for Bert and Norman to pass a chess board through so that they could play games against each other.

As well as this recreational pursuit, Bert and Norman were able to conduct Bible studies together and sing hymns. Norman remembered a group rendition of *Nearer my God to Thee* involving a fellow prisoner, Alfred Myers. In all, sixteen conscientious objectors who refused to co-operate with Non-Combatant Corps orders were taken to Richmond Castle. They had a variety of religious affiliations and numbered amongst them were Jehovah's Witnesses, Methodists, a Quaker, a Congregationalist and a member of the Church of Christ. Others had political reasons for their objection, mainly based on socialist principles.

The officers attempted to break Bert physically by trying to force him to march to order, pushing his arms and legs to make him do so, but Bert fell to the ground and stayed there when his legs were pushed. On the wall of his cell Bert began a series of drawings that have recently been preserved by English Heritage, the keepers of the castle. Firstly he drew his sweetheart from Conisbrough, Annie Wainwright, and signed it 'J.H. Brocklesby fecit 22.5.16'. Bert's is not the only graffiti drawn on the walls by the prisoners that survives to this day. One wrote, 'If you take a sword and use it to run a fellow through then God will send a bill to you'. Another wrote, 'Brought up from Pontefract and put into this cell for refusing to be made a soldier', and yet another wrote, 'Stand firm let the nation see that men should brothers be'. Perhaps the most moving piece is a drawing by Bert of a man lying on the ground struggling under the burden of a heavy cross, with the caption, 'Every cross grows light Lord beneath / The shadow Lord of Thine. Jesus Hominum Salvator'.

The military authorities grew to despair of their attempts to make the sixteen absolutist conscientious objectors at Richmond into soldiers. A decision was made to send them to France, the thinking being that as they would be officially part of a force in a war zone, their refusal to follow orders would then be a court-martial offence, one potentially punishable by death. An additional party of seventeen conscientious objectors from the south of England, including Howard Marten, were to be subject to the same challenge as the Richmond sixteen, as well as smaller parties from elsewhere, making forty-nine men in all. On 29 May 1916, the Richmond sixteen were taken to Darlington railway station and spent three hours singing hymns as they waited on the platform for their train to arrive. They entrained for London, then Southampton, where they were placed in handcuffs and taken on board ship. They were allowed on deck for an hour, a time they spent on further hymn singing and Christian fellowship.

Bert had managed to use a standard military postcard to cross out certain words and parts of words to relay the message home that 'I am being sent ... to ... b ... long'. From that his family worked out that he was being transferred to France.

The men were then taken by train to a camp at Henriville, near Boulogne. Told that they were now on active service, they were given twenty-four hours to think through the punishment for disobeying orders. However, the sixteen decided that they would, in the words of Leonard Renton, an International Bible Student (Jehovah's Witness) from Leeds, go 'to the last ditch'.[6] The following day an non-commissioned officer ordered them to parade, but when he found out they were conscientious objectors he decided not to carry on with the exercise as he wanted no part in them being shot for disobeying orders. On the next day they were taken down to the dock and each told to pick up a case of bully beef. In turn, each man refused and the group was taken to a guardroom to await the court martial.

Once again, Bert argued his case that killing was contrary to the Ten Commandments, and then waited to hear his sentence. Phil Brocklesby had promised his parents that he would look for Bert in Boulogne when he reached France. He finally found his brother, who had recently been deloused, and managed to use his rank of second lieutenant to negotiate thirty minutes that he could spend with him. Phil's visit was a welcome boost to the others too, as it made them realise that they were not entirely cut off from sympathetic peers. He later reported that Bert seemed cheerful and that the sentence for the first four objectors was to be announced shortly.

At 4.45 pm on 24 June 1916, hundreds of men of the Non-Combatant Corps and Labour Battalions were marched onto the parade ground and ordered to form three sides of a square. Phil had managed to delay his return to his battalion and formed one of the spectators. They watched four conscientious objectors – Howard Marten, Harry Scullard, Jack Foister and Jonathan Ring – be brought forward. Marten was called forward and told he was to suffer death by shooting. After a deliberately long pause, the adjutant then added that this had been confirmed by the commander-in-chief, General Sir Douglas Haig, but had been commuted to penal servitude for ten years. Phil Brocklesby felt his heart relax and his tension disappear. It was clear that the authorities were not going to execute those who had stuck relentlessly to their sincere beliefs.

Bert heard this news while sitting in the guardroom. He too experienced a great relief, and felt that ten years' imprisonment held no terrors for him. Phil managed to get some money through to Bert before he returned to his depot at Étaples. He found that his absence had been reported, but this misdemeanour was not followed up. Phil wrote to his father in the couched terms of a letter that was subject to military censorship, saying, 'I may say that up to the present the extreme penalty has not been carried out and I don't think it will be in Bert's case.'[7] He also wrote to Bert, expressing, 'I wish I had your faith, Bert, but your example even before the War has helped me tremendously. Adieu Bert, God guard and protect you. I pray God will open his mouth and stop these puny strivings of men.'[8]

The case of Bert and the thirty-four other men who had their death penalty commuted to penal servitude was raised in the House of Commons, with Prime Minister Herbert Asquith declaring that, from that point on, 'no soldier will be sent to France who we have good reason to believe is a conscientious objector.'[9] Some of them, including Bert, were taken to Rouen and then back to England. As they crossed the sea from France, the Battle of the Somme had begun behind them, with Phil Brocklesby in the thick of it. He had been appointed to command D Company of the 13th Battalion of the York and Lancaster Regiment, the Barnsley Pals. Their objective for 1 July, the first day of the battle, was to take the village of Serre. On the night before, Phil led his men in prayer that 'God's will be done', and at 7.30 am the next morning he led his men out of the trenches, pulling some up by the hand. He received a slight wound in the leg but did not feel the pain until he reached a forward trench. The advance was then called off due to the severe causalities the battalion had incurred. After three days in the trenches, during which they had to undertake the gruesome task of recovering what pieces of British bodies they could find, Phil and his men were relieved. They had suffered a 50 per cent loss. A fortnight later, younger brother Harold went into the same battle and was shot in the arm – a Blighty wound.

Remarkably, as 1916 ended, Bert had survived the death penalty, Phil had survived the carnage of the first day of the Battle of the Somme with a minor wound as the Barnsley Pals were being cut to pieces, and Harold had survived the same battle with a more substantial, but potentially life-saving, wound.

On his return to England, Bert was taken to Winchester Prison. Here a strict rule of silence was enforced for the prisoners. He encountered a different interpretation of his Christian faith from the Anglican prison chaplain, who told Bert he was 'a disgrace to humanity', and from another that Christ would have spat in his face.[10] The objectors were ordered to sew sacks, which they refused to do when they found they would be for military use, and were put on bread and water as a punishment. Bert was allowed just one visit from his father, mother and fiancée, Annie Wainwright.

At the same time that Bert was suffering punishment in prison, Phil was undergoing the suffering of the trenches as the war ground on into a third winter. At one point he wrote, 'GOD isn't in this war, it is the DEVIL, devilism.' Later in 1918 he wrote of the 'hell' he was experiencing, and of 'gradually losing faith in mankind'.[11]

Under the Home Office scheme to have the objectors doing work of national importance, rather than refusing to sew sacks, Bert was sent to Dyce Camp in Aberdeen, where Howard Marten and a group of other objectors were working. In a rebellious gesture, he left the camp without permission and caught a train to Conisbrough, being arrested six days later. The scheme was wound up shortly afterwards and Bert was sent to Maidstone Prison, where Phil and Harold were able to visit him. During a visit by the Methodist prison chaplain, The Reverend Robert Wardell, Bert heard words that sum up the widely varying reactions and experiences to the Great War contained in this book: 'It is very difficult to understand how conscience drives men in exactly opposite directions.'[12] Apart from these visits, a rule of absolute silence was observed, which was difficult for the intelligent, articulate and opinionated conscientious objectors to follow.

Early in 1918, Phil returned to England under an order that junior officers who had spent a long period of service abroad be replaced by those who had spent the majority of the war on home service. He was placed in the Huntingdon Cyclist Battalion to patrol the north-eastern coast of England. All four Brocklesby brothers were now in safe environments. On 12 April 1919, five months after the end of the war, Bert was released from prison and returned to Doncaster to be met by his three brothers and Annie Wainwright, whose brother Gilbert had been killed in October 1918.

Bert was offered his old teaching job by the headteacher of his school, but found himself resented by other people in the town who could never bring themselves to accept his decision. Therefore, he volunteered to serve in Vienna with the Friends War Victims Relief. This was too much for Annie, who accused him of feeding the people who had killed her brother. She broke off their engagement shortly afterwards. Bert briefly returned to England to teach and joined the Quakers. He then travelled to Russia to work in relief for the famine caused by the civil war there. His later career involved missionary work, more teaching and campaigning against nuclear weapons.

John Brocklesby died on Christmas Day 1927, widely respected by his local community. Phil went on to run a successful pharmacy business, firstly in Hull and then back in Consibrough, where he became chairman of the local British Legion and a major in the Home Guard in the Second World War, for which he was awarded the MBE.

The Brocklesby family had vastly different experiences of the First World War. Whilst two of them actively recruited for the military, and two fought steadfastly in appalling conditions, Bert stood out stubbornly to the point of being willing to sacrifice his life for his beliefs. What is striking is that despite the pressure on the other members of the family to disown Bert due to his stand, none of them did, providing another example of the centrality of their faith being love of their fellow man, which served to unite them.

Conclusion

'The Lord gave and the Lord hath taken away. Blessed be the name of the Lord'

This book has taken the reader on a journey from the home fires, hospitals and recruiting offices of Britain, through the Western Front in Belgium and France, on to Germany, through to the biblical lands of Salonica and Mesopotamia; from the prisoner of war camps of Eastern Germany to the military and civilian prisons of England and Scotland, and from the American Midwest to a German U-boat patrolling the Mediterranean. I would like to end that journey at a quiet English village church. Our parish churches collectively contain many thousands of memorials, in the form of tablets, brasses, windows, parchments, clocks and embroidery, to young men and women who paid the ultimate price for a cause. It is significant that so many chose to have their loved ones memorialised in their local church, emphasising the deep vein of Christian faith that ran through British society in the first decades of the twentieth century. (See plate 23.)

Mattersey is a village at the northernmost tip of Nottinghamshire, just a few miles from the borders with both Yorkshire and Lincolnshire. Prominent in the village is All Saints Church, which has stood on its present site since the thirteenth century. Opposite is Mattersey Hall, today a training centre for Christian ministers. The ruins of a former priory are a mile down a country track. As you enter the church, which is nearly always open, you are struck by a sense of timelessness and peace. Your eyes flit round to note the usual features of an English parish church: the altar, the clerestory and the pulpit. If you care to give attention to the eagle-shaped lectern you will notice a brass belt inscription:

To the glory of God and in grateful memory of William Huntriss of
Mattersey Hall
who died on 26th November 1912,
from his loving wife and three sons.

Move your gaze round further and your eyes eventually alight on a stained-glass window of vivid colour and breathtaking beauty, situated to the right of the oak door. The window depicts Christ surrounded by five soldiers, two of them kneeling, one with his foot on the cross of St George, and three of them standing. Christ is holding a crown in both hands and above him is the inscription from Revelation 2:10:

Be Thou Faithful Unto Death and I Will Give Thee a Crown of Life.

Beneath the images is a lengthy inscription:

IN EVER LOVING MEMORY OF LIEUT. WILLIAM HUNTRISS 3rd DUKE OF WELLINGTON'S WEST RIDING REGIMENT (ATTACHED TO GOLD COAST REGIMENT), BORN DECEMBER 16th 1886: DIED OCTOBER 23rd 1918 AT COOMASSIE, AFRICA. CAPT. HAROLD EDWARDS HUNTRISS. 1st BATTALION BEDFORDSHIRE REGIMENT; BORN MAY 23rd 1890; DIED OF WOUNDS AT FESTUBERT, FRANCE MAY 17th 1915. CAPT. CYRIL JOHN HUNTRISS, 1st BATTALION EAST YORKSHIRE REGIMENT; BORN JANUARY 29th 1893; KILLED AT FRICOURT, FRANCE JULY 1st 1916.

THE THREE SONS OF WILLIAM HUNTRISS LATE OF MATTERSEY HALL AND CHARLOTTE ELIZABETH HIS WIFE.

'The Lord gave and the Lord hath taken away.
Blessed be the name of the Lord.'

The three brothers – everything that the widowed Charlotte Huntriss had left in the world – were all lost to the war. Charlotte chose to formally and publicly commemorate their sacrifice in the church that stood opposite the house in which they had grown up. She chose words of comfort from the Bible.

Visit most churches in Britain and you will find memorials both inside and outside the buildings to men and women who paid the ultimate price during the Great War. In many of those churches their names are still read out each Remembrance Sunday. It is fitting to do so. They all fought the good fight, many enthusiastically, some reluctantly, but all faced the duty demanded of them by their country from 1914 to 1918. We can stand a century away from this time and wonder at the values that drove them to this duty, as well as the role played by Christianity in forming those perspectives. Although long dead, they should be forever remembered.

It is my hope that this book has stimulated thought and appreciation, not just of those men, but of others; those who served enthusiastically and survived, those who served reluctantly and survived, those who absolutely refused to serve, those women who served in the ways open to them in 1914 and those who saw their families torn apart by war. At the very heart of all their experience of war was their Christian faith. In an age that often seeks to deride religious faith, it is perhaps worth taking time to reflect on the achievements of a generation that did not so lightly dismiss Britain and Europe's Christian heritage.

Notes

Part I: Christian Britain in 1914

1. Philip Jenkins, *The Great and Holy War: How World War I Changed Religion For Ever*, p.28, Lion Books, Oxford, 2014.
2. David French, *Raising Churchill's Army: the British Army and the War against Germany, 1919–1945*, p.147, Oxford University Press, 2000.
3. Michael Snape, *God and the British Soldier*, p.5, Routledge, Abingdon, 2005.
4. Ibid, p.6.
5. Adrian Hastings, *A History of English Christianity, 1920–1985*, p.41, Collins, London, 1986.
6. R. Currie, A. Gilbert & L. Horsley, *Churches and Churchgoers: Patterns of Church Growth in the British Isles since 1700*, p.31, Clarendon Press, Oxford, 1977.
7. Adrian Gregory, *The Last Great War: British Society and the First World War*, p.159, Cambridge University Press, 2008.
8. Alan Robinson, *Chaplains at War: The Role of Clergymen during World War Two*, p.10, I.B. Tauris, London, 2008.
9. Quoted in Alan Wilkinson, *The Church of England and the First World War*, p.218, SPCK, London, 1978.
10. Ibid, p.27.
11. Robinson, p.11.
12. See for example S.C. Williams, *Religious Belief and Popular Culture in Southwark, c. 1880–1939*, Oxford University Press, 1999, and J. Cox, *English Churches in a Secular Society: Lambeth 1870–1930*, Oxford University Press, 1982.
13. Gregory, p.152.
14. Wilkinson, p.7.
15. *The Primitive Methodist Sunday School Hymnal*, preface, Primitive Methodist Publishing House, London, 1911.
16. *The Sunday Post*, Sunday, 21 February 1915.
17. *The Times*, 19 August 1916, p.9.
18. Wilkinson, p.61.
19. Quoted in John Wolffe, 'Protestantism, Monarchy and the Defence of Christian Britain, 1837–2005' in Callum Brown and Michael Snape (eds.), *Secularisation in the Christian World*, p.64, Ashgate, Farnham, 2010.
20. Wilkinson, p.153.
21. Richard Schweitzer, *The Cross and the Trenches: Religious Faith and Doubt among British and American Great War Soldiers*, p.31, Praeger, Westport, 2003.
22. *Nottingham Evening Post*, Saturday, 3 January, 1914, p.7.
23. *Bath Chronicle and Weekly Gazette*, Saturday, 6 February 1915, p.2.
24. *The Times*, 19 August 1916, p.9.
25. *Derby Daily Telegraph*, Tuesday, 3 October 1916, p.2.
26. *The Times*, 15 September 1917, p.9.
27. Ibid.
28. Archbishops' Committee of Inquiry, Reports, p.169, SPCK, London, 1919.

Chapter 1: John Reith
1. Ian McIntyre, *The Expense of Glory: A Life of John Reith*, p.3, HarperCollins, London, 1993.
2. Ibid, p.4.
3. Ibid, p.10.
4. John Reith, *Into the Wind*, p.6, Hodder & Stoughton, London, 1949.
5. Personal scrapbook, quoted in McIntyre, p.13.
6. Ibid, p.15.
7. Ibid, p.21.
8. John Reith, *Wearing Spurs*, p.33, Hutchinson & Co, London, 1966.
9. Ibid, p.65.
10. Quoted in McIntyre, p.36.
11. *Wearing Spurs*, p. 154.
12. Quoted in McIntyre, p.43.
13. John Reith, letter to father, 3 April 1915.
14. Ibid, 22 March 1917.

Chapter 2: David Jones
1. W.H. Auden, 'The Geste Says this and the Man Who was on the Field', *Mid-Century Review* 39, p.12, March 1962.
2. David Jones, *In Parenthesis*, p.166, Faber & Faber, London, 1961.
3. Quoted in Thomas Dilworth, *David Jones and the Great War*, p.116, Enitharmon Press, London, 2012).
4. Jones, *In Parenthesis*, p.183.
5. Dilworth, p.117.
6. Ibid, p.142.
7. Ibid, p.152.
8. Thomas Dilworth, 'Eliot for David Jones', in Benjamin G. Lockherd, (ed.) *T.S. Eliot and Christian Tradition*, p.285, Farleigh Dickinson University Press, 2014.
9. Dilworth, *Great War*, p.216.
10. Jones, *In Parenthesis*, p.vii.

Chapter 3: J.V. Salisbury
1. University of Leeds Special Collections, Liddle Archive, J.V. Salisbury Papers, GALL 90/1.
2. Ibid.
3. Ibid.
4. Ibid.
5. Ibid.
6. Ibid.
7. Ibid.
8. Ibid.
9. Ibid.
10. Ibid.
11. Ibid.
12. Liddle Collection, University of Leeds, J.V. Salisbury Papers, GALL 90 / 9a.

Chapter 4: Joseph Garvey
1. Joseph Garvey, *Fresh in my Memory Always*, p.9, PDG Books, Ilkley, 2012.
2. Ibid, p.22.
3. Ibid, p.69.
4. Ibid, p.91.
5. Ibid, p.99.
6. Ibid, p.170.

Chapter 5: Lewis Valentine
1. *Manchester Courier and Lancashire General Advertiser*, 27 January 1916.
2. *Brecon and Radnor Express*, 2 March 1916.
3. Lewis Valentine, *Dyddiadur Milwr A Gweithau Eraill*, 21 October 1916.
4. Ibid, 14 November 1916.
5. Quoted in http://daibach-welldigger.blogspot.co.uk/#!/2013/08/lewis-valentine-prophet-among-people.html <accessed 24 March 2015>.
6. Valentine, 21 July 1917.
7. Ibid, 30 July 1917.
8. Ibid, 4 August 1917.
9. Ibid, 8 August 1917.
10. Quoted in http://daibach-welldigger.blogspot.co.uk/#!/2013/08/lewis-valentine-prophet-among-people.html <accessed 24 March 2015>.
11. Quoted in http://daibach-welldigger.blogspot.co.uk/#!/2013/08/lewis-valentine-prophet-among-people.html <accessed 24 March 2015>.
12. Quoted in Arwel Vittle, *Valentine Cofiant I Lewis Valentine*, p.73, Y Loifa Cyf, Talybont, 2006.
13. Quoted in http://daibach-welldigger.blogspot.co.uk/#!/2013/08/lewis-valentine-prophet-among-people.html <accessed 24 March 2015>.

Chapter 6: Philip Bryant
1. Jonathan Greaves, *A Christian in Khaki*, p.28, Monk Street Publishing, Monmouth, 2014.
2. Ibid, p.166.
3. Ibid, p.51.
4. Ibid, p.65.
5. Ibid, p.69.
6. Ibid, p.71.
7. Ibid, p.84.
8. Ibid, p.98.
9. Ibid, p.111.
10. Ibid, p.44.
11. Ibid, p.111.

Part II: Three Chaplains and an Army Scripture Reader
1. Alan Wilkinson, *Dissent or Conform: War, Peace and the English Churches, 1900–1945*, SCM Press, London, 1986.
2. Michael Snape, 'Church of England Chaplains in the First World War: Goodbye to "Goodbye to All That"', *Journal of Ecclesiastical History*, Vol. 62, Issue 2, April 2011, p.318.
3. Ian Dobbie, *Sovereign Service The Story of SASRA, 1836–2013*, p.52, SASRA, 2013.

Chapter 7: Father Francis Gleeson
1. Dublin Diocesan Archives (DDA), Fr. Francis A. Gleeson Papers, P101/2, December 1914.
2. Robert Graves, *Good-bye to All That: An Autobiography*, p.241, Jonathan Cape, London, 1929.
3. *The Tablet*, 10 July 1915, p.3.
4. DDA, Gleeson, P101/4.
5. Mrs Victor Rickard, *The Story of the Munsters at Etreux, Festubert, Rue du Bois and Hulloch*, p.112, Hodder & Stoughton, London, 1915.
6. DDA, Gleeson, P101/4.
7. *Cork Examiner*, 9 June 1915, p.2.
8. DDA, Gleeson, P101/4.
9. Ibid, P101/4.
10. Ibid, P101/4.

Chapter 8: John Esslemont Adams
1. J. Esslemont Adams, *The Chaplain and the War*, p.30, T&T Clark, Edinburgh, 1915.
2. *Aberdeen Journal*, 28 December 1914, p.4.
3. Quoted in Malcolm Brown & Shirley Seaton, *Christmas Truce: The Western Front, December 1914*, p.87, Pan Books, London, 1994.
4. Ibid, p.89.
5. Adams, p.38.
6. Ibid, p.39.
7. Ibid, p.43.
8. Ibid, p.44.
9. *Aberdeen Weekly Journal*, 11 August 1916, p.7.
10. University of Leeds, Special Collections, Liddle Archive, J. Esslemont Adams Papers, GS/0527.

Chapter 9: Russell Barry
1. F.R. Barry, *Period of My Life*, p.15, Hodder & Stoughton, London, 1970.
2. Ibid, p.22.
3. Ibid, p.23.
4. Ibid, p.37.
5. Ibid, p.44.
6. Ibid, p.51.
7. Ibid, p.52.
8. Ibid, p.53.
9. Ibid, p.61.
10. Ibid, p.54.
11. Ibid, p.56.
12. Ibid, p.57.
13. Ibid, p.63.
14. *The Times*, 25 October 1976, p.15.

Chapter 10: Harry Wisbey
1. SASRA register.
2. Harry Wisbey, *Rough Journal*, Postscript, SASRA, 2014.
3. Ibid.
4. Ibid, 13 August 1914.
5. Ibid.
6. Ibid, 14 August 1914.
7. Ibid, 16 August 1914.
8. Ibid, 16 August 1914.
9. Ibid, 17 August 1914.
10. Ibid, 17 August 1914.
11. Ibid, 18 August 1914.
12. Ibid, 21 August 1914.
13. Ibid, 23 August 1914.
14. Ibid.
15. Ibid.
16. Ibid, 24 August 1914.
17. Ibid, 25 August 1914.
18. Ibid, 26 August 1914.
19. Ibid, 27 August 1914.
20. Ibid, 28 August 1914.
21. Ibid.

22. Ibid, 31 August 1914.
23. Ibid, 1 September 1914.
24. Ibid, 2 September 1914.
25. Ibid, 3 September 1914.
26. Ibid, 9 September 1914.
27. Ibid, Postscript.

Part III: Women in War
 1. Arthur Marwick, *Women at War, 1914–1918*, p.167–168, Fontana, London, 1977.
 2. D. Shaw, 'The Forgotten Army of Women: Queen Mary's Army Auxiliary Corps' in H. Cecil and P. Liddle (eds.), *Facing Armageddon: The First World War Experienced*, p.8, Leo Cooper, London, 1996.
 3. Elinor Lewis, *Hearts and Lives Given to Christ: Twenty-Four Bible Lessons for Young Women's Classes*, p.i, Society for Promoting Christian Knowledge, London, 1910.
 4. Ibid, pp.57 and 85.
 5. *Aberdeen Journal*, 5 January 1909, p.4.
 6. *Derby Daily Telegraph*, Wednesday, 26 February 1902, p.4.
 7. *Evening Post, Angus Scotland*, Wednesday, 15 March 1905, p.4.
 8. *Aberdeen Journal*, Monday, 17 January 1916, p.2.

Chapter 11: Lilian Hayman
 1. Imperial War Museum Department of Documents 948, Philip T. Bryant to Mrs Hayman, 21 March 1915.
 2. IWM 948, Bryant to Hayman, 27 March 1915.
 3. IWM 948, Tony Hewitt to Mrs Hayman, 17 January 1915.
 4. IWM 948, Hewitt to Hayman, 1 June 1916.
 5. IWM 948, Hewitt to Hayman, 11 February 1915.
 6. IWM 948, Hewitt to Hayman, 11 February 1915.
 7. IWM 948, Kenneth Eady to Mrs Hayman, 4 July 1917.
 8. IWM 948, Rex Harris to Mrs Hayman, n.d.
 9. IWM 948, Harold Little to Mrs Hayman, n.d.
10. IWM 948, L. Holland to Mrs Hayman, 30 December 1917.
11. IWM 948, W.F. Roberts to Mrs Hayman, 8 September 1917.
12. IWM 948, Roberts to Hayman, 19 November 1917.
13. IWM 948, Roberts to Hayman, 1 April 1918.
14. IWM 948, Charles Thomas to Mrs Hayman, n.d.
15. IWM 948, Thomas to Hayman, 4 May, n.y.
16. IWM 948, Bryant to Hayman, 21 March 1915.
17. Ibid.
18. Ibid.
19. IWM 948, Bryant to Hayman, n.d.
20. IWM 948, Bryant to Hayman, 27 March 1915.
21. IWM 948, Bryant to Hayman, n.d.
22. IWM 948, Bryant to Hayman, 20 October 1915.
23. IWM 948, Bryant to Hayman, 10 November 1916.
24. IWM 948, Bryant to Hayman, December 1916.
25. IWM 948, Eady to Hayman, 4 July 1917.
26. IWM 948, Hewitt to Hayman, 11 May 1915.
27. IWM 948, Hewitt to Hayman, 1 June 1916.
28. IWM 948, V. Leigh to Mrs Hayman, 7 July 1916.
29. IWM 948, George Marshall to Mrs Hayman, n.d.

30. IWM 948, Hewitt to Hayman, 16 April 1915; Marshall to Hayman, n.d.
31. IWM 948, Hewitt to Hayman, 26 August 1915.
32. IWM 948, A. Boreham to Mrs Hayman, 11 March 1915.
33. IWM 948, R.E. Davies to Mrs Hayman, 18 August, n.y.
34. IWM 948, Dorothy Barlow to Mrs Hayman, n.d., 1915.
35. IWM 948, W. Hall to Mrs Hayman, 6 April 1916.
36. IWM 948, Hall to Hayman, 22 September 1917.
37. *Bournemouth St Mary Parish Newsletter*, March 1944.

Chapter 12: Maude Royden
1. Quoted in Shelia Fletcher, *Maude Royden: A Life*, p.8, Basil Blackwell, Oxford, 1989.
2. Ibid, p.28.
3. Ibid, p.31.
4. Ibid, p.79.
5. Ibid, p.108.
6. Ibid, p.113.
7. *Daily Express*, 4 August 1915.
8. *The Times*, 17 July 1917.

Chapter 13: The Hon. Mrs Edith Lyttleton Gell
1. The Hon. Mrs Gell, *Under Three Reigns, 1860–1920*, p.30, Kegan Paul, Trench, Trubner & Co, London, 1927.
2. Ibid, p.152.
3. Ibid, p.157.
4. *The Times*, 19 December 1896.
5. Ibid.
6. *The Times*, 14 December 1904, p.10.
7. Edith Mary Lyttleton Gell, *The More Excellent Way: Words of the Wise on the Life of Love, A Sequence of Meditations*, p.1, Henry Frowde, London, 1898.
8. The Hon. Mrs Gell, *The Menace of Secularism: Addresses on the Nation's Need of the National Church*, p.iii, Wells, Gardner, Darton & Co, London, 1912.
9. *Under Three Reigns*, p.258.
10. Ibid, p.259.
11. Ibid, p.260.
12. Ibid, p.262.
13. Ibid, p.265.
14. Ibid, p.267.
15. Ibid, p.271.
16. Ibid, p.273.
17. The Hon. Mrs Gell, *The Happy Warrior: Daily Thoughts for all who are serving their country (whether on land, or sea, or in air)*, p.v., A.R. Mowbray & Co, London, 1915.
18. Ibid, p.ii.
19. The Hon. Mrs Gell, *Womanhood at the Crossroads*, p.7, SPCK, London, 1920.
20. Ibid.
21. *Derby Daily Telegraph*, 18 April 1944, p.4.
22. Ibid, 22 September 1944, p.5.

Chapter 14: Edith Cavell
1. A.A. Hoeling, *Edith Cavell*, p.7, Cassell & Co, London, 1958.
2. Quoted in Diana Southam, *Edith Cavell*, p.143, Quercus, London, 2010.

3. Thomas à Kempis, *Of the Imitation of Christ; The 'Edith Cavell' Edition*, Oxford University Press, 1920.
4. Quoted in Brand Whitlock, *Belgium under the German Occupation: A Personal Narrative, Volume II*, p.40, Heinemann, London, 1919.
5. Ibid.
6. Ibid.
7. *Imitation of Christ*, p.2.

Part IV: Christians from Other Nations
1. Philip Jenkins, *The Great and Holy War: How World War I Changed Religion For Ever*, p.6, Lion Books, Oxford, 2014.
2. Ibid, p.11.
3. Ibid, p.21.

Chapter 15: Louise Thuliez
1. Louise Thuliez, *Condemned to Death*, p.136, Methuen & Co, London, 1934.
2. Ibid, p.142.
3. Ibid, p.205.

Chapter 16: Martin Niemöller
1. Martin Niemöller, *From U-Boat to Pulpit*, p.1, Willett, Clark & Company, Chicago & New York, 1937.
2. Ibid, p.46.
3. Ibid, p.95.
4. Quoted in Dietmar Schmidt, *Pastor Niemöller*, p.57, Doubleday & Co, New York, 1959.
5. Ibid, p.63.

Chapter 17: Pastor Pieter-Jozef Dergent
1. Mgr. K. Cruysberghs, *Pastoor Pieter-Jozef Dergent: Een Priester-Martelaar*, p.9, N.V. de Vlaamse Drukkerij, Leuven, 1949.
2. Ibid, p.11.
3. Ibid, p.12.
4. Ibid, p.13.
5. Ibid, p.14.
6. Ibid, p.15.
7. *The Tablet*, 9 January 1915.
8. *Nottingham Evening Post*, 26 February 1915, p.3.
9. *Western Daily Press*, 7 January 1915, p.3.
10. *Exercise book of Samuel Ching* (see case study on Lilian Hayman).
11. Cruysberghs, p.2.

Chapter 18: Alvin York
1. Alvin York, *Sergeant York and the Great War: His Own Life Story and War Diary*, p.60, The Vision Forum, San Antonio, 2011.
2. Ibid, p.67.
3. Quoted in John Perry, *Sgt. York: His Life and Legacy*, p.27, B&H Publishing, Nashville, 1997.
4. York, *War Diary*, p.160.
5. World War I. United States Army Center of Military History, *Medal of Honor Recipients*, http://www.history.army.mil/html/moh/worldwari.html#YORK <accessed 28 Mar 2015>.

6. Douglas V. Mastriano, *Alvin York: A New Biography of the Hero of the Argonne*, p.156, The University Press of Kentucky, 2014.
7. York, *War Diary*, p.181.

Chapter 19: Francis Meynell

1. Francis Meynell, *My Lives*, p.43, The Bodley Head, London, 1971.
2. Ibid, p.47.
3. *The Herald*, 16 October 1915, p.2.
4. Meynell, p.95.
5. Ibid, p.96.
6. *The Herald*, 25 September 1916, p.1.
7. Meynell, p.102.
8. Ibid.

Chapter 20: Howard Marten

1. University of Leeds Special Collections, LIDDLE/WW1/CO/061.
2. *Harrow Observer*, 10 March 1916.
3. University of Leeds Special Collections, LIDDLE/WW1/CO/061.
4. Ibid.
5. Ibid.
6. Ibid.
7. Ibid.
8. Ibid.
9. Ibid.
10. Ibid.
11. Ibid.

Chapter 21: Laurence Cadbury and Corder Catchpool

1. Corder Catchpool, *On Two Fronts: Letters of a Conscientious Objector*, p.20, Headley Brothers, London, 1940.
2. Meaburn Tatham & James E. Miles, *The Friends' Ambulance Unit, 1914–1919: A Record*, p.vii, Swarthmore Press, London, n.d.
3. Catchpool, p.26.
4. University of Birmingham Special Collections, MS327/A/1/5, Laurence Cadbury letter, 26 December 1914.
5. Catchpool, p.44.
6. Ibid.
7. Ibid.
8. MS327/A/1/7, 20 January 1915.
9. MS327/A/1/14, 25 May 1915.
10. Catchpool, p.48.
11. Ibid, p.53.
12. Ibid, p.53.
13. MS327/A/1/29, 26 May 1916.
14. Ibid.
15. Ibid.
16. MS327/A/1/26, 4 March 1916.
17. MS327/A/1/26, 26 May 1916.
18. Catchpool, p.81.
19. MS327/A/1/44, 12 Apr 1917.

20. MS327/A/1/48, 6 June 1917.
21. Catchpool, p.96–7.
22. MS327/B/2, Letter from Norman Birkett to LC, 1 April 1915.
23. MS327/B/2, Letter from George Newman to LC, 25 March 1918.
24. *Evening Despatch*, 13 January 1917, p.3.
25. Catchpool, p.104.
26. Ibid, p.146.
27. MS327/B/4, Letter from John Van Schaick Jr, 28 January 1919.

Chapter 22: The Chavasse Family
1. *The Times*, Obituary – Dr Chavasse, 12 March 1928, p.8.
2. Peter Kennerley, *The Building of Liverpool Cathedral*, p.17, Carnegie Publishing, Preston, 1991.
3. *Manchester Guardian* – Bishop Chavasse, 12 March 1928, p.12.
4. John Thomas, 'The "Beginnings of a Noble Pile": Liverpool Cathedral's Lady Chapel (1904–10)', *Architectural History*, Vol. 48, 2005, p. 259.
5. Kennerley, p.16.
6. Selwyn Gummer, *The Chavasse Twins*, p.43, Hodder & Stoughton, London, 1963.
7. *Hull Daily Mail*, 5 November 1914, p.1.
8. *The London Gazette:* 24 August 1917.
9. *The London Gazette*, 3 October 1919.
10. Ann Clayton, *Chavasse: Double VC*, p.83, Pen & Sword, Barnsley, 2006.
11. Quoted in Clayton, p.78.
12. Ibid, p.96.
13. Ibid, p.131.
14. Ibid.
15. *The London Gazette*, 26 October 1916.
16. Clayton, p.171.
17. *Liverpool Echo*, 26 August 1917, p.3.
18. Quoted in Clayton, p.205.
19. *Liverpool Courier*, 16 August 1917, p.3.
20. Lord Derby to Francis Chavasse, 5 September 1917, Bodelian Library, 7/20.
21. *London Gazette*, 14 September 1917.
22. Gummer, p.64.

Chapter 23: The Brocklesby Family
1. University of Leeds Special Collections, LIDDLE/WW1/CO/011.
2. Alfred Salter, Faith of a Pacifist, 1914.
3. Quoted in Will Ellsworth-Jones, We Will Not Fight: The Untold Story of World War One's Conscientious Objectors, p.57, Aurum Press, London, 2008.
4. *Doncaster Gazette*, February 1916.
5. Ibid.
6. University of Leeds Special Collections, LIDDLE/WW1/CO/011.
7. University of Leeds Special Collections, LIDDLE/WW1/GS/0201.
8. Ibid.
9. Hansard, Vol. 83, p.1013, 29 June 1916.
10. University of Leeds Special Collections, LIDDLE/WW1/CO/011.
11. LIDDLE/WW1/GS/0201.
12. LIDDLE/WW1/CO/011.

Further Reading

Books

à Kempis, Thomas, *Of the Imitation of Christ; The 'Edith Cavell' Edition*, Oxford University Press, London, 1920.

Adams, J. Esslemont, *The Chaplain and the War*, T&T Clark, Edinburgh, 1915.

Atwood, Kathryn J., *Women Heroes of World War 1: 16 Remarkable Resisters, Soldiers, Spies and Medics*, Chicago Review Press, 2014.

Barry, F.R., *Period of My Life*, Hodder & Stoughton, London, 1970.

Bartelot, R.G., *A Book of Remembrance: Being a short Summary of the Service and Sacrifice rendered to the Empire during the Great War by one of many Patriotic Families of Wessex, The Popes of Wrackleford, Co. Dorset*, Chiswick Press, London, 1919.

Brown, Malcolm & Seaton, S., *Christmas Truce: The Western Front, December 1914*, Pan Books, London, 1994.

Burnham, Karyn, *The Courage of Cowards: The Untold Stories of First World War Conscientious Objectors*, Pen & Sword History, Barnsley, 2014.

Catchpool, Corder, *On Two Fronts: Letters of a Conscientious Objector*, London, Headley Brothers, 1940.

Clayton, Ann, *Chavasse: Double VC*, Pen and Sword Military, Barnsley, 2006.

Cruysberghs, Mgr. K., *Pastoor Pieter-Jozef Dergent: Een Priester-Martelaar*, N.V. de Vlaamse Drukkerij, Leuven, 1949.

Currie, R., Gilbert, A. and Horsley, L., *Churches and Churchgoers: Patterns of Church Growth in the British Isles since 1700*, Clarendon Press, Oxford, 1977.

Dilworth, Thomas, *David Jones in the Great War*, Enitharmon Press, London, 2012.

Dobbie, Ian, *Sovereign Service: The Story of SASRA, 1836-2013*, SASRA, 2013.

Ellsworth-Jones, Will, *We Will Not Fight: The Untold Story of World War One's Conscientious Objectors*, Aurum Press, London, 2008.

Fletcher, Shelia, *Maude Royden: A Life*, Blackwell, Oxford, 1989.

French, David, *Raising Churchill's Army: the British Army and the War against Germany, 1919-1945*, Oxford University Press, London, 2000.

Garvey, Joseph, *Fresh in My Memory Always: Joseph Garvey's Memoirs*, PDG Books, Ilkley, 2012.

Gell, The Hon. Mrs Edith, *The More Excellent Way: Words of the Wise on the Life of Love, A Sequence of Meditations*, Henry Frowde, London, 1898.

Gell, The Hon. Mrs Edith, *Under Three Reigns, 1860-1920*, Kegan Paul, Trench, Trubner & Co, London, 1920.

Gell, The Hon. Mrs Edith, *The Menace of Secularism: Addresses on the Nation's Need of the National Church*, Wells, Gardner, Darton & Co, London, 1912.

Gell, The Hon. Mrs Edith, *The Happy Warrior: Daily Thoughts*, A.R. Mowbray & Co, London, 1915.

Gell, The Hon. Mrs Edith, *Women at the Crossroads*, SPCK, London, 1920.

Graves, Robert, *Good-bye to All That: An Autobiography*, Jonathan Cape, London, 1929.

Greaves, Jonathan, *A Christian in Khaki*, Monk Street Publishing, Monmouth, 2014.

Gregory, Adrian, *The Last Great War: British Society and the First World War*, Cambridge University Press, 2008.

Gummer, Selwyn, *The Chavasse Twins*, Hodder & Stoughton, London, 1963.

Hastings, Adrian, *A History of English Christianity, 1920-1985*, Collins, London, 1986.

Hoehling, A.A. *Edith Cavell*, Cassell & Co, London, 1958.

Lewis, Elinor, *Hearts and Lives Given to Christ: Twenty-Four Bible Lessons for Young Women's Classes*, Society for Promoting Christian Knowledge, London, 1910.

Jenkins, Philip, *The Great and Holy War: How World War I Changed Religion For Ever*, Lion Books, Oxford, 2014.

Jones, David, *The Anaethema*, Faber & Faber, London, 1972.

Jones, David, *In Parenthesis*, Faber & Faber, London, 1978.

Jones, David, (ed. Rene Hague), *Dai Greatcoat*, Faber & Faber, London, 1980.

Kennerley, Peter, *The Building of Liverpool Cathedral*, Carnegie Publishing, Preston, 1991.

Kramer, Alan, *Dynamic of Destruction: Culture and Mass Killing in the First World War*, Oxford University Press, London, 2007.

Marwick, Arthur, *Women at War, 1914-1918*, Fontana, London, 1977.

Mastriano, Douglas V., *Alvin York: A New Biography of the Hero of the Argonne*, The University Press of Kentucky, 2014.

McIntyre, Ian, *The Expense of Glory: A Life of John Reith*, Harper Collins, London, 1993.

Meynell, Francis, *My Lives*, The Bodley Head, London, 1971.

Niemöller, Martin, *From U-Boat to Pulpit*, Willett, Clark & Company, Chicago & New York, 1937.

Pearce, Joseph, *Literary Converts: Spiritual Inspiration in an Age of Unbelief*, Harper Collins, London, 1999.

Perry, John, *Sgt. York: His Life, Legend and Legacy*, B&H Publishing, Nashville, 1997.

Reith, John, *Into the Wind*, Hodder & Stoughton, London, 1949.

Reith, John, *Wearing Spurs*, Hutchinson & Co, London, 1966.

Richardson, Neil, *A Coward If I Return, A Hero If I Fall*, O'Brien Press, Dublin, 2010.

Rickard, Mrs Victor, *The Story of the Munsters at Etreux, Festubert, Rue du Bois and Hulloch*, Hodder & Stoughton, London, 1915.

Robb, George, *British Culture and the First World War*, Palgrave, Basingstoke, 2002.

Robinson, Alan, *Chaplains at War: The Role of Clergymen during World War Two*, I.B. Tauris, London, 2008.

Royden, Agnes Maude, *The Great Adventure: The Way to Peace*, Headley, London, 1915.

Royden, Agnes Maude, *Downward Paths: An Inquiry into the Causes which Contribute to the Making of the Prostitute*, G. Bell & Sons, London, 1916.

Ryder, Rowland, *Edith Cavell*, Hamish Hamilton, London, 1975.

Salter, Alfred, *Faith of a Pacifist*, 1914.

Schmidt, Dietmar, *Pastor Niemöller*, Doubleday & Co, New York, 1959.

Shaw, D., 'The Forgotten Army of Women: Queen Mary's Army Auxiliary Corps' in H. Cecil and P. Liddle (eds), *Facing Armageddon: The First World War Experienced*, Leo Cooper, London, 1996.

Snape, Michael, *God and the British Soldier*, Routledge, Abingdon, 2005.

Snape, Michael, 'Church of England Chaplains in the First World War: Goodbye to "Goodbye to All That"', *Journal of Ecclesiastical History*, Vol. 62, Issue 2, April 2011, pp.318-45.

Souhami, Diana, *Edith Cavell* Quercus, London, 2010.

Tatham, Meaburn, and Miles, James E., *The Friends' Ambulance Unit, 1914-1919: A Record*, Swarthmore Press, London, n.d.

Thomas, John, 'The 'Beginnings of a Noble Pile': Liverpool Cathedral's Lady Chapel (1904-10)', *Architectural History*, Vol. 48, 2005, p.259.

Thuliez, Louise, *Condemned to Death*, Methuen & Co, London, 1934.

Weintraub, Stanley, *Silent Night: The Remarkable Christmas Truce of 1914*, Simon & Schuster, London, 2001.

Whitlock, Brand, *Belgium under the German Occupation: A Personal Narrative, Volume II*, Heinemann, London, 1919.

Wilkinson, Alan, *The Church of England & the First World War*, SPCK, London, 1978.

Wilkinson, Alan, *Dissent or Conform: War, Peace and the English Churches, 1900-1945*, SCM Press, London, 1986.

Wisbey, Harry, *Rough Journal: The Start of World War One, A Journal of August to September 1914*, SASRA, 2014.

York, Alvin, *Sergeant York and the Great War: His Own Life Story and War Diary*, The Vision Forum, San Antonio, 2011.

Newspapers and Periodicals

Aberdeen Weekly Journal
Brecon and Radnor Express
Christian Herald
Cork Examiner
Daily Express
Derby Daily Telegraph
Evening Despatch
Harlow Observer
Hull Daily Mail
Liverpool Courier
Liverpool Echo
Manchester Courier and Lancashire General Advertiser
Manchester Guardian
Mansfield Reporter
Sheffield Evening Telegraph
The London Gazette
The Tablet
The Times

Websites

www.spc.ox.ac.uk/content/chavasse-family-papers – provides a good overview of the Chavasse family and scans of some of the letters they sent and received during the war.
www.achristianinkhaki.co.uk/
firstworldwarsoldier.com/sitefiles/joe-garvey.html
www.ppu.org.uk/learn/infodocs/cos/st_co_wwone.html
daibach-welldigger.blogspot.co.uk/#!/2013/08/lewis-valentine-prophet-among-people.html

Archival Sources

Imperial War Museum Department of Documents
Letters to Mrs Hayman, Document 948.

Dublin Diocsean Archive
Papers of France Gleeson, DDA P101

University of Leeds Special Collections, Liddle Archive
Esslemont Adams, LIDDLE/WW1/GS/0527
Howard Marten, LIDDLE/WW1/CO/061
Phil Brocklesby, LIDDLE/WW1/GS/0201
John Hubert Brocklesby, LIDDLE/WW1/CO/011
J.V. Salisbury, LIDDLE/WW1/GALL/90

University of Birmingham Cadbury Research Centre Special Collections
Papers of Laurence Cadbury, MS327

Index